DOROTHY WEST'S
PARADISE

DOROTHY WEST'S
PARADISE

A BIOGRAPHY OF CLASS AND COLOR

CHERENE SHERRARD-JOHNSON

RUTGERS UNIVERSITY PRESS

NEW BRUNSWICK, NEW JERSEY, AND LONDON

LIBRARY OF CONGRESS CATALOGING-IN-PUBLICATION DATA

Sherrard-Johnson, Cherene, 1973–

Dorothy West's paradise : a biography of class and color / Cherene Sherrard-Johnson.

   p.   cm.

Includes bibliographical references and index.

ISBN 978–0-8135–5166–1 (hardcover : alk. paper)—ISBN 978–0-8135–5167–8 (pbk. : alk. paper)

  1. West, Dorothy, 1907–1998. 2. Authors, American—20th century—Biography. 3. African American authors—Biography. I. Title.

PS3545.E82794Z86 2012

813.'54—dc22

[B]

2011010854

A British Cataloging-in-Publication record for this book is available from the British Library.

Visit our Web site: http://rutgerspress.rutgers.edu

Manufactured in the United States of America

Typesetting: Jack Donner, BookType LLC

For Hayden and August

CONTENTS

ACKNOWLEDGMENTS

A project like this has been enhanced and enabled in so many ways by a very diverse group of people. First and foremost, I thank the Martha's Vineyard Museum and Historical Society, especially Linsey Lee, for the excellent work she continues to carry on as an oral historian of the island and its people. Without her interviews, through which I was first introduced to Dorothy West's distinctive and captivating voice, the seeds for the project would not have been planted. In addition to the Martha's Vineyard Museum, I express my sincere appreciation to the librarians, archivists, and library staff at Yale University's Beinecke Rare Book and Manuscript Collections, Emory University's Woodruff Library, the Schlesinger Library at the Radcliffe Institute for Advanced Study, Harvard University, University of Wisconsin–Madison's Memorial Library, and the Wisconsin Historical Society.

I acknowledge the ground-breaking early scholarship on black women's writing and the Harlem Renaissance; it was the recovery work of black feminist scholars like Nellie McKay, Mary Helen Washington, Deborah McDowell, Cheryl Wall, Valerie Smith, and Adelaide Cromwell that reintroduced West to the world. I also acknowledge Katrine Dalsgård, Lorraine Roses, Deborah McDowell, and Genii Guinier's priceless interviews with West. Finally, the scholarship of Verner Mitchell and Cynthia Davis made previously unpublished writings and selected letters of Dorothy West and her cousin Helene Johnson available in *Where the Wild Grape Grows* (2005) and *This Waiting for Love* (2000). The publication of West's letters made my work infinitely easier, and I gratefully acknowledge the editors' devotion to recovering West's writing and legacy.

I thank Adelaide Cromwell, Constance Williams, Anita Christian, Joyce Steward-Rickson, Elaine Weintraub, the late Della Hardman, and other incidental friends and neighbors I had the opportunity to speak with during the summers of 2005 and 2008 when I was researching this project in Oak Bluffs. I also thank the staff of the *Vineyard Gazette* and Nis Kildegaard at the Martha's Vineyard Public Library, who allowed me access to reams of *Vineyard Gazette* microfilm that contained West's columns. I thank my research assistants Kate Steinnagel and Mattie Burkert, graduate students at the University of Wisconsin–Madison.

I must thank colleagues at the University of Wisconsin–Madison and especially the fellows, staff, and the director of the Institute for Research in the Humanities (IRH). A Race, Ethnicity, and Indigeneity fellowship from the IRH allowed me the time off from teaching to write this biography in a supportive and intellectually vigorous environment. Visiting IRH fellows Daniel Birkholz and Julia Mickenberg from the University of Texas–Austin graciously hosted an impromptu screening of *Battleship Potemkin* while I was writing the chapter on West's visit to Russia, and Francine Hirsch kindly invited me to sit in her graduate seminar on Russian history. A Vilas Associate award provided invaluable travel support, and a Feminist Scholars Fellowship from the Department of Women's Studies extended my sabbatical year. An external faculty fellowship from Stanford University's Center for the Comparative Study of Race and Ethnicity provided space and support to reflect and refine the project in its final stages. I extend a special thanks to those who read this project in various stages and/or offered insightful references and observations: Amaud Johnson, Ethelene Whitmire, Craig Werner, Tejumola Olaniyan, Brenda Gayle Plummer, Francine Hirsch, Robert Nixon, Athan Biss, Julia Mickenberg, M. Giulia Fabi, Susan Friedman, Dale Bauer, Furaha Norton, Susan Bernstein, Jennifer Wilks, and Maureen Honey. At Rutgers University Press, Leslie Mitchner has always been a champion editor and sensitive reader; she believed in this biography before I knew for sure that I would write it. I also express my thanks to the anonymous reader who gave the book such an encouraging endorsement.

I thank Nancy Cott and the organizers, speakers, and participants of the Schlesinger Seminar on Gender History at Radcliffe Institute in 2007.

My thanks also go to the journals *African American Review* and *Letterature d'America* for publishing sections of chapters 3 and 6.

I send a very special thanks to Adelaide Cromwell and her impeccable generosity. Her words and scholarship continue to inspire.

I also thank those who provided encouragement and childcare at critical moments—my parents Martha and Fredric Sherrard. And I always acknowledge my first reader and life partner: Amaud Johnson.

Finally, I thank Dorothy West for writing, for living, and for giving me a chance to take my scholarly interests beyond the Harlem Renaissance. I hope that I have answered the question that appears as the epigraph to the introduction.

DOROTHY WEST'S
PARADISE

Introduction

Why would anybody write a book about me?

–Dorothy West (Genii Guinier, "Interview with Dorothy West")

It seems counterintuitive if not downright disingenuous to begin by explaining that this is not a traditional biography. Rather, it is a book about what the genre of literary biography and life writing can teach us about our society and our interior lives. How does the consideration of one particular person's life and art magnify our own? As a scholar of literature, I find writers' imaginations and the tools they use to craft the worlds that animate their writing fascinating. I must confess, however, that I am singularly uninterested in the plodding narrative of a life from birth to the grave. Biographies that begin "it was a dark and stormy October night when so-and-so was born . . ." rarely find their way onto my bookshelves or into my syllabi.

Am I now indulging in that tiresome biographers' habit of musing on their chosen forms and insisting that their books will be different, only to more or less begin on the second page with "so-and-so was born . . ."? I don't think so. If you pay close attention to the other words in the book's title, then you will already have an inkling of what you are in for. In the mid-1990s, the paradise alluded to in the title might have been placed in scare quotes to emphasize its relative interpretations and my skepticism toward establishing any authoritative definition. In any case, it is your first clue. This book is about a place both elusive and material. For the poetically inclined, paradise evokes John Milton's epic *Paradise Lost*; philosophers may turn to Thomas More's *Utopia*. The location of Paradise can be a theological conundrum or a firmly held religious belief. For leisure-minded consumers it is a term replete with the promise of colonial ventures and hedonistic vacations. It might simply be an Edenic retreat from the noise and overcrowding of urban industry and the monotony of suburban sprawl. The subtitle qualifies the inexhaustible interpretations of paradise by promising a biography of class and color. It would be less elegant, but more accurate, to say that I consider West's life and writing through the prisms of

1

class and color. I chose the word color over race to heighten attention to how racial identity works within African American culture. I acknowledge, however, that racial categorization and its Pandora's box of legal, social, economic, and existential issues are certainly implicit in, if not explicitly evoked by, the word color. This book, then, magnifies how Dorothy West's personal obsessions with the dynamics of class and color manifest in her writing. It is important to note that West is not alone; she shares her obsessions with others in the many social and artistic spheres she inhabited over the course of her life and career. I am interested in her preoccupations because they are the key to understanding how a group of people persevered against a system of oppression so pernicious that it remains a foundational site of identity formation in the United States of America.

Studying Dorothy West helps me to answer a slew of provocative questions: How did a small number of African Americans find a measure of success, equality, and psychological freedom in the town of Oak Bluffs on the island of Martha's Vineyard? How is that space representative of the anxieties and advantages of upper middle-class and elite black Americans? What is the cost of their success? And who bears the cost? Dorothy West's passionately rendered stories, entertaining novels, and occasionally perplexing nonfiction provide a complex schematic of the strategies diverse groups of African Americans use to pursue happiness as well as the rewards and ramifications associated with such maneuvers. *Dorothy West's Paradise: A Biography of Class and Color* examines the Harlem Renaissance writer's public and private life to reveal what her multigenre mythmaking can tell us about class, gender, and regional fault lines within African American culture throughout the twentieth century. To accomplish this task, I cast a novelist as a social historian and an island as a site of nationalist desire; thus, by illuminating a writing life I am able to probe the social and cultural geography of class representation.

The inspiration for this biography began in the right place with the wrong author. Dorothy West had always been on my radar. Indeed, like other Harlem Renaissance critics with a focus on women writers, I reluctantly left her out of my book, *Portraits of the New Negro Woman: Visual and Literary Culture in the Harlem Renaissance* (2007). West arrived in Harlem in 1926, but her first novel, *The Living Is Easy*, was not published until 1948. She did not fit neatly into the Harlem Renaissance or my first book. I shuttled her away to a journal article, but she lingered like the top note of a perfume I had tried but was not yet ready to purchase. Then, in the summer of 2005, I was researching the life history of an undervalued woman writer from the nineteenth century: Emma Dunham Kelley-Hawkins. Kelley-Hawkins was thought to be an African American writer, and her novels had been reprinted as part of the Schomburg Series of African American Women Writers. I was researching the early black presence on the island when the *Boston Globe* published an article revealing that Kelley-Hawkins was in fact Euro-American, findings later confirmed by an independent genealogist. Kelley-Hawkins wrote two novels with characters that might easily be confused with several of West's heroines. Many of West's central figures possess physical traits commonly associated with Euro-Americans, even though they are identified in her novels as black, colored, or Negro. Still reeling in astonishment of from the *Globe* announcement, I found myself quite literally on Dorothy West Avenue.[1]

Her cottage, an unassuming building in the campground style, sits on a quiet street in the Highlands area of Oak Bluffs, Massachusetts. I immediately imagined Dorothy working at her aqua blue desk, watching the ferries in the harbor "as anxiously as a lover" from her window.[2] In a tranquil wooded copse, across from the street sign that bears her name, sits a bench dedicated to her cousin, the poet Helene Johnson. Thanks perhaps to the restorative island air, both women enjoyed long lives; West died in 1998 at ninety-one and Johnson in 1995 at eighty-nine.[3] After trespassing on West's porch, I went to the Martha's Vineyard Historical Society in Edgartown, where I found hours of oral histories from West and other distinguished black residents. I revisited West's fiction while reading the columns she wrote for the *Vineyard Gazette*. Like Kelley-Hawkins, West wrote novels steeped in the specificity of place and the racialized inflections of class privilege. Her societal views and frequent light-skinned characters were also the subjects of much controversy. Listening to West's voice on the tape was like having tea in her parlor. That voice persuaded me to let go of Kelley-Hawkins and reinvest in West.

Though she is often considered a member of the last generation of the Harlem Renaissance, West's writing continues beyond the period usually defined by literary historiographers. She published her acclaimed first novel *The Living Is Easy* after she had left Harlem. This partially explains why her work has not been given the same prominence as that of Nella Larsen, Zora Neale Hurston, or even Jessie Fauset. She was not, for instance, one of Cheryl Wall's foundational *Women of the Harlem Renaissance*. Yet as an editor of the literary journal *Challenge* she had a hand in influencing both her peers and later generations of black writers. In 1926, at age nineteen, West arrived in "the magic city," Harlem, with Helene Johnson. Charles Johnson's journal, *Opportunity*, had awarded West a prize for the short story "The Typewriter." With that entrée, she became a part of the New Negro intelligentsia of artists, writers, and activists. As a result of her flirtations with the Communist Party, she was one of a select cadre of artists who visited the Soviet Union in 1932. West continued to publish her short fiction in a variety of periodicals during this period, but in 1945 she left New York. Oak Bluffs, Massachusetts, a longtime black bourgeois enclave, became the not-so-quiet retreat for the mercurial writer who chronicled the comings and goings of the insular community. With the publication of *The Wedding*, which was edited by her friend Jacqueline Kennedy Onassis and later made into a television miniseries produced by Oprah Winfrey, West resurfaced from her seclusion to a belated recognition. Before her death, a street adjacent to her home was christened Dorothy West Avenue, and in August 2008 her home on Myrtle Avenue was marked with a plaque and designated a stop on the African American Heritage Trail.

When I visualize Dorothy on her porch with her lap-desk, diminutive in form, delicate in everything but her voice, her mouth going a mile a minute, I do not think of her as either a grand dame of letters who used to be a "writer of the Harlem Renaissance" or an eccentric spinster with a fondness for cats and children. For me, she is "Miss West," the vivacious columnist for the *Vineyard Gazette*. Or perhaps "Aunt Dorothy," whose porch you must linger on once you open your house for the summer. When a person says to me, "I knew Dottie," or "I remember Miss West," the comment immediately communicates something about the nature of their relationship and the social realm of their encounter. "Miss West" suggests the respectful distance that characterizes a relationship between a younger person and a venerated elder; "Dottie," which is more often used by white residents rather than black, denotes not only an endearing tenderness but also a kind of diminutiveness that I find somewhat presumptuous, even patronizing. "Aunt Dorothy" or just "Dorothy" is used by close friends and her larger extended network of kin, none of whom are actual nieces or nephews as West was an only child. Throughout this biography I primarily refer to Dorothy West as West; however, when I am delving into the more intimate spheres of her life, I occasionally call her Dorothy.

Harlem Renaissance critics have sometimes considered West's work and life only in relationship to her more famous male contemporaries; the critics mention West as an aside: coeditor for the *New Challenge* with Richard Wright, the "little sister" of her adored Langston Hughes, and the sometimes romantic interest of poet Claude McKay. Such marginal treatment recalls Hermione Lee's observation in her biography of Edith Wharton—a writer much admired by West—that "to this day it is still rare for a book or an essay or a talk on Wharton not to mention [Henry] James" and some believe "that [Wharton's] relationship with James is the story of her life."[4] I do not want to lose sight of West; however, the personal and professional relationships that she shared with other Harlem Renaissance writers and midcentury American modernists deserve the same attention and scrutiny as the relationship between writers like Edith Wharton and Henry James. Moreover, the comparisons with Edith Wharton are not limited to West's social and artistic circles of exchange. Both West and Wharton viewed themselves as members of the East Coast aristocracy, albeit on different sides of the color line, and both sought to occasionally take up issues of the working class. Wharton was excruciatingly adept at the novel of manners and West emulates some of her narrative techniques. Also, like Wharton, West is capable of shifting her oeuvre into the realm of the pastoral; her brief literary sketch "Winter on Martha's Vineyard" manifests the cold lyricism of Wharton's local-color novel *Ethan Frome.*

Dorothy West's Paradise: A Biography of Class and Color captures the scope of her life against the unique topography of the black middle class in the Northeast from the turn into the twentieth century through the post–civil rights era. Immersion in West's fiction and family history provides a privileged glimpse into the insular world of the black elite. In interviews, Dorothy frequently referred to her mother, the formidable Rachel West, as one of the "Twelve Beauties of Boston," yet Rachel was actually born in the South. Rachel's light skin contributed to West's anxiety about her own appearance: she often described herself as the darkest member of her family and commented on her resemblance to her father, Isaac West. I follow Dorothy's experience growing up in the neighborhoods of Brookline and Oak Bluffs, Massachusetts, as the daughter of a popular beauty and the black banana king. The class terrain shifts when West moves to Harlem and exchanges the paradise of the island for the magical city that was the center of the artistic "renaissance" well under way before she arrived. In examining the class dynamics of the black bourgeoisie in each space, I approach the neighborhood enclaves and social circles characterized by West's fiction and nonfiction from a critical perspective that seeks to neither idolize the black elite nor disparage their material, if tenuous, success.

The question of West's sexuality is an unavoidable subject of much discussion and disagreement among scholars. Some saw her as asexual, her unrequited desire for Langston Hughes notwithstanding, while others cite her relationship with Marian Minus and her brief affair with Mildred Jones as proof that she was a lesbian. Despite evidence that supports West's long-term lesbian relationship with Minus, her fellow *Challenge* editor, I am not going to substantially reconsider her fiction in light of her "new" sexual orientation. Whatever her public or private orientation, her fiction maintains a clear investment in heterosexuality even as she demonstrates the potential dysfunction of heterosexual marriages. Her nonfiction writing, however, especially her social columns, evinces an attention to women's bodies and behavior that is somewhat ambiguous. This is partly because women often find themselves the subject of a panoptical gaze that alternately venerates and sexualizes their bodies as the bearers of culture and virtue. Be that as it may, West's gaze becomes almost rapturous when the female form, real or imagined, garners the attention of her pen.

Finally, the study of West's post-Harlem career also begins to redefine the era as a transatlantic (and transnational) moment. Her status as the only author from that era to publish a new novel in 1995 makes her a truly remarkable figure through which to analyze both the demise of the Harlem Renaissance and its lasting influence on American art and culture.

Remaking Respectability

Dorothy West inherited a particular understanding of entitlement, exclusivity, and birthright from her family, and she explored these concepts in her fiction and nonfiction. Close readings of how she represents African American upper-, middle-, and working-class subjects reveal the nefariousness of class boundaries and borders in the black community at a time when what it meant to be African American was in violent flux. The politics of respectability remains a nebulous yet persistent concept in African American studies and black feminism. Presumably, adhering to the behavioral tenets of respectability could counter some dangers posed by stereotypes of black women as sexually promiscuous. As such, ideas of respectability as they pertain to employment, speech, education, gesture, dress, and behavior may reflect fashion trends, legal/religious doctrines, and social customs. Some African Americans achieved or created higher-class status by "marrying up" in terms of class or skin color or through the acquisition of property and education. Without the kind of widespread socioeconomic change that would level the playing field for all blacks, such progress was tenuous, transitory, and always threatened by American racism's tendency to nullify individual gains in relationship to the collective.

What does it mean to perform class, or more precisely, to perform a class position that ameliorates or qualifies your racial identity? In 1841, Joseph Willson sought to answer this question in *Sketches of the Higher Classes of Colored Society in Philadelphia by a Southerner.* Willson, whose daughter Josephine became the wife of Senator Blanche K. Bruce, one of the nation's first black senators, defined the black upper class as "that portion of colored society whose incomes, from their pursuits or otherwise (immoralities or criminalities of course excepted), enables them to maintain the position of house-holders, and their families in comparative ease and comfort."[5] His narrative is acutely aware of the precariousness of class positions for people of color. Moreover, he is cognizant that once one reaches a certain class status it must be consistently affirmed if it is to be maintained. West's fiction, nonfiction, and interviews echo Willson's antebellum chronicle of a prosperous black community.

While the slave narrative proved the dominant genre of African American writing during the nineteenth century, a few authors wrote novels that dealt with the challenges of privilege and success in a society still held in the grip of white supremacy. Frank Webb's *The Garies and Their Friends* (1857) illustrated the challenges faced by free blacks in the North. Published in London and prefaced by Harriet Beecher Stowe, the renowned abolitionist and author of *Uncle Tom's Cabin* (1852), Webb's novel traces an interracial family's attempt to settle as free blacks in antebellum Philadelphia. The results of their endeavors are disastrous. The novel incorporates elements from narratives of passing, but literary historian Samuel Otter describes the style and content best as an "historical novel of urgent manners." The urgency emphasizes the vulnerability of "free blacks" in a country still invested in human capital. The race riot—the penultimate drama of the novel—is sparked by white desire to obtain black property. The protagonists "end up as targets for the machinations of George Stevens, an unscrupulous white lawyer who engineers a riot designed to drive blacks from their homes so that he and his cronies can reap a real estate windfall."[6] Webb's novel probes the intimate relationship between genteel behavior and violence in a way that prefigures, albeit with different outcomes, West's deployment of the novel of manners in her Harlem Renaissance fiction and her final novel *The Wedding*. That both Webb and Wharton may be considered West's literary ancestors underlines the potency of racialized novels centering on questions of class, legitimacy, and economics.

African American fiction published during the Reconstruction era often dramatized political discussions among highly intellectual groups of black activists. The views presented were diverse in method but singular in purpose: how best to achieve safety and success given the segregationist policies of Jim Crow. Within these postbellum, pre-Harlem writings the rhetoric of uplift, which demanded that a privileged few raise up the disadvantaged majority through philanthropic activism and individual achievement, set the stage for the New Negro movement.

Clubwomen, teachers, and activists of all shades and classes took refuge in performing respectability with the hope that it would contradict the sexual pathology associated with black womanhood. Their epidermal vulnerability required extreme measures to ameliorate the persecution, oppression, and presumed sexual availability that darker skin denoted. Respectable behavior may have included the choice to remain a spinster if an appropriate spouse could not be found, wearing excessively modest attire (black colleges often enforced dress codes upon their faculty and students), and following Victorian codes of true womanhood even after white American women were espousing the tenets of new womanhood. Despite the prevalence of these strategies, African American literature—from the black women's fiction of the 1890s through the Harlem Renaissance to Ann Petry's *The Street* and Toni Morrison's *Paradise*—is full of examples demonstrating how such tactics often backfire disastrously.

Like Harlem Renaissance writers Jessie Fauset and Marita Bonner, West's class-sensitive portrayals are particularly attuned to the symbolic roles actual women play in the social and familial order. Through this gendered framework we must first begin to view Rachel West and the many matriarchal characters based on her in West's fiction. West's characters struggle with the directives of the black women's club movement: to counter the public defamation of the black woman as sexually promiscuous and immoral by presenting positive examples of black women as ideal wives and mothers. As cultural critic Candice Jenkins observes, the club movement's "recuperative mission was explicitly tied to the emulation and promotion of bourgeois values."[7] In West's fiction and that of her contemporaries, performing respectability is a necessary step on the road to achieving and maintaining one's elite class status. Yet this performance has a certain price, one that West is not afraid to expose in her often searing portraits of social climbers and gatekeepers.

A Black Utopia

West achieved renown for early stories set in the urban settings of Boston or Harlem, but in later years she returned to her childhood vacation home. Through a column first entitled "Cottager's Corner" and later "Oak Bluffs," she chronicled and constructed a unique microcosm of the nation: the black colony on the island of Martha's Vineyard. West wrote of the island: "It is the closest to paradise I will ever come on earth."[8] Drawing on a rich archive of articles and taped interviews, I recover West's journalistic career, which spans several decades. West's preoccupation with intraracial divisions based on class and color marks much of her writing, regardless of genre, but I am also struck by a prescient, lyric sensibility in her writing about the natural topography of the island as well as its social landscape. Even more intriguing is her underlying desire for a black utopia, most evident when she writes in "The Legend of Oak Bluffs," that "nowhere else in America was there a place so favorable to the condition of being colored."[9] I argue that her nonfiction not only illustrates her fine grasp of societal relations and continued creativity but that it also directly informs the aesthetics and politics of her unpublished short fiction and sets the stage for her controversial final novel *The Wedding* (1995).

The experiment of a black oasis is not limited to Martha's Vineyard, although the island enclave with its center of Oak Bluffs is the most successful. Other "black edens" include Sag Harbor on Long Island, New York; Highland Beach in Maryland; Cape May, New Jersey; and Idlewild, Michigan, which lately inspired a musical called *Idlewild* starring the hip hop artists OutKast.[10] In 1921, philosopher, activist, writer, and race leader W.E.B. Du Bois wrote of Idlewild in the same terms that West does of the Vineyard:

> For sheer physical beauty—for sheen of water and golden air, for noble-
> ness of tree and flower of shrub, for shining river and song of bird and
> the low moving whisper of the sun, moon, and star, it is the beautifulest
> stretch I have seen for twenty years and then to add fellowship—
> sweet, strong women and keen-witted men from Canada and Texas,
> California and New York, Ohio, Missouri and Illinois—all sons and
> great-grandchildren (not of slaves, mind you but) of Ethiopia, all with
> the wide leisure of rest and play—can you imagine a more marvelous
> thing than Idlewild.[11]

Idlewild, like Highland Beach, fell upon hard times and now exists mostly as nostalgic memory.[12] Other attempts to establish black resort areas include boxer Jack Johnson's unsuccessful bid to purchase land in Lake Geneva, Wisconsin, a vacation spot for wealthy Chicagoans.[13]

Unlike Idlewild, Oak Bluffs has maintained a steady African American presence. In *African Americans on Martha's Vineyard*, Robert C. Hayden distinguishes the black community on Martha's Vineyard from other deliberately planned black resorts like Idlewild and Highland Beach that were designed as a direct response to racial exclusion and discrimination. In his view, Martha's Vineyard's black colony "developed alongside, parallel and in conjunction with the white community."[14] He describes the influx and growth of the community as a result of the same convergences of spontaneity and opportunity that made it popular for upper- and middle-class white vacationers. While I agree with his assessment in principle, it seems clear that the choice of where to live on the island is determined by a subtle design.

Novelist Stephen Carter opens his bestselling *The Emperor of Ocean Park* with a description of a Vineyard house bought "for a song back in the sixties, when Martha's Vineyard, and the black middle-class colony that summers there, were still smart and secret."[15] The invisibility of the black colony is both a point of consternation (we are here and have been here as long as you) and appeal (secrecy keeps the wrong sort out). Anxiety about the growth of the black community exists on both sides of the color line. Through her fiction and nonfiction, Dorothy West played a key role promoting the island, particularly Oak Bluffs, as a space of exclusivity, respectability, and interracial harmony. Whether it truly is such a place continues to be a matter of debate.

Happily ensconced in a cottage on Myrtle Avenue, adjacent to the street that will one day come to be known as "Dorothy West Avenue," West took on the role of cultural and regional historian by writing the column "Cottager's Corner" for the *Vineyard Gazette*. During my first visit to Oak Bluffs, I encountered the late Della Hardman on the porch of Ora McFarlane's guesthouse. McFarlane is a descendant of Oak Bluffs's two nineteenth-century black innkeepers, and Hardman, a longtime resident, inherited Dorothy West's column after she passed away. After I briefly explained my research interests, she recorded my information for Friday's column. She assiduously noted my name and my husband's, jotting down occupations, hometowns, and academic degrees. She also remarked on the verbosity of my two-year-old. As a result of this serendipitous conversation we were introduced and welcomed as newcomers to the Oak Bluffs community. The column still maintained its social influence, its power to both familiarize and legitimize, even after West's death. Shortly after our meeting, Della Hardman died in 2005 at age eighty-three. In true island fashion, residents celebrate a "Della Hardman Day" every July.

West and several other writers portray Oak Bluffs as a utopic space; it differs, however, from the black communal experiments studied in William and Jane Pease's landmark study *Black Utopia: Negro Communal Experiments in America* (1963). Although the black communities identified in the Peases' book resembled other contemporaneous, experimental utopian communities, they did not adhere to European ideas of socialism or communism. Instead, the Peases write: "if they partook of any specific social, economic, and political philosophy, it was the philosophy of the American middle class." These black utopias promoted the "virtues of self-reliance, individualism, and indepen-dence" combined with a devout espousal of "profit-making" capitalism.[16] The Peases do not study the aforementioned resort communities, because vacation homes are temporary abodes. They function as a refuge for African Americans who fully participate in mainstream (mainland) American society and economics.

The flexibility of the concept of utopia helps me to explain and establish the black community on the island of Martha's Vineyard as a collective character in this book, a place that embodies the tensions of race and class aspirations in both its natural and manmade architecture. Because it is an actual place, one might consider the black colony a heterotopia. In his essay "Of Other Spaces," Michel Foucault uses this term to describe "effectively enacted utopias." A heterotopia can take many forms. Foucault considers the Puritan societies of Early America to be heterotopias of compensation: "their role is to create a space that is other, another real space, as perfect, as meticulous, as well arranged as ours is messy, ill constructed, and jumbled."[17] The black colony in Oak Bluffs is a real space with a real history, but the idea of the colony, its potential, exists in another dimension that is always unreachable. After all, the etymology of the word utopia derives from the Greek root οὐ + τόπος, which translates as "not a place."

Class and Color Consciousness

The publication of West's unpublished writings in *Where the Wild Grape Grows: Selected Writing* illustrates how the intersections of class, region, and culture informed her concept of racial identity. The stories, which frequently recycle plots, characters, and themes, function as dress rehearsals for her novels. When considering that some stories were written much earlier than the oral histories and interviews, it is possible to read her short fiction as a kind of collective autobiography. Hermione Lee writes of Virginia Woolf, "Fiction is often [Woolf's] version of history." This concept definitely applies to West. The stories she tells her interviewers surface with little adornment in her fiction and vice versa. Her fiction might be fruitfully categorized as a type of "biomythography," to borrow an inventive term from Audre Lorde.[18] Like Zora

Neale Hurston, West is a trickster figure when it comes to telling the story of her life and her community. The slippage between the two is so frequent that it becomes difficult to determine when she is satirizing intraracial classism and colorism and when she is perpetuating it.

West's New England upbringing shaped how she viewed class and nurtured her investment in the politics of respectability. The anomalous figure of the black Yankee appears throughout West's fiction, often juxtaposed against the black New Yorker. West writes about class and the black bourgeoisie from the point of view of the "marginalized outsider," as Mary Helen Washington aptly observes. This peculiar, in-between status makes her a privileged and complex spectator in multiple spheres: first as young writer and editor in Harlem, and later as a mature journalist on the Vineyard. West's particularly New England understanding of class occasionally mirrors the perspective of a fellow New England writer, Ann Petry. In *At Home Inside: A Daughter's Tribute to Ann Petry*, Elisabeth Petry writes: "In some respects I believe what she saw as Yankee (or New England) characteristics were in fact attitudes or modes of behavior or mores attributable to the upper and upper-middle classes. Those she certainly tried to adopt." Yet Petry's daughter also maintains that her mother understood the contradictory position of the black New Englander as that of a maverick, and, for Ann Petry, ultimately "maintaining and acquiring the trappings of the upper class" did not increase her sense of belonging. Ann Petry came to believe that the idea of "a black middle class or a black upper middle class is a creation of white sociologists who refuse to acknowledge the existence of a caste system on the mainland—a caste system based on skin color."[19] Like Petry, West was something of a maverick. In testifying about the classism and colorism present among black Bostonians and black islanders, she began to construct, and even mythologize, her own definition of the black upper middle class, an endeavor Petry apparently remained skeptical of.

Considering West's writing from the Harlem Renaissance and beyond raises the following questions: How much of a radical was she? Can bourgeois exclusivity coexist with black nationalism? How does her life and life-writing exemplify the divisions of class and culture and the symbolic value of place? My approach to West's life and her fictions of race and class echoes Kevin Gaines's stance in *Uplifting the Race: Black Leadership, Politics, and Culture in the Twentieth Century*. Gaines writes: "I am less concerned with documenting the black elite's existence as an objective social group than I am in unpacking that group's ideology, and the extent to which that 'group' was itself socially and ideologically fragmented." Just as Gaines refuses to "contribute yet another study of a pioneering, persevering black middle class," I wish to turn a skeptical eye toward West's often flawed, yet eminently revealing, class consciousness. I'm not quite ready, however, to attribute all uplift endeavors to "unconscious internalized racism," as Gaines argues.[20] Instead, I wish to explore why West so eagerly documented the comings and goings of the black elite in her columns and then satirized the group in her fiction.

West's novels attempt to name, codify, and psychoanalyze the class divide in twentieth-century African America. Her explorations create a language that challenges white supremacist beliefs about black identity. At the same time, her writing reveals how intraracial class divisions have alternatively enabled and stifled progressive thought, collective achievement, and cohesive group identity. West's literary explorations of class hierarchies reflect national anxieties about the shifting categories of class in interwar and post–World War II America. In Flannery O'Connor's short story "Revelation" (1965), Mrs. Turpin demonstrates through nutty, self-aggrandizing estimations how befuddling such categories can be:

> Sometimes Mrs. Turpin occupied herself at night naming the classes of people. On the bottom of the heap were most colored people, not the kind she would have been if she had been one, but most of them; then next to them—not above, just away from—were the white-trash; then above them were the home-owners, and above them were the home-and-land owners, to which she and Claud belonged. Above she and Claud were people with a lot of money and much bigger houses and much more land. But here the complexity of it would begin to bear in on her, for some of the people with a lot of money were common and ought to be below she and Claud and some of the people who had good blood and had lost their money and had to rent and then there were colored people who owned their homes and land as well. There was a colored dentist in town who had two red Lincolns and a swimming pool and a farm with registered white-face cattle on it. Usually by the time she had fallen asleep all the classes of people were moiling and roiling around in her head.[21]

Mrs. Turpin's inability to concretize a fixed map upon which the classes were defined and confined is partly due to the murkiness of her slippery scale. In her mind, race should be a definitive marker of class, but it is not; wealth should also be a determining factor, but even "common" people seem to obtain money. The only logic governing her musings is perhaps the logic of contradiction. As I consider this passage I have to wonder if Dorothy also experienced such flights of fancy? Did the intricacies and relationships of her class scale—in which region, color, behavior, and education were all determining factors—keep her up at night? Of course West's primary concern would have been where to position Turpin's "colored dentist." For West, such a man was not an anomaly. She would have been intrigued by his appearance in Turpin's list as well as his identifiable markers of success. Who was this dentist, and how did he survive the brutal, dehumanizing system of slavery and the attendant racialized discrimination that followed?

Negotiating Whiteness/Preserving Blackness

In Dorothy West's fictional and nonfictional portrayals of black middle- and upper-middle-class communities it is possible to identify a series of coping strategies designed *not* to escape black culture, but to circumvent inconveniences resulting from social and legal practices. The coping strategies that emerge in West's imagined and real communities are not, however, unique to that community. A brief look at another community famous for its insularity and cultural particularity provides a helpful context for understanding the social forces at work in the black colony of Oak Bluffs and in West's fictionalized (and nonfictional) representations of the black elite and middle class.

It may seem strange to include a comparative discussion of the New Orleans community of Creoles of Color with the black colony in Oak Bluffs; however, similar discussions of property ownership, architecture, and nostalgia pervade both sites. Shirley Elizabeth Thompson's *Exiles at Home* traces the role Creoles of Color (specifically those living in the Faubourg Marigny and Tremé) played in shaping identity and belonging in a world divided by legal and social categories of race. As a result of its in-between and exoticized status within nineteenth-century America, the Creole city of New Orleans "functioned in various genres as a storyboard, its physical aspects enhancing fictional and symbolic narratives by providing the context in which New Orleanians performed the various components of their identities."[22] New Orleans is important because it is a place where a free community of color sought to shore up its free status by policing (culturally and legally) racial boundaries in the form of cultural practice, language, and neighborhood architecture.

The city of New Orleans and its people appear with stunning frequency in American literature, especially in the black-authored fiction of the 1890s. Pauline Hopkins's *Contending Forces* (1900), a novel obsessed with the possibility of transforming black womanhood from its historically maligned status to a place of legitimacy and respectability, moves between Boston and Louisiana. Hopkins alternately evokes New Orleans as symbolic shorthand for sexual exploitation and racial violence *and* as a space of spiritual recovery through her representations of the Sisters of the Holy Family, an African American order of nuns. The sisters were founded by Henriette Delille, a young Creole of Color woman who refused to follow her family's tradition of plaçage.[23] Beneath the surface of New Orleans' association with interracial sex runs a murkier discourse that hinges on class distinctions, ethnicity, and interracial relationships formed by neighborhood affiliation. Hopkins's novel gestures at those undercurrents by returning Sappho, the protagonist, to the site of her "deflowering" to find solace and renewal rather than keeping her in Boston, where enforced secrecy and rigid New England views of sexual transgression force her to flee.

Thompson's study of the Creoles of Color in New Orleans is an illuminating lens through which to view West's emphasis on social and regional geography; her examination of court rulings dealing with racial determination exposes the reliance in such cases on tenuous and often mythic fictions of racial identity. Witnesses called on both sides frequently offered their personal beliefs—they told stories—about race as concrete evidence. Novelists like George Washington Cable, and later Kate Chopin, picked up certain elements of these "testimonials," which included illicit and legitimate interracial love affairs, in their writing, thus shaping the image of New Orleans in American cultural and literary imagination. Property ownership was often at stake in these cases. One's legal racial classification could determine one's status as enslaved or free, marriageable or unmarriageable, heir to or part of the deceased's estate. Emerging from the litigation was the fact that visually identifiable features were not conclusive. Defendants could always produce witnesses that attested to their own expertise in detecting even trace amounts of African descent; witnesses often referred to the defendant's ancestors or introduced unrelated examples of similar racial "types." A defendant's occupation and acquaintances were as important as his or her physical appearance. The ability to perform according to racial expectations was a critical skill to master for free blacks hoping to circumvent the color line. Visual markers might "race" a person, but phenotypical evidence was always subject to "the eye of the beholder." Where one lived could also place an individual on the continuum of racial identity. The successful suits of those plaintiffs who demonstrated that regardless of appearance or ancestry they associated, behaved, and exercised rights synonymous with whiteness proved that it was possible to successfully attain legal whiteness through racial performance. What constituted legal whiteness evolved over time and depended on region, community, political climate, and a host of other complex factors. If the black bourgeoisie had a game plan for circumventing the color line, then it came from the idea that the so-called Negro problem could be mitigated by performing certain attributes of whiteness. As Monique Guillory suggests, the main appeal of the plaçées was that they performed the graces of white womanhood better than white women; in other words, they were trained expressly to be white women without the protection of the law. Similarly, in Ariela Gross's "Litigating Whiteness" she determines that the success of freedom suits often hinged on how successfully the plaintiff performed a given society's idea of white womanhood. Gross argues that "over the course of the antebellum period, law made the 'performance' of whiteness increasingly important to the determination of racial status."[24]

What if we bring a similar understanding of racial (and gender) performance to West's description of the socialites in her "Oak Bluffs" column? Is West's precise attention to feminine appearance in her articles a sign of her ambivalence regarding her own sexuality? Whatever her private sexual orientation, in her columns West positioned heterosexual marriage as a crucial and stabilizing aspect of black society, despite the tragically doomed unions that appeared in her fiction. The following excerpts from her column demonstrate a curious emphasis on racialized aspects of the female body.

> Mrs. Holloman is a striking beauty. From her blond mother—a blond of the black race—she has inherited enormous blue-green eyes. Her skin is not fair. Her coloring is one of the indescribable—olive, perhaps, coming closest. The unexpected blue eyes in the olive face with its lovely features, her projection of charm, complete her total appeal when she sings.[25]

The second describes a similar beauty.

> Lovely Joan Reppert, wife of Dr. James Reppert, English department head of Albright College in Reading, Pa. . . . Quite simply, Joan is beautiful. Her coloring is superb, an incredible shade of brown that comes nearest to bronze. She has that most difficult of all features to come by, a small elegant nose. She has a lovely brow. She hasn't time to fuss with her hair, and it is a tumble of soft curls. It is not surprising that she was inescapable to the young assistant's eye. It is no more surprising that he fell in love with her.[26]

West's focus on Reppert's "small elegant nose" or Holloman's "unexpected blue eyes" is strikingly similar to the language used to describe the plaintiffs studied by Gross and Thompson. In the case of *Alexina Morrison vs. White*, Morrison is repeatedly described as having a "light sallow complexion, blue eyes and flaxen hair." But her appearance alone was not enough to win her freedom; instead, Morrison had to "demonstrat[e] purity and moral goodness to her [white] neighbors" in addition to "showing [her] beauty and whiteness in court."[27]

In the Creole fauborgs of New Orleans, neighborhood architecture reflected the occupants' need for exceptional status within the city and culture. As Thompson writes, "facilitating this insularity and intimacy, the 'Creole cottage,' the dominant mode of architecture in the Creole faubourgs, mediated the ongoing transaction among official laws, public custom, and

private desires, freedoms, and transgressions." The architecture of the Creole
cottage was very different from the typical American-style house:

> Usually lacking a front gallery and set right on the sidewalk, the Creole
> cottage expanded towards the back, opening up onto an interior court-
> yard and focused toward the kitchen and rear quarters. . . . The floor plan
> of the typical Creole cottage, however, suggested a lack of privacy inside
> homes, featured multiuse walkthrough rooms, two to the front and two
> to the rear with no center hallway as that characterizing an American
> townhouse.[28]

Thompson's reading of George Washington Cable's short story "Madame Del-
phine" shows how he emphasizes the architectural particularity of the Creole
cottage to evoke and create an atmosphere of interracial mixing, "moral compromises made by those practicing plaçage," and the "dogged permanence of
these social relationships despite decades of codification and legislation meant
to undermine them."[29]

Can a neighborhood, through its architecture and social traditions, resist
Jim Crow segregation without threatening white supremacy? The convergence
of factors that created the Faubourgs' racial and cultural uniqueness is also
at play in the historiographical and fictional representations of the black
colony on Martha's Vineyard. In West's column, the location of the cottage,
its décor, and its occupancy (whether it is a new home, or one long held)
are as important as the physical attributes of the owners. Jill Nelson observes
in *Finding Martha's Vineyard* that paying less for a cottage (meaning it
has been in the family forever) is a mark of higher-class standing than
paying too much, a tendency of the *nouveau riche*. The acquisition and maintenance of property is a central feature of black bourgeois desire and an
essential prerequisite for passing on wealth in American society. For West,
mapping the insular Highlands neighborhood is as important as recording
the genealogy of the first families that settled there. In *The Wedding*, she
carefully situates the architecture, the landscape, and the inhabitants of the
Highlands in a way that reinforces the enclave's proud heritage and necessary privacy:

> The Oval was a rustic stretch of flowering shrubs and tall trees, desig-
> nated on the old town map as Highland Park. The narrow dirt road that
> circled it was Highland Avenue. But since in no islander's memory had
> there ever been signposts to bring these ambitious titles to life, the area
> had long ago been assigned to the descriptive name that better suited it.
>   A baker's dozen of cottages made a ring around the park. Some were
> small and plain of façade, others were bigger and handsomer (one, the

Coles place, was called a mansion), and all of them were spruced up for the summer, set back precisely on immaculate squares of green lawn. They formed a fortress, a bulwark of colored society. Their occupants could boast that they, or even better their ancestors, had owned a home away from home since the days when a summer hegira was taken by few colored people above the rank of servant.[30]

This lengthy description situates the Highlands neighborhood as a special point of pride for its black denizens, but it also intrinsically links the type of architecture—the gingerbread cottage—to the larger history of Oak Bluffs. The gingerbread cottages that evolved from the campground meeting tents in Wesleyan Grove (Cottage City) were uniquely portable. Chris Stoddard describes them: "because the cottages are so light and compact, and were not rooted by plumbing or webbed with wiring, it was a relatively simple procedure to jack them up and trundle the things all over the place by means of log rollers, pulleys, and horsepower."[31] That was how several cottages made it to the Highlands. Later developers, especially those who saw Oak Bluffs as a middle-class alternative to Newport, built cottages in a variety of styles, by placing Queen Annes and Greek Revivals alongside traditional Cape Cods. The distinctiveness of the Cottage City, which even today is like walking through a fairytale village, became more expansive and luxurious as citizens expanded outward. Similar to the Creole cottages in Fauborgs, the Highland cottages feel intimate and insular. The dense woods and unpaved roads maintain a sense of privacy from the outside world. The homes are situated close together so that neighbors are easily viewed from the front porch or backyard.

The communities West wrote about deployed coping strategies designed to circumvent "inconveniences" that arose as a result of social and legal practice, rather than to escape black culture. Thompson argues that "demonstrating historical grounds for ownership and developing a cultural aesthetic of place are strategies that reinforce title, and when skillfully interwoven, ascribe meaning to particular places."[32] West's fiction, nonfiction, and oral histories serve a function similar to one the literary, oral, and legal representations of New Orleans serve for that community. A cursory perusal of legal proceedings on racial determination shows that the definitions of race were inconsistent and fluctuating. As Thompson observes, witnesses' "personal narratives and social etiquette corresponded to their hopes and aspirations rather than to their legal classification."[33] A similarly complex narrative of desire appears throughout West's writing. She simultaneously describes what she sees and creates what she does not. That tendency explains how West is able to function as both an oral historian of Oak Bluffs' black community and a writer who deftly uses the novel of manners as a successful genre for satire, entertainment, and above all social critique.

In my first chapter, "A 'Legend of Oak Bluffs'" I address the significance of Martha's Vineyard in West's life and life writing by excavating her numerous stories about how the "New Yorkers" "lost the beach for the Bostonians." Tracing the evolution of this story reveals how West simultaneously preserves and invents the social, historical, and racial geography of Oak Bluffs. In looking at how an incident peculiar to the unusual socioeconomic configuration of Martha's Vineyard gets recycled in West's interviews, fiction, nonfiction, and oral histories, I illustrate the social, economic, and cultural factors that converge, often violently, on the contested space of the beach.

Chapter 2, "A Charmed Childhood," examines West's protected, insulated girlhood and the crucial role her mother, Rachel West, played in her artistic development. West continually dramatizes her mother as a central figure in her formative life. Rachel appears as both a fictional character, most notably as the inspiration for Cleo Judson in *The Living Is Easy*, and a glamorous ideal in West's autobiographical writings. Does West's portrayal of her mother as young Brahmin socialite contradict Rachel's former identity as a migrant from South Carolina? West's mythologizing of her mother is in concert with her vague identification of the twelve black families that became regular "summer people" on the Vineyard. Were there really "Twelve Beauties of Boston" or "Twelve Families"? Or are these stories a myth-making exercise, part and parcel of West's desire to create and/or chronicle a black elite particular to the Northeast? If the "Twelve Beauties" did exist, then they may have been part of a concerted effort to identify particular black women as the feminine ideals of the race, a representative strategy reinforced by the regionally organized photographs of black socialites that regularly appeared in periodicals like the *Crisis*, *Messenger*, and *Opportunity*. This chapter also traces Dorothy's Brookline childhood as both the scion of the "Black Banana King" and part of a coterie of cousins raised within a matriarchal compound of aunts led by her mother. Dorothy's memories are of a domineering mother, a self-made father, and cousins with whom she is close but often unfavorably compared. Mr. West appears as the railroaded husband bankrupted by his wife's excesses in *The Living Is Easy*. West acknowledges that "her father was born a slave" but "that it meant absolutely nothing to me, because when I saw my father he was a businessman."[34] As West positions her family as one of the founding twelve, she considers her father to be a self-made man who models his strategy for success after Horatio Alger and Booker T. Washington. In actuality, her family existed in a liminal social space, not quite on a par with other black elite families either on the island or in Boston. This in-between position made West acutely attentive to class distinctions.

Chapter 3, "Dorothy West's 'Typewriter,'" follows her early career as a short story writer in Harlem. In the 1920s, Harlem was a "magic city." For black intellectuals and artists, it embodied the utopic ideals of the New Negro vanguard.

An analysis of West's early stories—namely "The Typewriter," "An Unimportant Man," and "Hannah Byde," which were published in three different New Negro periodicals—provides insight into her development as a writer and her public persona as a young ingénue in the Harlem Renaissance era. These stories manifest West's astute understanding of the interconnections of class, race, and gender hierarchies. Read collectively, they also reveal her recurring interest in dysfunctional marriages and how the black middle class negotiates domestic and urban spaces. This chapter also explores her relationships with other Harlem Renaissance figures, such as Wallace Thurman and Zora Neale Hurston. Rather than offering an exhaustive recap of the Harlem Renaissance, this chapter imagines how West and her cousin Helene Johnson might have experienced the city. Arriving late to the party in 1926, the cousins represented to established artists both the promise and the transience of the movement. This chapter also examines West's relationships to her literary mentors and the problem of patronage within the Harlem Renaissance. For female authors like West the plums bestowed on young, male prodigies like Langston Hughes were often out of their reach.

In chapter 4, "To Russia with Love," I follow West's excursions abroad and examine the influence of transatlantic exchange on Harlem Renaissance writers. Drawing from letters (primarily to her mother) and West's impression of London, Moscow, Leningrad, and Berlin, which she pronounces a "thrilling city" this section builds a unique travel narrative that is punctuated by her infatuation with Langston Hughes and her love affair with Mildred Jones. These letters contain whimsical observations like "Russians are like colored folks, slightly crazy."[35] Her letters offer an interior glimpse into West's complicated sexuality. Historians and critics are split on the question of West sexual orientation. Adelaide Cromwell denies that West had any sexual interest in women, while others, like Verner Mitchell and Cynthia Davis, see a clear indication of both fleeting, unrequited passion and long-term commitment. I read West's passionate, often embarrassing offers to Hughes to bear his child as somewhat performative and disingenuous. Like Hughes, she may have felt compelled to act out a veneer of heterosexuality. Or perhaps her understanding of her own sexuality was more fluid, and she felt attracted to both men and women. Whatever the case, her time in Russia leads to a period of sexual exploration and artistic maturity. This chapter also places West's personal relationships and politics within a larger body of meditative memoirs about Russia. I draw upon the memoirs of Nancy Prince, Claude McKay, Langston Hughes, Andrea Lee, and Louise Thompson to identify the Russian sojourn as a common feature of black artists' coming-of-political-age narratives. Russian society acts as an experimental milieu for black writers to explore the particular position of minority groups within societies structured according to class, regardless of societal proclivities such as communist, socialist, or democratic.

Chapter 5, "New Challenges," follows West's tumultuous tenure as the editor of the black literary journal *Challenge*. At the young age of twenty-five she not only published work by well-established writers such as Langston Hughes and Zora Neale Hurston but also provided an opportunity for newcomers like Ralph Ellison. Similar to Jessie Fauset, whose fiction for many years played second fiddle to her editorial role as a "literary midwife," West's editorial pursuits temporarily sidelined her own art. When Richard Wright, who took the literary world by storm when he published "Blueprint for Negro Writing," became coeditor of the journal, its name changed to the *New Challenge*. Aesthetic differences lad to the *New Challenge*'s demise. Also during this period West became romantically involved with her coeditor, Marian Minus.

Chapter 6, "The Living Is Easy," focuses on the writing, reception, and criticism of West's largely autobiographical masterpiece: *The Living Is Easy*. Part bildungsroman, part novel of manners, *The Living Is Easy* centers on the relationship between Judy, the young dark-skinned protagonist, and her mother, Cleo Judson, a beautiful, selfish ice queen. This chapter deals with the difficult placement of the novel within the Harlem Renaissance. Published in 1948, almost ten years after the era of artistic exploration and activism presumably ends, the novel's brutal satirizing of the black bourgeoisie and the failure of racial uplift prompts comparisons with Ann Petry's *The Street* and the naturalist novels of Richard Wright. Once again issues of class stratification coalesce around gender. The antiheroine in this novel closely resembles Edith Wharton's social-climbing vixen Undine Spragg in her novel *The Custom of the Country*. Like Undine Spragg, Cleo Judson reinvents herself and manipulates class definitions to suit her whims. I argue that one reason a novel that so successfully critiques capitalism and its values falls short of offering an alternative socioeconomic model is directly linked to the communist witch hunts undertaken by the federal and local governments following the passage of the 1940 Smith Act. This chapter also discusses how the publication of this novel complicates the periodization of the Harlem Renaissance and counters the assumed dearth of black fiction written between the first and second Black Arts movements.

In chapter 7, "Cottager's Corner," I ask an important question: What was West trying to achieve in her newspaper column that she could not confront in her fiction? Her *Vineyard Gazette* column began with a focus on black life on the island before expanding to broader topics. As in her fiction, the column illustrates how region, a sense of "old guard" entitlement, and a preoccupation with skin color and hair texture arising from miscegenation profoundly shape West's musings on class identity. As she tells Linsey Lee, "Black people of a certain class live better, talk better, and behave better than . . . All right. So that therefore my point is that they are often mistaken for rich people when they are not."[36] The intersections of these aspects of identity shape both her early fiction, which was much more sensitive to working-class issues, and her involvement in organizations like "The Cottagers."

Chapter 8, "Two Weddings" examines West's final novel and its transformation into the television miniseries that draws West back into the spotlight as the last surviving artist from the Harlem Renaissance. What appeal does *The Wedding* have for late twentieth-century audiences? Why does Oprah Winfrey choose to film *this* novel and not the more critically applauded *The Living Is Easy*? I examine the significant alterations to both the novel's plot and character descriptions (with regard to casting) as evidence of how difficult it is to legibly render racial ambiguity to a contemporary audience. Shelby, the novel's heroine, has "blond, sun-bleached tresses" and "beautiful blue eyes"; however, in the television adaptation, she is played by Academy Award–winning Halle Berry.[37] Unlike Shelby, whose African heritage is visually undetectable, Berry has copper skin and dark hair. In this case, casting decisions subtly change one theme of the text: the ironic situation of visually ambiguous African Americans who choose to live as black. Finally, given West's personification of the island's geography in the novel, the substitution of Wilmington, North Carolina, for Oak Bluffs in the television adaptation further distances the movie from its literary reference.

My coda, "Winter on Martha's Vineyard," considers one of West's unpublished essays as a meditation on her contribution to African American art and letters. Because this is an unconventional biography, the first chapter begins not with an examination of West's formative years and family history, but with the history of a place—a legend told and retold by West until it became a kind of truth that is stranger than fiction. In a way, *Dorothy West's Paradise* begins where it ends, on the beach.

1

A "Legend of Oak Bluffs"

The [New Yorkers] lost the beach for the Bostonians. That beach like no other, that tranquil spot at that tranquil end of the Island. All one summer the Bostonians saw it coming like a wave they could not roll back. It came the next summer. The beach became a private club, with a gate that only dogs could crawl under, and a sign that said, "For members only."

–Dorothy West, "Fond Memories of a Black Childhood"

The title of my biography intentionally evokes Toni Morrison's novel *Paradise*: a book that probes the viability of a radically exclusionary black nationalist enclave. Candice Jenkins argues in "Pure Black: Class, Color, and Intraracial Politics in Toni Morrison's *Paradise*" that African American class privilege and associated questions of skin color and racial authenticity are central to the novel.[1] Incidentally, Morrison published *Paradise* in 1998, three years after *The Wedding* (1995). Although both novels were published in the midst of debates around multiculturalism, this timing is important because the novels' "present times" return to that post–civil rights moment when unprecedented numbers of blacks were joining the middle class. To explain, justify, and historicize their fictive presents, both narratives also venture further back in time to the Reconstruction era.

If *Paradise* presents readers with what Jenkins describes as a "deeply flawed model of African American community building, driven by what is undeniably a black nationalist impulse,"[2] what elements of that community might be useful to think of in conjunction with West's portrayal of Oak Bluffs? One definition of "Ruby," the second town founded by the "8-rocks," references a term describing the very dark skin of the town's founding families:

> Unique and isolated, his was a town justifiably pleased with itself. It neither had nor needed a jail. No criminals had ever come from his town. And the one or two people who acted up, humiliated their families or

threatened the town's view of itself were taken good care of. Certainly there wasn't a slack or sloven woman anywhere in town and the reasons, he thought, were clear. From the beginning its people were free and protected. A sleepless woman could always rise from her bed, wrap a shawl around her shoulders and sit on the steps in the moonlight. And if she felt like it she could walk out the yard and on down the road. No lamp and no fear. A hiss-crackle from the side of the road would never scare her because whatever it was that made the sound, it wasn't something creeping up on her. Nothing for ninety miles around thought she was prey.[3]

The salient features of Ruby are a study in contradiction. It's a place of safety and isolation, where women are free and protected only within its boundaries and only if they adhere to its behavioral standards. Though Ruby is named after a woman, the narrator reiterates twice that it is "his town."

Just as gender and place are at the heart of Ruby's class dynamics, issues of class, color, region, and respectability underscore the many versions of what I call West's "lost beach story." This tale appears in nearly every genre of her writing, including the autobiographical sketch "Fond Memories of a Black Childhood," the unpublished novella *Where the Wild Grape Grows* that evolved into *The Wedding* (from which this story is conspicuously absent), and numerous interviews. I excavate West's story of how the "New Yorkers" "lost the beach for the Bostonians" in Oak Bluffs, Massachusetts, as a point of departure for this biography because it places the major thematic concerns in West's writing in conversation with the overall concerns of my book. Her recounting of this beach story through multiple mediums reveals how her journalism, fiction, and storytelling simultaneously preserved and invented specific aspects of Oak Bluffs' social history and racial geography. In tracing the literary and oral iterations of an incident peculiar to the unique location and population of Martha's Vineyard as it is recycled by West and echoed by her peers in interviews, pictorial archives, unpublished and published writings, I illustrate the social, economic, and cultural factors that converge, often violently, on the contested space of the beach.

The first version is taken from the transcript of an interview with Linsey Lee. Over the course of my research I listened to approximately thirty hours of oral interviews with West. Some interviews had already been transcribed; others I transcribed myself with the help of a research assistant. It is a challenge to transcribe West accurately because some tapes have corroded over time and she speaks very quickly. Still, the written text conveys her dynamic personality and precise diction; you can almost hear the Bostonian accent. Here is the pertinent excerpt:

The New Yorkers came, they had never, they will kill me for this, they had never had such freedom because you see you had the whole island here, if you understand, whereas the various beaches they had come from, Harlem Beach, they had section, I mean somebody owned a house, not one of them, but some year around Black person owned a house and therefore they went to the stretch of beach in front of that house. But here you could drive up to Gay Head, you could go all over, you could go to South Beach and one thing and another, so they had never had such freedom, and they wouldn't like that expression but the women wore, they were good looking women in good looking clothes and I'm sure they looked good, but they had paint on their faces and only sporting women I think was the phrase, only sporting women, a euphemism for kept women, smoked cigarettes, but even worse than that, they carried—you see they were boarding and they wanted to stay on the beach all day so they had food in baskets, and mostly chicken. Chicken I think travels well in baskets, but you see, we have a reputation for eating chicken so that there they were, and we said they are going to lose the beach for us, they are going to lose the beach and I swear to God, one summer we came down and it said Private, East Town Beach Club, Private.[4]

The general question to which West provides this extended narrative response is: "What are your earliest memories of the Vineyard here as a child?"[5] Just prior to the telling of this story West refers to one of Lee's earlier comments: "You speak of the division of Black and White." West's story is less about the division between black and white than it is about the unspoken, intraracial divisions between black and brown, Boston and New York, North and South. This story expresses the dichotomies between the Bostonians and the New Yorkers, separating us from them and identifying respectable women who were "quiet" in contrast to sporting women who publicly ate chicken, smoked cigarettes, and wore too much make-up. It is significant that West also identifies the New Yorkers as "boarders," rather than homeowners. This identification was a key distinction. To be a "Cottager," a member of an association of African American women on the island, you had to own your vacation home. Moreover, as author Jill Nelson describes it, such divisions persist: "Sometimes 'Us' is used by black homeowners with years of roots here, who refer to 'Them' as the weekend visitors, newcomers, who presumably lack the requisite longevity and black bourgeois credentials that would entitle them to the peaceful enjoyment of the island that is a public right."[6]

The recycling and refashioning of West's personal history is intimately intertwined with the complicated history of the blacks in Boston and on the island. The African American presence on Martha's Vineyard dates back to the late 1700s. The first blacks who came to the island included both enslaved Africans and free people of color in the service of their white employers. Although the island had a strong history of antislavery activism, Massachusetts did not abolish slavery until 1783. Probate records reveal that some landowners left land to their manumitted slaves. By the mid-nineteenth century the black community included indentured servants, skilled workers, laborers, and domestics. One of the earliest references to the African presence on the island in the *Vineyard Gazette* was Nancy Michael's obituary, dated January 2, 1857. Known as "Black Nance," Nancy Michael (1772–1857) was the daughter of Rebecca, an enslaved woman who was described as a "public pauper" and "looked upon as a witch."[7] Michael's descendant, William Martin, was a renowned whaling captain. The maritime culture and native (Wampanoag) population who intermarried and cohabited with the free black population shaped race relations on the island. William Martin was highly respected for his skills as a whaler and captained several voyages throughout his thirty-year career. Whaling was a dangerous business. Aboard ship, racial and ethnic hierarchies could be subverted or replaced by hierarchies based on skill level and experience. Despite his professional success, Martin did not live in an austere colonial in Edgartown with the white whaling captains;[8] instead, he built his house on Chappaquiddick among the native community.

Prior to the opening of Shearer Cottage in 1917, visitors stayed with friends on the island or in one of the few guesthouses run by enterprising black women innkeepers. Ora McFarlane, whom I met on my first trip to the Vineyard, still occupies the home purchased by Miss Louisa Izett in 1899 at what is now 121 Lower Circuit Avenue. Miss Izett and her sister, Georgia O'Brien, provided housing for seasonal workers in the inhospitable Edgartown and for vacationers in Oak Bluffs.[9] In 1868 the Vineyard Grove Co. designed the area known as the "Highlands," where West lived. As at Wesleyan Grove—the site of the Methodist campground known as Cottage City—at the heart of the design was a circular park, or "oval."[10] The Highlands' proximity to the coveted oceanfront in question is a critical part of the lost beach tale.

West's story is more than a nostalgic anecdote; this narrative line in the sand also appears in her later fiction with a less critical edge. Her oral recounting of the story is even more revealing when juxtaposed with fictionalized accounts of the same event. Looking at this event through each subsequent lens reveals how West illuminates the nuances of class stratification within the African American community. Her specific representations of the black elite explain how a small group prospered and successfully negotiated racial barriers to education and economic stability, while a majority of Americans of African descent remains economically disadvantaged and continues to struggle to reach a level playing field. Historian Kevin Gaines argues "through uplift's bourgeois evolutionism, black elites tried to alchemize elite status out of cultural narratives whose primary material was, and remained, ideologies of race."[11] West, then, engages in a kind of alchemy as she both recounts and invents the history of the black beach. For better or worse, she presents an imperiled black aristocracy whose environment is endangered by the shadow of the unrefined Negro brought to life as a New Yorker with "diamonds," "paint and powder," low-cut dresses, and "high heels."

I privilege the story of the lost beach because it occurs in a public terrain that allows for an extraordinary convergence of anxiety around interracial, interclass, and mixed gender interaction, the environment, ecological pollution, and ideas of social contagion. As contested spaces in transatlantic discourse of the African Diaspora—private or public, national or international, human or nonhuman—the beach and its waters exist as sites where the local becomes the global. I am thinking here of issues of access and ownership dramatized by the fact that these islands in the sun can be both "places of our own," to borrow from the title of Stanley Nelson's documentary, and spaces of rampant capitalism, sex tourism, and overdevelopment. As critical studies of the segregationist policies that led to the formation of American Beach in Florida and Highland Beach in Maryland can attest, the privatization of beaches involves various national, social, legal, economic, political, and ecological factors.[12]

In *Contested Waters: A Social History of Swimming Pools in America*, Jeff Wiltse examines how U.S. swimming pools were transformed from interracial, single-sex spaces in which class and gender were more important than race to "leisure resorts, where practically everyone in the community except black Americans swam together." His study then follows what he calls the second social transformation—"when black Americans gained access through legal and social protest" and "white swimmers generally abandoned them for private pools."[13] The various iterations of West's story, which discuss the span from 1950 to 1980, fall between these two moments in social and legal history. I am particularly intrigued by how the national history of segregated bathing areas informs the local, particular event described by West. Does the exclusion of blacks from the high beach parallel the segregation of public pools? In the early twentieth century, public bathing spaces were notoriously violent. The Chicago Riot in 1919 was touched off when white bathers threw rocks at black teenagers who had drifted into a white beach on Lake Michigan. Northerners' use of pools during the Progressive era reinforced class and gender but not racial distinction.[14] Working-class folk did not swim with the upper classes, but they were not as concerned about color. Following the Great Migration, the concerns about intimacy and sexuality that have always been latent in conversations about public space (in particular the public space of the pool) were directed at blacks. The peculiar democracy of the beach—in bathing suits it is more difficult to determine class—worked against black Americans. Wiltse marks this shift between the years of 1920 and 1940. The social changes that took place during this period shape West's complex politics.

Given that Wiltse marks gender integration as the "watershed in the history of municipal swimming pools," it is not surprising that all versions of West's story dress down the women.[15] It is possible that West emphasizes the improper behavior of the women so as not to further pathologize black men, who were read in interracial bathing spaces (as elsewhere) as sexually aggressive.[16] Her castigation of the "sporting women" also echoes black nationalist views on racial conservation and purity. In a nod to propriety she peculiarly offers a misleading definition of the term "sporting woman," a vernacular euphemism for prostitute, and substitutes the less pejorative "kept women." In his examination of black nationalist literature and the writings of turn-of-the century novelist Sutton Griggs, Kevin Gaines writes: "to ensure racial integrity and respectability, and to counter widespread accusations of black women's unchastity, black nationalists promoted fidelity to marriage and family ideals."[17] Similarly Gaines affirms "for educated blacks, the family, and patriarchal gender relations became crucial signifiers of respectability."[18] I'm not sure that West literally believes these women were "unchaste," but she certainly implies that they are tricked out in a manner that provokes such comparisons.

West's investment in surface indicators of female respectability is a persistent element in her oral history interviews and published writings. Remembering the preparations for her mother's funeral, West recounts when the undertaker told her "your mother is so beautiful I would like to leave [the coffin] open," she asserted that her mother preferred a closed casket. West then pointedly objected to the undertaker's application of makeup: "I knew that the man had painted the pink on her cheeks . . . and I didn't want my mother painted."[19] West did not want her mother to resemble the painted ladies on the beach in any way.

In her oral history West tells her interviewer that the "[New Yorkers] had never known such freedom" as they experienced on the high beach. Similarly, she described the same New Yorkers in her sketch "Fond Memories of a Black Childhood" as "brown" and "freedom drunk." West is not referring to the intoxicating quality of the island air. Instead, she points out how this group of interlopers "show color" through undisciplined behavior, conspicuous consumption, and their brown skin.[20] For the presumably lighter-skinned Bostonians, Martha's Vineyard beaches, including Gay Head (Aquinnah) and South Beach, appear to be exempted from the strife facing public bathing areas throughout the nation. In 1936 in Harlem, for instance, the "Thomas Jefferson Pool" was used almost exclusively by whites despite its proximity to neighborhoods of color whose inhabitants were deterred by white lifeguards and encouraged to patronize the "Colonial Park Pool" further uptown at 146th Street. Perhaps West's invocation of "Harlem Beach" is meant to contrast the Vineyard's natural beauty with the industrialized concrete design of the urban bathing areas many cities rushed to construct in the 1960s in out-of-the-way locations in order to pacify and "essentially quarantine angry black citizens."[21]

In West's unfinished novella *Where the Wild Grape Grows* (circa 1950), the New Yorkers' arrival is dramatized when islander Essie Carlson rents a bedroom in her home to a New Yorker who pays an exorbitant amount:

> That was the year the New Yorkers began their infiltration. Though one swallow does not make a summer, a dozen foreigners do seem to constitute a swarm. When they show color their number is multiplied ten times over in that strange arithmetic applied to dark minorities. One of the longest and loveliest beaches had, by its location, become the almost exclusive property of the wealthier whites and the colored Bostonians, who considered themselves in the same scale of society even if the same yardstick could not be applied as measure.
>
> To this sacred strand came the colored New Yorkers with the natural assumption that they were no different from the colored Bostonians. But they were.[22]

There are several ways to read this fictive rendering of a beach incident. The repeated dramatizations of the story show that it is more than anecdotal history; it is also a mythmaking and disciplining text. Those who claim West as an astute satirist of black capitalist desires (a precursor to Stephen Henderson or a sister of E. Franklin Frazier) might read this as a humorous mockery of regional distinctions or a critique of white liberal New Englanders who benevolently tolerate difference only when it is virtually invisible, when successful mimicry renders the black beachgoers almost indistinguishable and therefore recognizable and therefore nonthreatening. West suggests that by choosing to sit together rather than in discrete parties of two or three, the New Yorkers "showed their color." In other words, they made themselves conspicuous to such an extent that their small numbers were amplified in the minds of whites by a bizarre racial arithmetic. Such statements illustrate West's belief that moderating behavior promotes racial tolerance and exceptionalism. In fact, she dramatizes this particularly New England attitude in *The Living Is Easy* when she describes two main characters on a streetcar: "[the White Bostonians] did not stare at Cleo and Judy, but they were discreetly aware of the pair, and appreciative of their neat appearance. Boston whites of the better class were never upset or dismayed by the sight of one or two Negroes exercising equal rights. They cheerfully stomached three or four when they carried themselves inconspicuously. To them the minor phenomenon of a colored face was a reminder of the proud role their forebears had played in the freeing of the human spirit for aspirations beyond the badge of house slave."[23] The irony of the incident is more pronounced because the reader is meant to be skeptical of New England benevolence.

Another way to read West's odd delineation is that it constitutes not so much a mocking critique of white liberal views as a policing of intraracial class lines. The "New Yorkers" "show color" by being darker-skinned, congregating in large rather than in small numbers, and engaging in excessive behavior that is directly at odds with thrifty New England values by paying exorbitant amounts for lodging and wearing diamonds. This story had meaning for West; otherwise, she would not have continued to mine it for its fictional and nonfictional potential during a forty-year period. With each repetition the tale becomes denser. Each version adds a layer that is only rendered visible when they are placed side by side. Note the difference between how this scene constructed in "Fond Memories" contrasts with the oral history recounted to Linsey Lee: "The New Yorkers did not talk in low voices. They talked in happy voices. They carried baskets of food to the beach to make the day last. They carried liquor of the best brands. They grouped together in an ever increasing circle because what was the sense of sitting apart?"[24] In short, they had a good time, and they were conspicuously wealthy, whereas the Bostonians "left [their diamonds] at home."[25] This scene resembles a minstrel tableau. Popular vaudeville sketches featured blackface performers who mocked the very idea of a black elite, which they viewed as a hopeless attempt to ape the Euro-American aristocracy. Given the migratory patterns of southern blacks, the appellation "New Yorker" might also have meant southerner. West is not the only Oak Bluffs resident who notices how regional differences overdetermine class perception and performance. The sociologist and historian Adelaide Cromwell observes that the opening of Shearer Cottage and the influx of famous New Yorkers like Adam Clayton Powell drew vacationers from beyond the Boston area. In contrast to the New Yorkers, who liked to party and socialize, Cromwell explains: "Bostonians, they were very dull. And they didn't have much money to spend, and they didn't believe in spending what they did have that way."[26]

The underlying anxiety of the narrator underscores the reality that the black elite's position (on and off island) is necessarily precarious as it is dependent on the cheerful, good-natured tolerance of whites. This is why, as Kevin Gaines writes, early twentieth-century urban migration was not always advocated by the black elite, as it posed an imminent threat to their own precarious status in the city. West's characterization is commensurate with Gaines's argument that "although numbers of elite blacks had migrated, other black elites opposed migration and resorted to pejorative minstrel representation to describe black migrants to the city." In a more pointed observation, the kind of behavior exhibited by the New Yorkers "represented the antithesis of black progress and respectability."[27]

Another example of this outlandish behavior revolves around the New Yorkers' choice and consumption of food. In various versions of the story West and/or her narrator object to how they transport and eat their meals. West tells her interviewer in a slightly joking voice that "we have a reputation for eating

chicken." In another fictive example she writes that after the New Yorkers visited the beach "chicken bones littered the sand."[28] Why is chicken an important
reference here?

Chicken, otherwise known as "the gospel bird," has a particular resonance in African American culture as a comfort food, a conveyer of culture
and essential nutrition; it is also a nuanced marker of class. Psyche Williams-
Forson argues for the centrality of the "gospel bird" within African American
food culture.[29] Segregation laws denied black travelers access to the whites-
only dining car. To eat they had to travel with their own food. The main dish
packed in these box lunches was frequently fried chicken, hence the moniker
"Chicken Bone Express." Aboard the railway system, chicken provides vital
nourishment for travelers moving to and through the South. When Dorothy
West refers to the chicken eaten on the beach, she invokes a context that
Williams-Forson examines in detail in her book: the notion that chicken is
uniquely portable. West tells her interviewer: "you see they were boarding
and they wanted to stay on the beach all day so they had food in baskets,
and mostly chicken. Chicken I think travels well in baskets, but you see, we
have a reputation for eating chicken so that there they were."[30] For West,
chicken becomes anathema precisely because it is expected. She recognizes
chicken's resiliency and its ability to provide mobile nourishment, thereby
admitting to an understanding of its role in black culture; however, she is
well aware of the array of negative stereotypes associated with chicken that
appeared in advertisements and minstrel shows.

In her fiction, West uses food to mourn cultural loss and illustrate the
process of assimilation into a new, urban space. In the short story "The Typewriter," the narrator regrets the northern substitution of Boston beans and
franks for southern delicacies such as cornbread and fried salt pork. Williams-
Forson scrutinizes the menu Cleo Judson serves at a charity dinner in *The
Living Is Easy*. She notes the absence of chicken and correctly argues that Cleo
"holds the party to impress upon her neighbors and friends that she has indeed
learned the behaviors and comportment necessary for inclusion in their social
set."[31] Also missing from the menu are the dishes that Cleo relishes: "peaches
and cream, butter-soaked muffins, chops, hashed-brown potatoes, broiled
bananas, sliced tomatoes and pie for whoever had the capacity."[32] Instead, Cleo
seeks to impress her guests by offering a lavish spread that includes lobster,
grapefruit, Welsh rarebit, and tea sandwiches. Williams-Forson argued that the
absence of chicken from Cleo's table is glaringly indicative of her self-denying
social aspirations.

West's ambivalent invocation of chicken in the lost beach story affirms
both its practicality and its problematic status. Williams-Forson observes that
"having good food that traveled well was clearly essential given that some
journeys could take hours and even days."[33] For West, however, the New York-

ers' need to preserve their foods only emphasizes their lack of entitlement and propriety. "Nice people," West tells interviewer Nancy Safford, "should eat at home." And that is precisely the point she uses her story to make. New Yorkers are boarders: a transitory group regionally distinct from the black Brahmins who should not be allowed to permanently alter the environment.

In *Transcending the Talented Tenth*, Joy James shows that despite Du Bois's eventual repudiation of the talented tenth theory of racial uplift, black intellectuals maintain a symbolic investment in the flawed notion that a privileged few can save the majority of African Americans. That symbolic investment is evident in Lawrence Otis Graham's biography of Blanche K. Bruce, *The Senator and the Socialite: The True Story of American's First Black Dynasty*. Graham traces the Bruce family's rise to social and political prominence. Their ascent ultimately alienated them from both black and white communities and ended in a tragic, downward spiral. Although West's fiction often satirized the black elite and poked fun at the idea of a black dynasty similar to the family chronicled in Graham's book, by setting the New Yorkers apart from the Bostonians she actually affirms intraracial class divisions. Moreover, her repeated memorialization of the lost beach places blame on the shoulders of invading New Yorkers who could not or would not perform respectability, rather than on club owners who privatized a formerly public space.

The Lost Beach

It is a challenge to reconstruct in time and space the exact tranquil strip of paradise to which West refers. While not exactly cosigning West's characterization, historian Adelaide Cromwell confirms that "High [Highland] Beach was purchased for the Yacht Club to which no Black could belong, thus forcing them to use the beach closer to the wharf, just below Ocean Park."[34] This beach, later known as Inkwell Beach, is located just off the area known as the "Gold Coast," "the area roughly between Circuit Avenue and the Sound, from Tuckernuck Avenue to Ocean Park."[35] According to Robert Hayden, the Gold Coast turned from white to black in the 1950s and 1960s.[36] Another longtime Vineyard resident, Eloise Downing Allen, explains that in 1947, when she first came to the island, "There were no signs saying white or colored, but it was understood" that the "ten cents beach" was "for the white people."[37] By 1947, the racial harmony of the beach had been lost, a loss that West memorializes again and again in her fiction and prose. It is more than a loss of access, because there are always other beaches; rather, it is the loss of the ideal of hard-won interracial harmony, of a nostalgic space where black and white cohabitated in "that tranquil spot at the tranquil end."[38] The privatization of the beach and the inauguration of the Inkwell are fissures that subtly undermine social and artistic constructions of the island as an interracial paradise.

Martha's Vineyard's historic black presence is often left out of histories like Dona Brown's *Inventing New England,* even though it is well known in local circles and has been documented in fiction, film, memoirs, and lay histories of the island. From Oak Bluffs' beginning as a Methodist camp meeting site called "Cottage City," the town combined the secular and sacred. Visitors expanded beyond those who came to worship at the Iron Tabernacle at Wesleyan Grove. According to Brown, Martha's Vineyard became an alternative to the more elite areas of Newport or Saratoga by appealing to families "poised at the edge of the middle class."[39] That position aptly describes some early black families who settled in the Highlands area, where West lived, in contrast to the "newcomers" living in the Gold Coast.

Acting as island historiographer, West writes about the first settlers of the black colony: "They numbered no more than a dozen, and they were mainly Bostonians. That gave them a group identity and a cohesiveness that established them as solid members of the larger community. Because they were few in number, their contacts had to spread outward. A harmony resulted that set the pattern for years to come. On occasion that harmony may sag, but it never shatters."[40] The loss of the beach definitely disturbed that harmonious pattern. The proximity of the beach to the Highlands' colony was a key element of the area's desirability. Once the beach became privatized, how the residents experienced Oak Bluffs changed. To access the water, they now had to walk a significant distance to the pay beach. Through West's retelling the incident becomes almost mythic. Although she does not directly connect it to the origins of Inkwell Beach, others do. For West, the significance of the story is the *loss* of Highland Beach, rather than the gaining of Inkwell.

To borrow a term from Toni Morrison, West constructs Highland Beach as a site of "disallowing." In Morrison's *Paradise*, when the light-skinned blacks of the aptly named "Fairly, Oklahoma," reject the 8-rocks on the basis of their skin color, the moment acquires a mythic significance: the trauma of the "disallowing" provides the glue that holds their tight-knit community together and solidifies their own embrace of exclusionary practices. Ironically, the image that lingers and is ascribed a skewed value in the town fathers' memory is a photograph of "nineteen negro ladies" in "summer dresses" "with creamy, sunlit skin."[41] Why were these particular women singled out to be photographed? Why did their images imprint so vividly on the patriarchal shepherds of black womanhood in Ruby? And what does this have to do with West's fond recollection of her mother as one of the "twelve beauties of Boston"? In Martha's Vineyard's visual archives and in histories of the island blacks a certain noticeable aesthetic prevails over the beachside shots collected from family albums. Stanley Nelson's film *A Place of Our Own* explores the predominance of light-skinned blacks in the community. Nelson interviews residents who remember feeling or being excluded on the basis of skin color in their youth. Such experiences, seemingly the exception rather than the rule, can be ameliorated by family name, occupation, and education. An obvious distinction between the loss of the beach for the black colony in Martha's Vineyard and the disallowing of the 8-rock pioneers in *Paradise* is that the white club owners erected the gates on Highland Beach; however, West's implication of the "The New Yorkers" makes it both an intraracial and an interracial incident.

I have not yet been able to pinpoint the exact date of the founding of the East Chop Beach Club; employees told me they celebrated their sixty-fifth anniversary in 2005. The club was most likely established in the early 1940s, a date commensurate with the conditions described in the oral histories. The acclaimed painter and longtime Vineyard resident Lois Mailou Jones acknowledges: "we did have some problems at the Highland bathing beach. I mean there began to be restrictions that blacks could not swim there and that was very upsetting because we had been swimming there for years, and then for it to be claimed as a beach for the East Chop Beach Club was quite an affront."[42] Jones also attributes her artistic success to a formative conversation on Highland Beach with artist Meta Vaux Warrick Fuller and composer Henry Burleigh. Burleigh said, "you're not going to make it in this country," and inspired Jones to go to France. Barbara Townes, another resident, remembers: "When I was a young child we went to . . . Highland Beach. . . . We all went together and you walked. . . . I remember when they told the people that used Highland Beach that they could not use it anymore. It had been a public beach, but now they were leasing it to a group of people from East Chop. . . . They refused to have any black people on the beach."[43] Unlike West's story, these accounts do not attribute the beach's loss to either a lack of respectability or a failure to adhere to Bostonian standards of behavior. They do hint, however, at the problem of black visibility. Neither Townes nor Jones suggests that allegedly darker-skinned blacks from New York had anything to do with the beach's privatization, but they also do not necessarily contradict West's insistence that "unobtrusiveness" had held the beach. From West's perspective, the injustice resulted from improper manners.

It might be more than a coincidence that in 1947 another beachside retreat for African Americans was founded in Sag Harbor, New York. Azurest, a small community nestled on the bay side of the Hamptons, celebrated its fiftieth anniversary in 2007. Just as Coles' Corners and Dorothy West Avenue honor the names of established residents in the Oak Bluffs' Highlands, Terry Drive in Sag Harbor's Azurest neighborhood honors the woman whom novelist Colson Whitehead calls the "spiritual architect of the developments" in his semi-autobiographical novel *Sag Harbor* (2009).[44] Whitehead sums up the historic land grab in a neat paragraph:

The twenty acres belonged to a man named Mr. Gale, who'd been trying
to unload them for some time. No one wanted the parcel. It wasn't on
the Atlantic, like the prime acreage of Bridgehampton, South Hampton,
etc. Terry hatched a plan where she'd sell the lots for him—to her friends,
to her friends' friends, and so on, the middle-class black folk of their
acquaintance—$750 for an inside lot, $1000 for a beachfront lot. The
word went out. One by one the houses went up.[45]

The unanswered question remains: "What incident put the idea in her head,
what kind of day or evening did she have to make her hope and scheme, think
up such a thing?"[46] A perusal of the *Chicago Defender*'s social columns reveals
that African Americans were visiting Sag Harbor as early as 1923, prior to the
formal development of Azurest. An article entitled "Return from Sag Harbor"
lists Regina Anderson (a socialite, playwright, and librarian) and Charles
Johnson (a sociologist whom historians credit as one architect of the Harlem
Renaissance) among the vacationers returning home to Philadelphia, Newark,
and Brooklyn.

It takes a visionary consciousness to tap into a collective desire, circumvent segregation and restrictive covenants, and build a separate, but viable,
alternative community. In the case of Oak Bluffs, it is possible that the survival
strategies developed over time by black Bostonians provided the blueprint
for development of the island's black colony. George Levesque in *Black Boston:
African American Life and Culture in Urban America, 1750–1860* does not touch
on the island blacks; however, his analysis of black life in Boston illuminates
the psychological mindset of the pioneering vacationers. Levesque writes: "The
survival strategies devised by nonslave blacks to cope with their unenviable
condition were subtle and complex and if we would uncover and understand
these strategies, we must be prepared to look at present formalisms in a new
light and to jettison their use altogether if their use conceals the social reality
they were intended to reveal."[47] Levesque focuses on churches and schools, and
his examination reveals that the tensions between separatist and assimilationist tendencies are very complex. He argues that "elements from both cultures
were so inextricably bound and black ambivalence toward each so ingrained
that the end result was the creation of a hybrid third-culture. The key of this
middle way was physical survival—an objective endorsed by accommodationists
and segregationists alike."[48] One wonders how Levesque would respond to the
arguments that postintegration "bright flight"—when those African Americans
who could afford to live in newly desegregated neighborhoods fled—resulted in
the destruction of primarily black communities and their internal economies?
The constitution of the Vineyard enclave is so unusual because early Bostonians
and other African Americans who settled there seemed to be flying to what
would become a black, utopic space. Subsequently, the post–civil rights resi-

dents continued to arrive in a kind of second (temporary in the case of summer residents) flight from predominantly white neighborhoods.

The visionaries who bought property and opened guest houses at the turn of the century followed a version of Levesque's middle way to create a hybrid culture that existed alongside mainstream resort settlements. The Oak Bluffs community, older and more established than Long Island's Azurest, also enjoys national popularity. President Barack Obama's family vacationed on the island in the first and second years of his presidency, though he did not rent a house in Oak Bluffs, but in Chilmark. Yet which tradition was the president following? Martha's Vineyard was also a favorite with the Clintons, and the island became infamously associated with the Kennedys, especially following the incident with Senator Edward Kennedy on Chappaquiddick.[49] Local lore credits (or blames) the Clintons for the island's inflated real estate values and increased popularity. President Obama's choice to spend his Augusts on Martha's Vineyard replicates the travel patterns of many affluent blacks who vacation on the island, traditionally in the month of August, to enjoy paradise among their peers. The definition of peer, as we can see from West's example, is certainly subject to interpretation. African American political icons like Adam Clayton Powell (1908–1972) and Senator Edward Brooke were some of the island's first nationally prominent visitors. The island may not be a racial utopia; however, providing a vacation home for the family of the first African American president does quite a bit to bolster its reputation as such.

During my tenure as one of Oak Bluffs' summer people, day-trippers and weekenders frequently asked me about the Inkwell. Some approached with curiosity; others with apprehension. For some, it was a welcome experience to relax on a beach that was truly interracial. Others appeared uneasy, as if the self-segregation on the beach recalled the legal and social practice that necessitated its founding. A woman and her partner asked me in surprise, "Is this the Inkwell?" They seemed disappointed that on that particular afternoon the site did not live up to its name. Another visitor sought confirmation that blacks were "welcome" on other beaches on the island. The Inkwell exists as a bittersweet site of commemorative nostalgia. There is a celebration of leisure on Oak Bluffs; the ability to relax on one's seaside porch is in itself a breaking of racial barriers. A tour bus often passed by our rented cottage, aptly named "The Sea Horse," at the noon hour. At one point, the bus was full of predominantly African American passengers. Upon seeing my husband in repose upon the porch, several tourists gave him a Black Power salute, which he returned. Why offer an impromptu, outdated, nationalist response to affirm an ultimately bourgeois act? That the twenty-first-century spectacle of a black man engaging in a leisure activity on a porch within sight and steps of the Inkwell prompts not condemnation, but affirmation, illustrates that black nationalist desires manifest a complex tension among separatism,

self-determination, and assimilation. The persistent return of black vacationers is not a demand for integrationist inclusion. It is a claim of entitlement.
Historian and island resident Manning Marable explains: "Part of what racism does in the U.S. is deny black folks notions of celebration, of leisure,
of creative cultural space to do your own thing. I think what black folk for
several generations have tried to do is to carve out those niches where they
can find their own voice, where they can celebrate with their friends, and
where you don't have to explain a damn thing."⁵⁰

In "The Legend of Oak Bluffs," West ascribes a mythic quality to the "Black
colony," with its "little pockets" of "acceptable people." Of necessity that select
group excludes immigrants from the Deep South not just because they pack
chicken in baskets like the New Yorkers but also because they "might bring
their attitudes and uncertainty to a place where blacks did not hang back to
let the whites go first."⁵¹ There is no satirical language in "Legend." Sentimental phrases like "the Island was the home of my heart" are commonplace. The
historiographical writing is seductively pastoral and very similar to the lyric
sensibility that West brings to "Winter on Martha's Vineyard," a short essay
about the natural topography of the island. When she writes "there was a magic
in island living," you believe her.

Other African American artists who resided on the island, such as Lois
Mailou Jones, echoed West's tendency to revel in the island's picturesque
qualities. Both the Joneses and the Wests were longtime summer residents. In
a 1909 photograph both families pose in front of the Joneses' residence. At one
time, the Joneses' grandmother, Phoebe Ballou, actually owned several acres in
both Edgartown and Oak Bluffs. Lois Mailou Jones taught art at Shearer Cottage
before she went on to international acclaim for her portraits and landscapes.
Several of her paintings showcase the island's ethnic heritage, maritime culture, and sublime vistas. The impressionistic *Indian Shops, Gay Head* (1940),
which won the Robert Wood Bliss Prize for Landscape in 1941, captures the lumi-
nescent quality of the afternoon light off the cliffs. Her inclusion of a large tent
with the wooden storefronts gives the piece a sense of timelessness and marks
the space as native land. Wampanoag-owned commerce is still present at Gay
Head, or "Aquinnah" (Wampanoag for "land under the hill"), as it is now known.
That Jones's visual archive includes paintings from every corner of the island's
public space, from Oak Bluffs' *Flying Horses* carousel to *Fishing Shacks, Menem-
sha, Massachusetts* (1932), suggests that black vacationers were not restricted to
the Inkwell. Jones recalls:

> I'll always remember finishing school in June as a child and getting the
> trunks packed and ready to go. It was a delight to take the train to Wood's
> Hole, where we boarded the ferry. Looking out on the ocean—smelling
> the salt air and seeing the seagulls flying and the big boat coming—was

breathtaking. It was the most wonderful experience of my life to get on that boat. When we arrived, we would take the horse-drawn buggies up the hill to 25 Pacific Avenue.

The fields of daisies and buttercups and the beauty of the landscape and the ocean were overwhelming. This beauty affected my life to the extent that I am to this day a great lover of nature. I think that my experiences on the Vineyard interested me in painting and have motivated me to paint the beauty of the island even to this day.[52]

Jones's memories document the historical experience of black vacationers on the island. She pays sharp attention to the ecological topography of the island—the features that set it off from the mainland United States, literally and figuratively. The language she uses to describe the journey and the arrival is hyperbolic, a remembrance replete with utopic diction. The island scenery is "overwhelming," and the sensory details are "breathtaking." Most important, Jones positions the "most wonderful experience of her life" as the genesis of her artistic talent.

"Where do you summer?" is a question heavy with geographic presumption. You would never ask it of a Los Angeles native. It is a question that immediately evokes a privileged vocabulary linked to the eastern seaboard. Like many insular communities with a transient population, the island has its own vocabulary to define, describe, and distinguish. "To summer" reverberates with cultural and economic expectations. It conjures a social network that operates just beyond the strata of the everyday by implying that people, like birds, still migrate with the change of seasons. Of course, a colony has more implicit meanings than those inscribed by an ornithologist. That novelists and historians refer to the occupants of the Highlands in Oak Bluffs as the original black colony invokes a cluster of early settlers willing to purchase property through white go-betweens and even more determined to live without reminders of the hoops through which they had to jump to acquire their land. In Stephen Carter's novel *The Emperor of Ocean Park*, the narrator maps out the Highlands:

> I start at East Chop Drive, which leads up to the old lighthouse and what used to be called the Highlands. At the foot of the bluffs is a private beach club. In the middle of the Chop is a private tennis club. East Chop, for all its crisp New England beauty, has a whiter feel than the rest of Oak Bluffs. Not many of the summer residents seem aware that East Chop was once the heart of the Island's black colony.[53]

Because of the Highlands' proximity to "Eastville," an area that had the largest population of blacks from the late 1780s through 1835, it was a logical black settlement.[54] In this passage, the imperialist connotations of "colony" have a disturbing resonance on an island that still includes Native American sovereign territories and whose street names, like "Pequot Ave," recall its indigenous heritage.

Once on-island, the black colony did not want to be reminded by whites or blacks of the racial divisions that existed "off-island." Visitors did not want to be flies in the buttermilk, nor did they have a particular yearning for an all-black beach. A major attraction of the island was that it fulfilled the desire for a space where race could become secondary to class. Until very recently, there were two mailboxes in Oak Bluffs: one for "On island" and the other labeled "America." In the minds of black summer colonists, this critical distinction rang with a certain hard truth: coming to the island was not merely a vacation from work, but an escape from the structural racism and social segregation that plagued late nineteenth-century America through the civil rights era. The island also proved the persistence of unequal social and economic policy that continues to beleaguer the country in the twenty-first century. For this utopic space to exist, one must follow the blueprint and avoid the fractures and fault lines that exist, even in paradise.

In an age in which environmentalism has begun to supplant social justice on the liberal agenda, issues of ecological conservation overshadow racial conservation. Jill Nelson maintains that the "the Vineyard is not a racial utopia."[55] The tensions evident in West's story of the beach reemerged when an influx of newcomers flooded the islands in the late 1990s. The vocabulary of "us" and "them" returned. I focused on the lost beach story because it exemplifies how a close reading of West's life and life-writing illuminates the nuances of class stratification among African Americans. The enduring question remains: how does one perform a class position that ameliorates or qualifies racial identity? The fictions of entitlement and exclusivity staged and restaged in West's fiction and nonfiction reveal the nefariousness of class boundaries in the black community at a time when African American identity and citizenship was in violent flux.

2

Childhood Sketches

The house that I grew up in was four-storied, but we were an extended
family, continually adding new members, and the perpetual joke was, if
we lived in the Boston Museum, we'd still need one more room. Sur-
rounded by all these different personalities each one wanting to be first
among equals, I knew I wanted to be a writer. Living with them was like
living inside a story.

—Dorothy West, "Rachel"

Taking an inspirational cue from West's description of her childhood home
at 478 Brookline Avenue, this chapter traces "four storie[s]" that repeat in
nearly every form and genre of writing she undertook.[1] Instead of providing
a linear chronology of West's childhood or recapitulating what can be found
in her own life-writing, this chapter follows the myths West relates to various
audiences while explaining and fashioning her persona as a writer. These
stories manifest the tension literary critic Sidonie Smith identifies as latent in
much of women's autobiography: "that 'truthtelling' and 'lying' lie close to one
another, affectionately and contentiously intermingling with and intervening
with one another."[2] My intent is not to prove these stories factual or false;
instead, I seek to probe their impact on West's self-presentation, explore how
they inform her understanding of her position in her family, and discuss how
she relays that position to her many readers. Similar to the permutations of the
lost beach story, as each tale is recycled through various genres and interviews
its significance accrues.

West never wrote a formal autobiography; however, from the extensive
interviews she gave during the course of fifty years, her published and unpublished "sketches and reminiscences," and the autobiographical elements that
appear in her fiction, one could compile an autobiography from what appears
to be, on the surface, a massive amount of personal and historical information.
Several factors complicate this task: the repetition that occurs throughout

West's papers and writings, her resistance to direct questioning, and her tendency to intertwine her familial history with that of a place or a people. Her famous digressions have prompted interviewers to take creative license with their presentation of the interviews in written form. Genii Guinier, her interviewer for the Black Women's Oral History Project in 1978, made almost no alterations. Her lengthy interview is not only the most comprehensive but also the most frustrating and impenetrable. For example, consider West's typical response to a direct question: Guinier asks where she attended college, and West pontificates, remarking that Harvard, which she did not attend, is the only respectable college. Her nonresponse echoes a line from *The Living Is Easy*. In the novel, Cleo Judson's young nephew Tim "expected to go to Harvard. He had never heard there was any other university."[3] In contrast to Guinier, feminist scholar and literary critic Deborah McDowell compressed her interview into a tidy package that primarily illuminated West's role in the Harlem Renaissance. Katrine Dalsgård falls somewhere in between, and the bulk of the interviews done by Linsey Lee—the oral history curator at the Martha's Vineyard Museum—focuses on West's relationship to the island and her self-appointed, *Gazette*-sanctioned role as the social historian of the black colony.[4] Still, enough of a pattern, or rather a thematic cluster, emerges to allow me to trace common themes and stories that repeatedly surface in West's life-writing and oral histories about her childhood.

After my reading transcripts and listening to hours of West's interviews, following her abrupt transitions and appreciating her recurrent interjection of "Dahlin'" as almost a caesura in the unimpeded flow of conversation, a few distinct phrases stand out; these assertions appear with a curious frequency in her interviews and published life writings. The first, "My mother was one of the twelve beauties of Boston," provides a point of entry into the life of the person who most influenced West's writing and character development: Rachel Pease Benson West (1878–1954).[5] In perusing her autobiographical writings it is difficult to remember that West was an only child. Throughout the short stories "Rachel" and "Fond Memories," she uses the first person plural. That an only child would write about her mother from the perspective of "we" says a great deal about the closeness of her extended family. In "Rachel," West slips back and forth between "my mother" and "we who had been the children under her command."[6] If we take West's view at face value, the matriarchal household headed by Rachel West was one in which she reigned supreme. Who was Rachel West? Without her mother would West have become a writer or created Cleo Judson—one of the most captivating antiheroines in African American fiction?

The next assertion is West's identification of her father as "the Black Banana King," a way of emphasizing her father's unique entrepreneurial role in the family and black Boston economic scene. In the oral histories her father is a legendary figure with a supernatural ability to ripen fruit. Her paternal stories reflect enticingly on her parents' marriage and the unusual power dynamic in her family, the source of narrative tension in many of her short stories and the novel that, as Abigail McGrath (Helene Johnson's daughter) recounts, includes the only "written version" of the West family's financial history.

The proliferation of late twentieth- and early twenty-first-century memoirs and autobiographical fictions have thematized the complex identity of mixed-race individuals to such an excess that the identity conflicts of biracial children have become familiar, hypertheorized, and occasionally stereotypical. But what of intraracial color conflicts within the same family? As a young girl whose position in the family is both favored—she is the only child of Isaac West and Rachel Benson—and marked as "the only dark child," West struggles with her darker complexion.[7] Two examples of autobiographical stories from women of color provide a helpful context for West's constant reflection on her color and position in her family. The first is from Cherrie Moraga's groundbreaking memoir *Loving in the War Years* (1983). In her familial structure Moraga is the light-skinned daughter of a brown mother. To claim her identity as Chicana, Moraga has to eschew her fair skin to claim her mother's racial identity. Sidonie Smith notes, "being 'fair skinned' or 'white' becomes the 'lie' of identity for [Moraga] as she negotiates the dialogical and polylogical implications of her position as a lesbian Chicana feminist in Anglo culture."[8] The spatial and ethnic context of Moraga's autobiography (the border[s] between Mexican America and Anglo America) is markedly different from black Boston; however, the language of light and dark and the fusion of class status/societal position with skin color is a transnational inheritance of colonialism that crosses borders. Another poignant example of the rifts caused by intraracial colorism appears in Michelle Cliff's poetry collection, which is aptly titled *Claiming an Identity They Taught Me to Despise* (1980). Cliff's prose poems provocatively underline the difference in skin color in her family as a violent fracture. In contrast to the harmonic notion that there is "no color foolishness" in her family—a concept that West attempts to sell to her readers and interviewers—Cliff writes: "in my family I was called 'fair'—a hard term. My sister was darker, younger. We were split—along lines of color and order of birth."[9] Here the word "fair" is not a complement but a pejorative category that "splits" the sisterly bonds of Cliff's family. Again, the Jamaican context is not the same as West's Bostonian/Vineyard upbringing, but West's desire to assure her audience that there was no difference in terms of how she was treated in her family has a false note that sounds clearly in the accusations she levels unfairly at her mother.

West's obsession with color and class can certainly be traced to her childhood, but not all family members share that obsession. McGrath notes that "much has been written about our being 'Boston Brahmins' and people of privilege" but that it was Dorothy, as opposed to her cousin Helene, who seemed most invested in such distinctions—"Helen[e] never aspired to be rich, that was Dorothy's thing."[10] The fact that West inherits neither her mother's beauty nor light complexion hangs over her childhood stories. Abject poverty and systematic racial discrimination, factors that burdened many black children born at the turn of the century, do not appear to have haunted her childhood. West may not have been born with a silver spoon in her mouth, but her family stories deviate sharply from the standard up-from-slavery trajectory. In the class-based hierarchies of Black Boston and the Martha's Vineyard enclave of the Highlands, West defines her family as one of the "genteel poor"—a somewhat ironic and precarious category. Abigail McGrath seems to concur with West's assessment of their position; she affirms that they "were a family of substance," but "shabby gentility" at best.[11]

West's position as an outsider within the black Brahmin set allows her such a privileged and reflective perspective on the social maneuverings, complexities, and struggles of Boston's black elite. In *The Souls of Black Folk* W.E.B. Du Bois uses his personal experience of his first realization of his blackness, of "how it feels to be a problem," to formulate a theory of race consciousness for African Americans.[12] No such moment seems to arrive dramatically for West. Instead, her family unit seems to have forthrightly prepared her and her cousins for the roles they would play in the white world. Rachel fostered a defiant stance predicated on exceptionalism among both whites and blacks who did not meet her standard of excellence. What made the Wests exceptional? How were they able to circumvent the pitfalls of racial apartheid and discriminatory practices? With excellence and humor Rachel sought to shield her brood from a "world that outranked" and "outnumbered" them. One of her many strategies was a comic sense of provocation. Knowing that her multihued family would be a source of speculation, she heightened those differences by "dressing the blond child and [Dorothy] alike." She would then say: "come on children, let's go out and drive the white folks crazy."[13] Rachel was fond of stating "we Bensons only like Bensons," and that sense of self-contained individualism made the Wests' enclave atypical as well as representative within and outside the black Brahmin community.

West's frequent use of the first-person plural in her sketches suggests a collective consciousness, but it is not necessarily a representative consciousness. In this she mirrors some of the life-writing strategies that have fascinated the readers of her friend and mentor Zora Neale Hurston's many autobiographical narratives. Elizabeth Fox-Genovese, writing on Hurston's *Dust Tracks on a Road, an Autobiography* (1942), observes:

> All of *Dust Tracks* must be taken with caution. Hurston became an accomplished "liar" who also spun her tales to suit her purposes, became

an accomplished artist who also crafted her work to satisfy her imagination. Poised between two worlds—the black South of her childhood and the white North of her education and adulthood—she constructed the statue of herself that she permitted the world to see.[14]

Was Hurston lying or "signifying"? Signifying is a key strategy in the African American vernacular tradition of the double-entendre, sometimes known as playing the dozens. Signification can be tricky to define, but there is no denying that Hurston was adept at the constitutive elements of the black folk tradition: in-group humor, exaggeration, and misdirection.[15]

Critics who study African American autobiography argue that it occupies a primary, if not originating, genre within the African American literary canon. James Olney affirms that "the mode specific to the black experience has been autobiography," precisely because through autobiographical narratives one could access and unlock unrecorded and deliberately suppressed histories.[16] Truth telling has been an important aspect of the African American autobiographical tradition; it was the singular authenticating note of the slave narrative. The authors directly affirmed their slave narratives as both factual and representative: I wrote this account of my life as a slave and my escape. In Harriet Jacobs's *Incidents in the Life of a Slave Girl*, which she published under the pseudonym of Linda Brent, she explicitly states that she reveals the details of her enslaved life to help her sisters in bondage. Scholars and readers, however, acknowledge that autobiographical narratives come in many forms and employ a diverse field of literary and representational strategies. What constitutes a truthful rendition, especially a self-reflective, truthful rendition, cannot be taken at face value.

African American autobiographical narratives often possess a "communal, consciously political self," a self we might be tempted to identify in West's plural references. In approaching West's autobiographical writings I apply the same caution that Alice Deck (paraphrasing Hurston biographer Robert Hemenway) urges:

that we read *Dust Tracks* not so much for its biographical facts (which present an image of its author that fails to conform with her public career or her private experience) or for its racial politics (which were suppressed at her editor's insistence in the interest of promoting racial harmony); we should read Hurston's memoirs as a cultural celebration of her life and career (Introduction). . . . *Dust Tracks* consists of an intricate interplay of the introspective personal engagement expected of an autobiography and the self-effacement expected of cultural descriptions and explications associated with ethnography.[17]

The term autoethnography, describing what Alice Deck calls the shifting nature of both autobiographical narratives and ethnographical studies,[18] suits Hurston's many autobiographical narratives perfectly, and it also illuminates West's fragmented narrative of her life as told in her interviews and published sketches. Autoethnography, according to Alice Deck, applies particularly to those self-reflective narratives in which the authors consider and examine themselves as native to the environment of examination.[19]

Like Hurston's, West's autobiographical voice is communal, but not conventionally political. She speaks for herself, her cousins, her immediate community—black islanders and Bostonians—and only then, sparingly, of the black community at large. I am intrigued by what is completely omitted from West's fiction and life-writing and only hinted at in her private letters and public interviews: a full discussion of her sexuality or her adolescence. Little from West's childhood sheds any light on her sexuality or the sexual repression Wallace Thurman later read into her writing and her virginal condition among her peers in Harlem.

In writing about the stories told by lesbian women of color in the ground-breaking collection *This Bridge Called My Back*, feminist scholar Biddy Martin writes:

Lesbianism ceases to be an identity with predictable contents, to consti-
tute a total political self-identification, and yet it figures no less centrally
for that shift. It remains a position from which to speak, to organize, to
act politically, but it ceases to be the exclusive and continuous ground
of identity or politics. Indeed it works to *unsettle rather than to consolidate
the boundaries* around identity, not to dissolve them altogether, but to
open them to the fluidities and heterogeneities that make their rene-
gotiation possible. At the same time that such autobiographical writing
enacts a critique of both sexuality and race as "essential" and totalizing
identifications, it also acknowledges the political and psychological
importance, indeed the pleasures, too, of at least partial or provisional
identifications, homes, and communities. In so doing, it remains faithful
to the irreducibly complex and paradoxical status of identity in feminist
politics and autobiographical writing.[20]

I do not attempt to categorize West's writings as lesbian autobiography, but I am intrigued by the interplay between her virtual silence in her autobio-graphical sketches about sexuality and her intimately revealing letters from Russia, letters which "unsettle rather than consolidate" our understanding of black women's sexuality and the gay/lesbian/bisexual communities that existed during the Harlem Renaissance. Even if West never explicitly recounts her emergence out of the proverbial closet, she does live relatively openly with Marian Minus, a woman whom Margaret Washington and Joyce Rickson affirm was lesbian identified: "And we knew, we always knew. We called them queer then. But she wasn't queer in the sense that 'ooo' you know, it was just the way it was. . . . And we always knew that [she and Marian] were together, and it didn't make any difference to us, it was just the way things were."[21] West is similar to several subjects of feminist biography. Consider, for example, Elizabeth Barrett Browning, who openly opposed what we think of as proto-feminist ideals like suffrage or free love but in her life resisted traditional roles and redefined her sense of womanhood against patriarchal, heteronormative gender roles.

West can be forthright describing the slippage between what she remembers about her family life and what she has fictionalized. Katrine Dalsgård attempts to get at the truth behind "Prologue to a Life" by observing: "it seems to be a study for *The Living Is Easy*. It is about a Southern woman coming North. She runs into this man, and he runs her over on his bicycle." West responds: "I'll go to my grave not knowing whether I made it up or not. . . . I wish I knew how my mother and father met, but I can't remember because I've written so many versions that I don't know whether I made them all up, or whether one is true."[22] In "Prologue" the male protagonist rides the bike; in *The Living Is Easy*, Cleo is riding the bike. That West throws doubt on her own memories of childhood may unsettle a skeptical reader, but to my mind it only enhances our understanding of a practice Toni Morrison describes in "The Site of Memory" as "literary archeology." What distinguishes Morrison's fiction from biography is the focus on the image, the imaginative act that conveys the feelings and interior experience of an action or a character. For Morrison the critical distinction is not between fact and fiction, but between "fact and truth."[23] I offer a case in point: her novel *Beloved* conveys to readers a meaningful rendition of historical trauma. For West, the imaginative image, the "site of memory" that locates her parents' first meeting, is the bicycle. In addition to its central imagistic function within the story the bicycle is first and foremost a mode of transportation adopted as a representative symbol of the New Woman's enhanced mobility. Images of athletic women on bicycles in bloomers proliferated within the popular press at the turn of the century on both sides of the Atlantic. On the bicycle the New Woman "exercised power more fundamentally, changing the conventions of courtship and chaperonage, of marriage and travel."[24] The intricate weave of life-writing does not provide definitive explanations or obvious connections between West's personal history and fiction. Instead, the productive tension between her imaginative acts and the sites of memory she uses to create and record her personal history reveals a unique family that produced a terrific writer who did not inherit her mother's beauty but certainly manifests her aptitude for signifying, in the Hurstonian sense.

"My mother was one of the twelve beauties of Boston"

West's mythology about her mother's beauty informs how she aestheticizes fair-skinned, European-featured African American women in her texts. In this she is not so different from many nineteenth- and twentieth-century writers who created the many ambiguously raced heroines who populate slave narratives, narratives of passing, and tragic mulatta stories.[25] West's persistent reference to her mother's exceptional beauty is often coupled with a critical appraisal of her own appearance. West was not unattractive, but from an early age she defined herself as the family intellectual, the creative one. At times, West intimates that to be beautiful was also to be vapid or unintelligent, yet her portraits of Rachel suggest no such intellectual failings. She knew that brains and beauty could go together, and they did so with her mother. Joyce Rickson suggests that West developed her strong personality to surmount any color discrimination she might have experienced: "you could not be around her and not pay attention to her. And I think this was her way to compensate for being so dark. Because her father was very dark, and Rachel was probably about my complexion or a little darker but could still be considered light skinned, but not light light skinned." She describes Dorothy as "quite animated and vivacious," "very expressive," "a typical Bostonian."[26]

Naming Rachel as one of a dozen women singled out for their beauty in Boston severs her from her Carolina roots and positions her as a true Bostonian. Who were the other eleven beauties? Certainly another was Edna Thomas, a fair-skinned actress whom Bostonian readers believed was the template for the Duchess in *The Living Is Easy*.[27] Another was Bessie Trotter, the wife of Monroe Trotter, the editor of *The Guardian*. Yet in Adelaide Cromwell's sociological study *The Other Brahmins: Boston's Black Upper Class 1750–1950* there is no direct mention of a group of debutantes or socialites that bore that particular moniker. Perhaps West magnified her mother and her friends in her imagination precisely because they formed a brilliant constellation that she struggled to emulate?

In "The Purse" West describes her mother as a fearless, sassy beauty who wore her "gold-colored, pink-cheeked beauty" "like a banner."[28] As the daughter of an extraordinarily beautiful woman West may have felt a singular inadequacy. The question here is not whether Rachel West was exceptionally beautiful—black-and-white photographs of West's mother in her youth reveal that she was attractive in the context of accepted beauty at the time—but how West saw her mother in relationship to herself. Physical beauty is highly subjective. Unless the photographer is very skilled, a black-and-white photograph cannot capture the animation, spirit, and elegant manners that make up a legendary beauty.

Joyce Rickson, one of West's "cousins," remembers "Aunt" Rachel as "an older woman, like a grandmother type, so you don't say 'oh what a beauty' because of the age alone, an older woman."[29] Rickson reflects that it took her some time to understand color distinctions because what is considered light or dark skin is often based on individual perception. Family photographs reveal that while West is certainly darker skinned than her mother, others in her large extended family had complexions similar to West's. Adelaide Cromwell maintains that standards of beauty in the Northeast differed from those in cities like Washington, D.C. She remembers Barbara Townes as having a very attractive mother but did not see Rachel as particularly remarkable outside of her light skin. In fact, Cromwell suggests that light skin might be synonymous with attractiveness in the North, but she felt that these standards were parochial: "If [Dorothy] had ever spent a season in Washington or Altanta or even any other place . . . she would have realized how very many pretty women made up that group . . . who didn't just look one way."[30]

The story that West tells of her mother's transformation from a spirited southern girl to one of the twelve beauties of Boston resembles Zora Neale Hurston's award-winning story "Drenched in Light." The heroine of the story—Isis Watts—is too much for her grandmother and the constrictions of the South. Her exploits attract the interest of a northerner who says, "I want this brightness—this Isis is joy itself—why she's drenched in light." The story is a self-reflective commentary on Hurston's own journey from Eatonville, Florida, to Harlem and the relationship she developed with Charlotte Osgood Mason. Many critics have commented on the similarity between Isis Watts and young Cleo Judson, who is every bit as insolent and hoydenish as the irrepressible Isis. West presents her mother as a woman who was just too much for the South and her family.

Rachel Benson West was the daughter of Helen Pease Benson and Benjamin Benson. She was one of nineteen children, and her siblings frequently argued about the number and birth order of Mama Benson's many children.[31] She was neither the eldest nor the youngest, but she took on the authority of an elder child. West's aunts (not her uncles) figure prominently in her oral histories and her fiction. Most often we hear of Minnie, or Ella, Helene Johnson's mother. Mama's household was proud. West tells interviewers that above all her grandmother resented the charity of outsiders.

While West amplifies the pride of Cleo's foremothers in *The Living Is Easy* as women who preferred to die rather than suffer insult, she stresses the pride her grandmother took in her domestic sphere. In "The Purse" she writes: "The sum of my grandmother's pride was the lace that decorated her little girls' drawers in those days when little girls wore long-legged drawers that showed beneath their dresses. The lace that my grandmother made by hand and sewed on all those homemade drawers was her way of showing those noseybodies who minded her business that nobody went in want at her house, not for bread, not for meat, not for lace on their drawers."[32]

This was what was ingrained in Rachel Benson: a pride in deportment, the sense that cleanliness was next to godliness, but also the idea that her charges (Dorothy and the cousins) would not "worry her to death the way she worried Mama to death."[33] Mama Benson was born in slavery, the daughter of her master. All too soon she was "bound again," this time in marriage and then to a "batch of babies." After an enslaved childhood, her "girlhood" was over before it began. Like many daughters with numerous siblings Rachel did not want to be enslaved to motherhood and so, not surprisingly, West was an only child. The boys, her uncles, West tells us, "never had to nurse any of the babies" but her mother was told to look after her little sister Minnie from the age of seven and no doubt help out with the others as well.[34]

As in many African American narratives the last association of Rachel with the South of her youth was broken by train travel: "my sixteen-year-old mother stood with Mama alongside the tracks where the Jim Crow train would stop." She "heard its mournful whistle" and "never saw Mama alive again."[35] Under the auspices of her northerner mentor Mrs. Tewksbury, Rachel was sent North where presumably her beauty and spunk would not get her into too much trouble. It seemed that there were "too many woods in the sultry south."[36] Apparently the North was the only salvation for beautiful and/or intelligent African American women. In *Their Eyes Were Watching God*, Hurston explored the "remedies" for endangered black womanhood in the South; in this novel, the moment Janie becomes aware of her own sexuality her Granny believes the only solution is to marry her off to a much older man. West does not speak directly of the rape and sexual violation that many black women experienced in the South, but she does explain how her mother obtained her fair complexion: "My grandfather, my mother's father, came out of slavery; he was the child of his master. My grandmother, my mother's mother, came out of slavery; she was the child of her master, and evidently there had been some before because my grandmother was very fair. I think maybe like is attracted to like." West also attributes her grandmother's scrupulous rearing of her children to the fact that she was descended from house servants. Her observation that "like is attracted to like" also extended beyond color to class, or perhaps through color to class. She rationalizes that the children of house servants were not "going to marry a shoe shine man."[37]

If West circumvents the history of sexual exploitation that bequeathed light skin to the Bensons, then her mother seems to be in an even more dramatic state of avoidance. "My mother lived and died without ever admitting she had a drop of white blood in her," West tells Lee. Instead, Rachel would tell West that she was descended from a "white tribe of Indians." West told several interviewers that she was writing a novella about this very issue, which is a common phenomenon in African American families. Rather than attribute a particular genetic trait like green or blue eyes and straight or wavy hair to a white progenitor, who may have been a sexual aggressor, some oral family histories claim the anomalous features come from an Indian ancestor. This is not to say that there is no evidence of interracial marriage or sexual relationships between African Americans and Indians, but family oral histories sometimes create romanticized narratives to obscure more unpleasant truths, like the idea of romantic relationships between enslaved Africans and their owners, or stories of Native Americans hiding and intermarrying with fugitive slaves.[38] When West's mother tells her daughter that her light skin came from a "white tribe of Indians," she was participating in a rewriting of ancestry not unlike the practices of many other ethnic groups in the United States.

And yet, while Rachel Benson escapes the fate awaiting her in the woods of the South, once she arrives in the North she too is quickly "bound in marriage" to a another southerner: Isaac West. Born in slavery in Henrico County, Virginia, Isaac West (1860–1933) was emancipated at the age of seven, but his connection to slavery at a young age ingrained an interest in "buying and selling."[39] His mother had been a cook in the big house, and one of his first ventures as a businessman was to open a boarding house. Then he migrated (with his mother) to Springfield, Massachusetts, where he opened an ice cream parlor before finally opening a fruit store specializing in bananas. Apparently, Rachel traveled to Springfield to teach around 1894. Whether she met Isaac in Springfield or Boston is unclear. Perhaps one of them was riding a bicycle, perhaps not. Either way, the fateful meeting resulted in a marriage in Boston, where they apparently reconnected some time later. Their marriage was both advantageous and typical for couples within Boston's upper class. It linked a woman "poor as a church mouse," but beautiful, with a man whose mother rode around in a carriage bought with her son's success.[40] They were not exactly a May and December pairing, but Rachel always called Isaac "Mr." There is no indication, however, that she ever called him "Mr. Nigger," which is how Cleo Judson frequently refers to her husband.[41]

West maintained that her parents represented two different generations: her father was a workaholic concerned primarily with the acquisition of capital and indifferent to marriage until he reached middle age. The short story "At the Swan Boats" plays up the age difference between Jude, and Lila in a way that is almost disturbing. Lila is a "cream-colored child" in braids and bloomers. Her youth and inexperience is not lost on Jude, who feels as if he was "robbin' the cradle." The courtship proceeds in fits and starts and is finally consolidated around a bicycle, which they take turns riding until they are "thoroughly spent and ravenous." Jude's efforts to perform tricks on the cycle convince Lila that Jude "was not really old." If the difference in age is played up in "At the Swan Boats," the chemistry—though tinged with mild pedophilia—is more passionate and sincere than it is in the other imagined meetings. Lila declares that she "almost" loves him and sees him as "her own kind." Jude hopes that she will sense his "bold ambition" to become a wealthy tycoon and bear him a "soft-haired son" as an heir.[42] Subsequent versions of this meeting are more one-sided. After the collision that occurs between Cleo and Bart in *The Living Is Easy*, she is distraught by the loss of her bicycle and indifferent to the love-struck Bart; she impulsively marries him only to escape the lecherous designs of her benefactor's son.

"My father was the Black Banana King of Boston"

"I was my father's daughter," West writes in "The Gift," one of the many sketches in which she tells the story of her father's life.[43] Her identity as the daughter of the black banana king was fundamental to her sense of entitlement within both the Boston and Vineyard communities. Unlike the children of tailors, butlers, and caterers that made up the Black Brahmins, she was the daughter of an entrepreneur rather than a man in service. Isaac West, a shrewd and intelligent businessman, was the archetypal self-made man. According to his daughter, Isaac West, the only black wholesaler in Boston Market, was well respected by his fellow merchants and bankers. His business—"Imported and Domestic Fruits and Vegetables, Bananas a Specialty"—was situated in a prime location directly across from the famed Faneuil Hall. West describes him as an extraordinary man who "had taught himself to write in a Spencerian hand, to read whatever was set before him, to talk with a totally literate tongue, and most of all, perhaps most importantly of all, to figure like a wizard."[44] As the "heiress" to a great beauty and a financial wizard West had everything she needed to exceed her parents in distinguished endeavors. But she was not a boy and could not succeed her father in business. In any case, by the time she was ready to make her start in the world his business was on the decline, as was her parents' marriage. Just as she inherited neither her father's business acumen nor his blue eyes, she also failed to claim her mother's light skin, which meant that she could not capitalize on the capital of her body. Instead, through her imagination and her writing skills she built a unique path for herself.[45]

How accurate is West's narrative about her father's role as the black banana king? The story that appears in *The Living Is Easy* bears a strong resemblance to the history of several Jamaican-born "banana kings" who challenged United Fruit for a piece of the banana market at the turn of the century. Leslie Goffe and his Italian American partner also claimed the title of the "banana king" at the very time that Isaac West would have been building his business in Boston.

The notion of multiple black banana kings suggests a tantalizing confluence between West's oral family histories and the pernicious, global history of corporations like United Fruit, which was preceded by Boston Fruit: a company run by a man named Captain Baker.

West remembers plentiful food during her childhood: "My father was a fruit man, because when I was a child I didn't know you could buy anything by the pound, and he would take a basket of peaches, which might be worth a dollar and a quarter no more, I mean, but they were the best peaches, beautiful peaches, then he would get a loin and the meat man would give him a loin of meat, do you see. And so that, as I said, this friend said to me—I said, 'Our food was free.'"[46] West continually explains her family's status as one of the "genteel poor" in a way that evinces a Bostonian dismissal of wealth.[47] No Bostonian, she asserts, would describe themselves as rich. Instead, they, like her father, would say, "I'm not poor." According to West, real wealth was money that would never be frivolously squandered: a substantial nest egg that one could fall back on. Without generations of wealth to bolster his business, West's father was vulnerable to the fluctuations of the market. His business, like other independents, ultimately succumbed to the chain stores that underbid his contracts with the Navy and the department stores.[48]

While we have much more evidence of West's correspondence with her mother than with her father, his death in February 1933 brought her home from her sojourn in the Soviet Union and forced her to forgo trips to Paris and Berlin. His death prompted her to finally grow up. Before leaving New York for Russia, she apologized for her mother's failure as a wife and told her father: "I know she has not been a good wife to you." Her father's reply, "I understand your mother," stayed with her for all of her life. Despite its difficulties and rumors about her father's extramarital affairs, West ultimately seemed to feel that her parents' marriage if not ideal was inevitable: "I cannot imagine either one married to anyone else."[49]

"I was the only dark child"

One of the most painful moments in West's interview with Genii Guinier is the moment when she relates how she once accused her mother of not passing on her father's blue eyes or her own beauty: "You wouldn't give me your beauty and you wouldn't give me my father's blue eyes."[50] If not conventionally beautiful by mainstream black or white standards, West was not unattractive: she was petite, brown-skinned with dark curling hair, and obviously talented. Certainly she did not lack for suitors as evidenced by several marriage proposals and her liaisons in Russia. Still, she carried her color (not her race) as a chip on her shoulder that was connected less to the divide between black and white, which her mother had prepared her to subvert with aplomb, than it was to the fractures between black and brown and yellow. She explored and theorized these persistent and elusive barriers in her fiction and nonfiction for the entirety of her writing-life.

West relays a story to Linsey Lee that poignantly captures both her vulnerability and confusion about her complexion and self-worth. West rarely responds directly to her interviewers' queries, but in this case the story she offers to answer Lee's question—"When you were growing up, did you think of yourself as beautiful?"—is important because of its manifestation in *The Living Is Easy*. In fact, like the story of her parents' courtship, it is hard to determine which version is true. In response to Lee's question West replies, "No. Wait a minute. If I may tell you another charming story." Precisely when West is asked questions about her personal life she most frequently retreats into storytelling mode. Though she first offers a direct, negative response—she immediately qualifies it with a segue into "another charming story." The next sentence introduces one of her many cousins, "a little boy in the family, very blonde kid, and he loved me." Very likely this child is Bertram Arnold Jackson, who is often called "Melvin," just as West referred to Joyce Rickson's father.[51] Rickson remembers that "some of the stories [in *The Richer, the Poorer*] were about my dad, who is referred to as a golden haired boy."[52] Once again, West emphasizes the presence of unexpected, presumably Anglo attributes in her family. She slips into the third-person plural voice that she uses in the sketches that appear in *The Richer, the Poorer* and then proceeds to express her ambivalent feelings about the boy's admiration. Because he was six years younger than Dorothy, he pestered her and the other children. He asked, "Can I go with Dotsie?" Then West would defy the others and look after him. At one point the group—the boy, Dorothy, her cousin Eugenia who West describes as resembling a "French doll" with "delicate features" and "curly hair," and another unnamed cousin—encounters a person who excessively praised Eugenia's (Minnie's daughter) good looks. At this point in her story West pauses to emphasize relevance of the tale: "this is in answer to your question. . . ." She then relates how the boy, overhearing Eugenia praised, begins crying and subsequently asks Rachel, "Why did that lady say [Eugenia] was beautiful. I think Dorothy is beautiful." Rachel gives the little boy the answer West would "remember forever": "Dorothy is beautiful. I'm glad you know that . . . she is beautiful on the inside."[53] From here the story rebounds to West's typical discussion of color, class, and maternal issues, and the storyline of the little boy is lost.

The import of the story—that is, an Anglo-identified child finding Dorothy more lovely than her conventionally pretty cousin and her mother's affirmation "I'm glad you know that . . ."—finds its way into *The Living Is Easy*. In the novel, when Cleo's baby sister Serena and her young son Tim come to live in the Judson household, the "bright haired" Tim immediately fixates on the "cocoa-brown" Judy.[54] While at the breakfast table Tim "ate with his eyes on Judy" and "would not wear bibs because Judy" did not. The fact that she "is not a beauty like her mother" defines Judy's relationship to her parents. She is a deeply moral child with "no funny bone," an attribute that leads Cleo to sometimes wonder "where she had got Judy." West uses the same descriptive language to describe the household of children run by Cleo that she uses in her interviews: "vari-hued, from very dark Bart to very blond Tim." The mother-daughter relationship in *The Living Is Easy* is the most intensely autobiographical. Yet, like all fiction, this meditation magnifies certain aspects of West's rich and complex upbringing. West explains that the germ for *The Living Is Easy* came to her while she was on a walk with a friend. They were speaking of Rachel, and West said, "To her the living was easy." From there she began to write a story. After twenty pages of writing the "character began to have a life of her own, and went her own way."[55]

West's identification with her father resembles the myth of Pallas Athena, whose father Zeus supposedly birthed her—the Greek goddess of wisdom and war—in full armor out of his head. According to West, "father could have spit me out of his mouth."[56] Within her family she was the odd one out, and strangers, both white and black, frequently misidentified her relationship to her mother. She admits that her mother was "horrified" with her complaint about her father's eyes, given that she was twenty-five years old and there was no way for her to return to her mother's womb.[57] It is perhaps significant to remember two things: Isaac West was rarely with the family in her early life, and, given her age, this conversation must have taken place shortly after his death. Perhaps West felt a bitter irony that she had inherited everything from her father except the one feature she and society saw as unequivocally desirable: blue eyes.[58] Even if *The Living Is Easy* reads like a referendum on Rachel's mothering abilities, the interviews exonerate her. Though fond of comic pranks that befuddled white observers, she did not make a difference between the cousins based on color. She found her husband attractive and considered her daughter beautiful inside and out. In this Rachel diverges from West's portrait of Cleo Judson and her hypercritical treatment of her daughter, which includes forcing her to wear a clothespin to straighten her nose. West did not feel alienated within her home, but outside her home, especially in Boston where "we were inspected like specimens under glass," West was made to feel her difference.[59]

The Genteel Poor: West and the Brown Brahmins

While West described her family as part of the "genteel poor," her cousin Helene Johnson's daughter Abigail McGrath uses a similar term, "shabby gentility," to describe the communal living arrangements of the West clan. McGrath describes the family as similar to a kibbutz that traveled back and forth between the "big house in Boston and the beach house at Martha's Vineyard."

Though she admits that the description of the family's financial situation in *The Living Is Easy* included some factual evidence about West's father, who McGrath refers to as the self-proclaimed Banana King of Boston, she feels West omitted from the novel that "the sisters (all nine of them) pitched in together in a communal way in order to maintain a lifestyle which had the façade of the real Boston Brahmins."[60] McGrath's comments reinforce the in-between position that West occupied in the tenuous category of the black middle class, which can encompasses individuals with a wide range of educational and economic backgrounds. According to McGrath, "Dorothy's version" of the family history as represented in the novel "caused such a catastrophic uproar that in the family most members stopped speaking to Dorothy."[61] Given the portraits of Cleo as a controlling, selfish matriarch obsessed with status and material acquisition, and the characterization of her three sisters as co-independent supplicants, it is not surprising that there would have been family fallout once West's relatives read the novel.

The Rachel that emerges from the personal reminiscences of McGrath and Rickson was a complex individual with a big heart, an open door, and an inclusive understanding of family ties—all characteristics that sharply distinguish her from the novel's protagonist. Rickson remembers Rachel primarily as a "kind of ya'll come person. She always wanted family, all her sisters to come and visit and be with her and they should all be together." The family came to include Rickson, who was not a blood relative to the West family but the child of a neighbor in Boston.[62] Rachel invited Rickson and her brother to the island for consecutive summers, essentially adopting her into the family; Rachel was "the grandmother I [Rickson] never had." Rickson recalls spending time with Dorothy—she is the model for the character of Sis in West's story "The Sun Parlor"—and Marian Minus, who also came for frequent visits. This was typical behavior for the Wests and explains the complex, extended network of kin. It also reflects the closeness of the ties among Highlands residents. "Those fabulous summers" with Aunt Rachel no doubt also influenced Rickson's decision to purchase a home on the Vineyard.[63] Mitchell and Davis observe, "West's Rachelesque characters are never merely one-dimensional shrews"; they are complicated women negotiating the particular constraints of their times.[64]

What was the Boston community in which West grew up like? In Adelaide Cromwell's *The Other Brahmins*, she addresses the difficulty of analyzing social class among African Americans. Race has been and continues to be such an overwhelming discourse that it almost precludes other forms of group identity. Additionally, because the urgent problems of the working class and poor blacks are more pressing, those needs and the causative factors and communal dynamics of the underclass have preoccupied the majority of sociological studies of African Americans. Shades of skin color indicated class status, especially for particular groups like the blue vein society; however, these groups were small, to the point of obscurity. Families like West, where the shades ran the gamut, were more common.

Cromwell relies on John Daniels's *In Freedom's Birthplace* (1914), a study modeled on W.E.B. Du Bois's *The Philadelphia Negro* (1899) and his strategy of dividing his subjects into various categories; however, Eugene Gordon's "Negro Society" provides the most prescient insider account. Given West's relationship with Gordon through the Saturday Evening Quill Club they clearly occupied intersecting circles. Gordon, a Howard University graduate, was one of the few black reporters for the *Boston Post*.[65] No doubt his experiences at Howard provided him with an interesting perspective on Washingtonian society as well. With his wife, Edythe, also a writer, Gordon started the Saturday Evening Quill Club, and Dorothy and her cousin were members. Gordon's journal, the *Saturday Evening Quill*, published "Prologue to a Life" and "An Unimportant Man." Gordon's article is a satirical, impressionistic report embedded with many intriguing insights about "Negro Society." The article's publication in *Scribner's Magazine* puts it in the same category with other revealing, tell-all ethnographic treatments that purport to enlighten white Americans about this particular class. As with the later studies produced by Gatewood and Cromwell, Gordon has a difficult time defining exactly who is included in the societies of well-to-do African Americans throughout the country. He writes: "The occupational diversions of Afro-America are too congolomerate, reaching from the sewer to the cathedral spire." Moreover, there is no "social register," and so "it's left to the hostess's intuition and rather doubtful sense of values to determine who shall and who shall not grace her board."[66] Economic advancement among the black elite has been a topsy-turvy business. A man elected to the Senate during Reconstruction may have had an enslaved grandfather and a Harvard-educated son working as a bellhop. For this reason, Gordon explains, "in any large gathering of Afro-American elite, the sheep are found rubbing noses with the goats. . . . The goat just happens to be the big ram's father or brother or some other close relative." Gordon does not focus on Boston, except in his opening description of a lavish wedding that took place at a friend's "cottagelike house near Boston"; instead, he examines in detail "Negro Society" in Washington and Harlem.[67]

The satirical edge of Gordon's account indicates another problem with examining how public and artistic spheres, as well as sociological studies, represent the black middle and upper classes. Most seem to approach the group as purely imitative of the European and Anglo-American upper class. Cromwell's title, *The Other Brahmins*, references this tendency. The long history of mocking and parodying upper-class society through the figure of the uppity Negro who appeared in vaudeville and minstrel shows made it difficult to take such studies seriously. Empirical studies shifted the focus of class firmly toward the poor and disenfranchised, by dismissing the elite as impotent and invested only in maintaining a "make-believe lifestyle having status without substance."[68] E. Franklin Frazier's *Black Bourgeoisie* probably put the final nail in the coffin by depicting the black elite as a brainwashed minority not worthy of study or emulation.

Because privacy and secrecy were valued within subgroups like the brown Brahmins in both Boston and Martha's Vineyard, it is difficult to get accurate data about class divisions. Cromwell's study, in its geographic specificity and chronological approach, helps to locate West's family life, especially between 1875 and 1890, a period identified by early twentieth-century chronicles of the brown Brahmins as a "golden age." J. Walter Stevens writes: "Colored society and its customs in Boston in the 1890s had a certain orderliness which is missing now. Boston had a quality which made its inhabitants completely at home and content in their own social group."[69] West's portraits in *The Living Is Easy* of Thea Binney and Miss Eleanor Elliot, the dance instructor who sees Thea as an ideal representative of the old guard who is nevertheless endangered and in need of the new money of recent migrants like the Judsons, amplify the idea of "Old Bostonians" as social isolationists holding on to a decaying ideal.[70] This representation is similar to the overwhelming sense of decay and nostalgia that pervades Edith Wharton's novels, especially *The House of Mirth* and *The Custom of the Country*. Both books contain characters who are completely unable to negotiate the rapidly changing social geographies of New York.

In considering West's life-writings as a lay history of black Boston we see the dimensions of the make-believe world of the Brown Brahmins as one that is not necessarily supported by empirical data. When asked about Boston, West tends to talk about the Vineyard. When asked about her earliest memories of the Vineyard, she gives a precise answer entirely about Boston:

LEE: What are your earliest memories of the Vineyard here as a child?
WEST: All right. I lived on Brookline Avenue. That doesn't mean anything to you, but my point is, it was the dividing line, Brookline Avenue was about the last street in Brookline because every once in a while they rezoned it and it was Boston and then they would rezone it back, and so my point is, in back of us we had Mission Hill and in front of us, it was a true dividing line.[71]

Why this reversal? Divisions, boundaries of neighborhoods, borderline streets all play a role in how West maps both her childhood and her movement across social, racial, and national lines. The realities of implicit and explicit segregation left her with an acute sense of spatial inaccessibility. To explain why she had "Fond Memories" of her childhood on the Vineyard she had to introduce the circumstances that propelled them across the water to an island refuge: the intense class divisions and ethnic clashes in Boston. These were not just black/white conflicts—those terms were too simple—but between recent black southern migrants and well-established free communities of black Boston, between Jewish European immigrants, Irish immigrants, and the "old Yankees" who first inhabited her early childhood homes on 10 Cedar Street and later her mother's house at 23 Worthington Street (now considered the Roxbury neighborhood).

West has little to say of her primary and secondary education beyond her admittance into Girls' Latin, a school founded in South Boston in 1878. We know that as a young girl she had a "Finnish governess" and attended the dancing school commemorated in her novel.[72] In contrast to her first experience at a school with Irish children who called her "nigger," at Girls' Latin the other students were polite, white middle-class girls, and she was very happy at the school. Given the virulent history of Boston's fight over school desegregation, her comments are somewhat surprising. Joyce Rickson's memories of the school several decades later dramatically differ from West's:

> I went to Girls' Latin junior high years, and I was miserable, because it's a very hard school and it's very demanding. I mean this is like your top academic school but you get the feeling that if you're a little colored girl, you ain't gonna make it, you're gonna fail. Because we don't want to see you succeed anyhow. You just feel this hatred thing of white Bostonians, so for high school I left Girls' Latin. I went to Girls' High, and I had a good time because I had my buddies. And suddenly I started getting better grades. I get my A's then, but Girls' Latin was hard because some of that bad energy just kind of sucked your energies or whatever. But the interesting thing is about, and this really has to do with the mindset growing up in that kind of environment and where Dorothy may have gotten some of her thoughts from, because it's so subtle. You have to try very hard to be proper and better than, and to meet the white standards. And no matter how you stroll they ain't gonna like you anymore. And she had a lot of white friends here because that's what happens here. You cannot live here and not develop white friendships. Because we're only 10% and we're kind of spread out, so if you're going to live on the Vineyard, you need to be open, because it's that kind of place anyhow.

Rickson identifies the insidiousness of Boston racial climate as a covert, polite resistance, and she believes that West's ideas about black achievement must have come from her experiences growing up in that environment: "if [she] tr[ied] very hard [she'd] be better accepted, so she's constantly dealing with it through her stories, and it's a part of racism that's not well known or thought about or considered. And it's certainly part of racism that white people by and large don't understand."[73] Rickson's comments also point once more to the idea of the Vineyard as a more open accepting space, especially in contrast to Boston, where it is harder to assert exceptional status.

Comparatively speaking, West did appear to have the charmed childhood she remembers in her sketches and interviews. Her family dynamics, the circumstances of her parents' marriage, the matriarchal household of extended family, and their particularly defiant way of countering racial discrimination provided all the material she needed for a prolific writing career. Moreover, West's fiction, nonfiction, and oral histories, like early histories such as Joseph Willson's *Sketches of the Higher Classes of Colored Society in Philadelphia* (1841) and John Daniels's *In Freedom's Birthplace*, provide an invaluable archive of the particularities of the African American elite and middle class at a time when empirical data was either elusive or not quite capable of capturing the full spectrum of class stratification among black Bostonians.

When asked about who would be an ideal biographer West is utterly dismissive of her longtime friend, sociologist Adelaide Cromwell. Cromwell wrote the Afterword for the Feminist Press 1982 reprint of *The Living Is Easy,* and West claimed that her old friend "drove her mad" with her questions about her age, the age of her father, and the precise details needed to paint an accurate biographical portrait. "Those things are very important to [Cromwell]" as a sociologist, but West was entirely resistant to such factual interrogation.[74]

Given West's resistance to a sociohistorical approach to her biography, I imagine she would be equally opposed to a psychoanalytic reading of her relationship with her mother, and I shall not attempt one here. I do find it interesting, however, that while Dorothy West never becomes a mother she reproduces in her fiction a series of maternal characters that magnify certain aspects of her mother's real life experiences and personality traits. In Nancy Chodorow's excellent study, *The Reproduction of Mothering,* she traces how mothering is reproduced across generations. Not only was Rachel the template for Cleo Judson, but West also intended to write a second novel that dealt with her mother's later years, although that novel was never fully realized. It's also intriguing that the white matriarch of the African American family featured in her last novel, *The Wedding,* is actually based on the mother of her longtime partner, Marian Minus. Although there are numerous similarities between West's childhood sketches and her fiction, the interplay of personas and characters that repeatedly emerge from her life-writing and fiction is part of what makes her a complicated, but fascinating, storyteller.

3

Dorothy West's "Typewriter"

By nature I am a short story writer. Because you can finish a short story.
–Dorothy West (Interview with Linsey Lee, 5 May 1994)

Next to Dorothy West's early years growing up in Oak Bluffs and Boston, the most formative period in her artistic life was the time she spent in Harlem as the darling of the New Negro vanguard. In *The Richer, the Poorer: Stories, Sketches and Reminiscences*, she describes an encounter with *The Crisis* magazine in Boston in the mid-1920s as the spark that fueled her entrée into the Harlem Renaissance. West recounts the incident:

> In my sixteenth year an aunt who shared our home was waiting for the trolley that would take her there when a personable young black man approached her, summarily informing her that he was working his way through medical school and thereupon entreating her to buy a subscription to a black magazine called *The Crisis*. Though my aunt had never heard of a magazine so named she believed in ambition and opened her purse.
>
> My mother, who had heard of *The Crisis*, was dismayed when the magazine appeared in our mail slot. The young members in our extended family, all born and raised in Boston, had little if any knowledge of lynching and other obscenities. To see them graphically depicted might discourage us from pursuing our ambition in a world stacked against us.[1]

For West's mother, providing her gifted daughter with a sheltered upbringing in a middle-class household insulated from the extreme racial violence that had become commonplace in the South was critical to West's achievement. The larger question of what nourishes and stifles black ambition is paramount in this passage. The sixteen-year-old West is not riveted by reports of southern brutality; instead, what catches her eye is an advertisement for the magazine's "third or perhaps its fourth literary contest, persuading [her] to assume that the preceding contests had reaped such a yield of black talent that the contests were on-going."[2]

The promoters of what would be known as the Harlem Renaissance, Black Renaissance, or New Negro Renaissance felt that artistic activism and the positive representation of black life and culture through the arts would have a transformative effect on American society and the status of blacks in the United States. To this end, they included and promoted the arts in the pages of their little magazines through contests supporting literary and visual culture. Alain Locke emphasized that the cosmopolitan nature of the New Negro movement was fostered by "a Negro newspaper carrying news material in English, French and Spanish, gathered from all quarters of America, the West Indies and Africa has maintained itself in Harlem for over five years. Two important magazines, both edited from New York, maintain their news and circulation on a cosmopolitan scale."[3] Locke may have been referring to the NAACP's *The Crisis*, edited by W.E.B. Du Bois, but he also might have been singling out the *Opportunity*, *The Messenger*, and Marcus Garvey's *Negro World*, the publication of the United Negro Improvement Association, commonly known as the UNIA. Through the broad circulation of New Negro periodicals, short fiction had the potential of reaching a diverse group of readers. In fact, several promising writers from the era—including Gwendolyn Bennett and Marita Bonner as well as almost complete unknowns such as Anita Scott Coleman and Eloise Bibb Thompson—never wrote book-length novels. That West's aunt purchased the paper from an aspiring medical student speaks to how black communities collectively conceived of and supported progress. Employing students to sell the periodicals not only disseminated the publications' political and aesthetic agendas, but direct financial contributions or subscriptions also enabled readers to participate actively in the uplift endeavors the publications endorsed. Although Bostonians like West's mother may have been somewhat skeptical about the brouhaha in Harlem, her aunt's small act of activism had a great impact on the direction of West's life and that of her cousin, poet Helene Johnson.[4]

West recalls submitting her short story "The Typewriter" to a contest sponsored by *The Crisis*; in fact, in *Opportunity*'s contest, she won second prize, which she shared with the now legendary Zora Neale Hurston.[5] On May 1, 1926, she and her cousin attended *Opportunity*'s Second Annual Literary Awards dinner at the Fifth Avenue Restaurant. These parties showcased the work of emerging artists, but they were also social occasions for the vanguard of the New Negro movement. For Dorothy West the prize introduced her into the era with which she would always be associated. Less than a year later, she and her cousin moved to Harlem.

It was no secret that Harlem was the place to be if you were an artist, a writer, a musician, or an average citizen seeking freedom from segregation and sharecropping. The Great Migration of African Americans from the South to the North, Midwest, and West Coast had been happening since the turn of the twentieth century. At the end of the nineteenth century, when blacks saw the gains of Reconstruction fall away only to be replaced with Jim Crow segregation, disfranchisement, increased racial violence, and a neoslavery system that persisted until the civil rights movement, the stirrings began of what became known as the New Negro movement. In Alain Locke's era-defining manifesto "The New Negro," he wrote "the pulse of the Negro world has begun to beat in Harlem."[6] For Locke, the idea of Harlem represented an end to the stereotype of the plantation Negro and the emergence of an emancipated, modern black subject. The "pulse," the call for transformation, echoed throughout the United States and abroad, propelled in part by the era's key periodicals. Most historians cite the "red summer of 1919"—a period in which record numbers of black men and women were lynched and killed in race riots following the end of World War I—as the beginning of the Harlem Renaissance.

Over the course of her writing career, West published numerous short stories that exemplify the often-contradictory aesthetics of the time. They also underscore her interest in class, labor, and color distinctions. Popular representations of Harlem in the 1920s highlight its flashy, bohemian side: the Harlem of speakeasies and interracial rent parties. West's imaginative stories strike a sharp contrast to what we might presume were her experiences as a nineteen-year-old in the "magical city of New York."[7] In their introduction to West's selected writings, Cynthia Davis and Verner Mitchell note that her early stories reflect a cynicism "unusual in a young woman in her late teens"; they point to her family life, especially her parents' complicated marriage, as a source of inspiration.[8] West's intimate and professional relationships with writers like Wallace Thurman, Langston Hughes, and Zora Neale Hurston shaped her persona in the Harlem Renaissance—first as a young ingénue and later as an editor and social columnist. They laid the foundation for her writing beyond the era. Exploring these friendships and the writing produced during the prolific twenties allows me to identify and trace the evolution of West's trademark focus on class, gender, and race hierarchies in African American culture.

As a result of the publicity surrounding *The Wedding*, West was "rediscovered" as the last surviving participant of the Harlem Renaissance, and a resurgence of popular and critical interest sparked the reprinting of her published and unpublished short stories. The availability of these short stories allows them to be read collectively. Laurie Champion argues for their value as a whole:

West's short stories illustrate much more when read collectively than when read individually—the whole is much richer than the sum of its parts. Attitudes of characters as well as consequences of various economic positions can be compared and contrasted both within individual stories and against other stories. When read together, these stories provide powerful statements about America as a sort of social text. They survey results of unequal distribution of power that leads to oppression based primarily on class, while also demonstrating ways race and gender are affected by social hierarchies.[9]

Three stories by West published in the mid-to-late 1920s can be read as a collective social text that sets the stage for her future creative and editorial work. "The Typewriter" (*Opportunity*, 1926), "An Unimportant Man" (*Saturday Evening Quill*, 1928), and "Hannah Byde" (*Messenger*, 1926) appear in distinct publications that have particular audiences for which West's writing is uncommonly suited. In each story, she uses the domestic sphere as a recurring site to explore class and color, ambition and desire. West's tendency to recycle character types such as the frigid shrewish wife, the melancholy husband, and the ambitious mother anticipates her critiques of marriage and the social conventions and aspirations of the black middle class in her most memorable and satirical work of fiction, *The Living Is Easy*.

"The Typewriter," the most anthologized of all West's stories, was first published in *Opportunity*. Edited by sociologist Charles Johnson, *Opportunity* featured less inflammatory material than *The Crisis*. The style and content of "The Typewriter" appears to be particularly in line with the publication's emphasis on uplift and integration. Gwendolyn Bennett designed a provocative cover for July 1926; the image features three female silhouettes caught in a variety of titillating poses. One of the silhouettes wears an ensemble that resembles Josephine Baker's iconic banana skirt. The images evoke the musical sensibility of the jazz era and the iconography of Africa. The playful, seductive cover is somewhat at odds with the featured articles, such as E. Franklin Frazier's "Three Scourges of the Negro Family" and William Harmon's "Skilled Negro Workmen." Poems from Helene Johnson and Wallace Thurman also appeared in this issue.

In its portrayal of the yearnings of a working-class father and husband in a way that universalizes one man's particular struggle in the modern city, "The Typewriter" reads like a product of the literary Left. Its themes foreshadow West's later involvement with black radicalism and communism. The protagonist is most likely patterned after her father. Although Isaac West was a successful businessman, the character "J. Lucius Jones" embodies the work ethic, values, and inner turmoil West sees as constitutive of her father's personal and professional life. In fact, Jones is a precursor, or perhaps the original template, for several of West's masculine characters, who are stoic and hardworking, yet frustrated by their inability to be effective patriarchs.

In the story, the father invents the persona of "J. Lucius Jones" to help his daughter perfect her typing speed. At first, the noisy "clatter clatter" and the cost of the rented typewriter annoy him; however, once he begins dictating letters the instrument becomes the vehicle for his imaginary life as a financial tycoon communicating with J. P. Morgan and Henry Ford about fictitious business ventures.[10] His fantasy life is both pathetic and sympathetic. He acts out the dream of success that many American workingmen of all colors share; the confines of his apartment expand into the penthouse suite of the office building he cleans. Once his daughter finds a job—"Twelve dollars a week to start with!"—his dream comes to an abrupt halt. Rather than pride in his daughter's achievement, the void left by the returned typewriter creates: "Silence. That crowded in on him, engulfed him. Blurred his vision, dulled his brain." The blinding despair he feels is too much; Jones dies of a heart attack foreshadowed by the "inhuman, strangled cry" he suffers earlier in the story.

"The Typewriter" provides a sharp portrait of the difficulty black southern migrants faced in the North. The reader first meets the protagonist as he, lost in thought, trudges down a cold Boston street: "He was cold, and he hated the North, and particularly Boston, and saw suddenly a barefoot pickaninny sitting on a fence in the hot, Southern sun with a piece of steaming corn bread and a piece of fried salt pork in either grimy hand." The immediacy of this recollection is as startling as the contradictions it embodies. The image should be a wishful counter to all Jones hates about Boston, yet the child is a pickaninny on a fence: a blatantly derogatory character, the staple stereotype of blackface minstrelsy. The food, while delectable to Jones who has tired of the "beans, and frankfurters, and light bread" that composed his evening meal, is held in the child's "grimy hand[s]." Neither dish suggests affluence. It is ironic that the family's migration has altered their geography, but their class status has remained stagnant. The novelty of the new dish does not represent the kind of transformation Locke prophesies in his manifesto.

Although an atmosphere of entrapment and disappointment undergirds "The Typewriter," West does not necessarily name racial discrimination as the overt cause of Jones's thwarted dreams and untimely demise. Rather than provide a schematic or simple explanation for his predicament, the story slowly explores various internal and external factors familiar in American naturalist fiction, with its debates over nature versus nurture and the struggle of the individual against the social forces of his environment. West's narrator wryly classifies him: "he was not the progressive type." Neither his education nor his jobs—"bell boy, porter, waiter, cook, and finally janitor"—prepared him for an office with a "real mahogany desk" and "plate-glass windows." Yet generations of readers recognize his universal plight. In her sensitive treatment of how Jones transforms himself into "that enviable emblem of American life: a businessman," she offers a profound glimpse into his inner life.[11]

While an inaccessible American dream haunts the protagonist of "The Typewriter," the prescriptive requirements of uplift and the politics of respectability preoccupy the namesake of "An Unimportant Man."[12] In this story West introduces multiple themes and character types that meander backward and forward in a man's life in order to explore the connections between social, economic, and sexual desire and the necessary sacrifices that enable middle-class achievement. The story was first published in the *Saturday Evening Quill,* a publication produced by a Boston organization of black writers who met in the home of Eugene and Edythe Gordon. This "Club" was similar to the literary salons held in other urban centers; for example, poet and playwright Georgia Douglas Johnson hosted the "Saturday Nighters" in Washington, D.C., and novelist/editor Jessie Fauset held literary teas in Harlem. These spaces provided crucial opportunities for the kind of social and artistic exchange that nourished creative production.

Also set in the domestic sphere, the first line of "An Unimportant Man" immediately places class aspiration in direct conflict with romantic and sexual fulfillment. The protagonist Zebediah "awoke to the dig of his wife's sharp elbow in the tender flesh of his side."[13] While sleeping next to his wife Minnie with her "dry" breasts and "long ropes of hair," Zebediah dreams of a "phantom woman," with "dark flesh," and "hot, thick, sensual lips" "more terribly real than the passionless woman who lay every night by his side." That dark woman is Wanda, his first love who "bound him eternally to him with her darkly beautiful body." Wanda, however, was antithetical to success. With Wanda, Zebediah "had never seen beyond a two-room cabin" in the South. Zebediah's mother, Miss Lily, views Wanda as a jezebel.[14] In contrast, Zeb's wife Minnie—a light-skinned woman possibly named for West's white-looking aunt—recalls Jean Toomer's imagistic poem "Portrait."[15] In this poem, Toomer infuses the imagery of lynching into a compact description of the woman: "Hair—braided chestnut, coiled like a lyncher's rope/Eyes—fagots/Lips—old scars, or the first red blisters/Breath—the last sweet scent of cane."[16] While not quite as accusatory or graphic as Toomer's allusions, Minnie's alluring attributes are the very instruments of Zebediah's psychic destruction: "the long dark hair of his golden bride was the silken coil that had trapped him."[17] She is a succubus stripped of all sensual appeal.

Zebediah's frustration with his marriage and his inability to pass the bar recalls J. Lucius Jones's melancholy; however, "An Unimportant Man" is more concerned with how restrictive ideas about success and happiness are passed down from parent to child. As he tries to make sense of his choices, Zebediah concludes that allowing his mother to determine the course of his life was a mistake, and he is anxious to prevent his wife's and mother's suppression of his daughter Essie's dreams in service to what he has come to believe are false values. Class and racial hierarchies consistently and ironically frustrate his efforts to either support Essie or mentor his young friend Parker. Just as Zebediah dreams of becoming a "Darrow for his race," Parker wants to "go just as high as a white man—and then just a little higher."[18] Like Zebediah's mother, however, Parker sees an advantageous marriage as a prerequisite for joining the ranks of the black middle class and marries "into the cream of Washington society" for his "children's sake."[19]

Although we often presume that patriarchy endows men with the power to enforce behavioral standards of respectability upon women, in "An Unimportant Man" two generations of women, Miss Lily and her daughter Minnie, suppress Essie's desire to become a dancer. Her father is sympathetic to her artistic nature and her wish to do or create something beautiful. His empathy for her aspirations triggers memories of his first love Wanda, who embodies creative expression, folk culture, and sensuality—all things absent from Zebediah's current life.

In Candice Jenkins's study of intimacy in black culture she identifies an impulse called the salvific wish that partially accounts for Zebediah's conflict and clarifies Miss Lily's and Minnie's motivations. Jenkins defines the salvific wish as "the desire to rescue the black community from racist accusations of sexual and domestic pathology through the embrace of bourgeois propriety."[20] Because this impulse carries with it the unintended consequences of intraracial hatred, classism, and colorism, Jenkins views it as an untenable position that does not achieve its proposed goal. Miss Lily's and Minnie's Victorian beliefs equate performing on the stage with prostitution. A more contemporary association would be the dancers at the jazz clubs like the Cotton Club or vaudeville's all-black revues. The women adhere to antiquated behavioral standards; they believe that a woman's primary role is to educate the next generation. Miss Lily's equation of dancing with sin is problematic, but her cautionary advice—"They's too many good-looking girls in the gutter. Let your brain work for you, chile, not your face"—is understandable.[21] The problem focuses on the limited roles available to black women. Even if the salvific wish does not entirely explain Parker's marriage, it is certainly in play when he informs Essie that "all nice colored girls are teachers. . . . There's nothing else for a real nice colored girl to do." No career option allows Essie autonomy and self-expression. A series of fateful events brings her father in line with his wife. He acquiesces to the women's plans for Essie and decides that "the race [is] too young . . . for whimsical indulgence."[22]

West's male characters seem destined for sexless unions in which the carnal act is only allowed for procreation; however, in "Hannah Byde" West presents the female point of view from these doomed, calculated marriages in which women perform their marital duty rarely, grudgingly, and, once the desired heir has been produced, never again. These wives' defining emotion toward their husbands is contempt; they are completely unappreciative of the material goods their men provide. "Hannah Byde" portrays black women not as the nurturers of the race but instead associates them with slavery's most pernicious instrument of torture: "[Hannah] had learned to whip him out of a mood with the lash of her scathing tongue." Hannah accuses her husband "with rising hysteria": "You feed me. You clothe me. You've bought me a player piano which I loathe—flaunting emblem of middle-class existence—Oh, don't go to the trouble of trying to understand that—And a stupid victrola stocked with dreadful noises of your incomparable Mamie Waters."[23] Hannah scorns the markers of middle-class identity, yet these "emblems" determined her marital partner. Her accusations also introduce the now familiar contrast of male desire for the dicty, asexual respectability of the wife in contrast with the low-down sensuality of the blues woman. "Mamie Waters" represents the same nostalgic longing for the passionate and sexually fulfilling relationship proffered by Wanda in "An Unimportant Man."[24]

West's stories generalize about the universal condition of women through the particular lens of the black middle class. The problems affecting Hannah Byde seems to be those that also afflict Edna Pontellier in Kate Chopin's *The Awakening* (1899) and Helga Crane in Nella Larsen's novel *Quicksand* (1928). "The tentacles of awful despair" frustrate West's female characters as much as they pull at Edna and Helga, who see themselves trapped in a meaningless existence. Hannah's abstract, inarticulate depression drives her to stage her own murder (or suicide), but she faints before she can follow through. As Doctor Jim examines her (and diagnoses pregnancy as the cause of her fainting spell), he thinks, "How different would have been her life, how wide the avenues of achievement, how eager the acclaiming crowd, how soft her bed of ease, had this glorious golden woman been born white."[25] The doctor's observation, however, does not elicit much sympathy for Hannah. By creating an unlikable character West diminishes the story's exploration of how women experience a stifling marriage.

Effective in "Hannah Byde" is the acute awareness of how gender interacts with spatial relations. In each of her stories West imagines how exterior space influences a character's interiority, how the family domicile and neighborhood constrain or enable mobility. Frequently, her family dramas unfold in the domestic space of the apartment. Regardless of size—Hannah Byde lives in a four-room flat—many of her characters feel constrained and suffocated by the narrowness of their lives. The kitchen, which traditionally represents a place of community and comfort in black culture, functions as a site of confusion and constriction. After all, four heavy kitchen knives prompt Hannah to imagine staging her own murder.

West's fellow Bostonian, writer Marita Bonner, elegantly expresses the perplexing containment women experience in public and urban space in her 1925 essay "On Being Young—a Woman—and Colored." Marita Bonner was educated in Brookline, Massachusetts, and taught in Washington, D.C. Although her prizewinning essay did not lead her to Harlem, she encountered the New Negro Renaissance through attending Georgia Douglas Johnson's S Street salons. Bonner's experimental essay captures the intensity of the urban landscape while deftly articulating the limitations imposed by gender and color:

"For you know that—being a woman—you cannot twice a day or twice a year, for that matter, break away to hear or see anything in a city that is supposed to hear and see too much. That's being a woman. A woman of any color. You decide that something is wrong with a world that stifles and chokes; that cuts off and stunts; hedging in, pressing down on eyes, ears and throat."[26]

Bonner's depiction of a woman hedged in by her sex echoes the suffocation experienced by Hannah Byde. Hannah's "four-room flat" reinforces that sensation, as does the inevitable proximity of her husband: "One comes upon Hannah in her usual attitude of bitter resignation, gazing listlessly out of the window of her small, conventionally, cheaply furnished parlor. Hannah, a gentle woman crushed by the environment, looking dully down the stretch of drab tomorrows littered with the ruins of shattered dreams."[27] Though the exact view from her window is withheld, below her "holiday crowds [are] hurrying in the street," drunks encounter policemen, and "proud black fami[lies]" mingle. Unlike J. Lucius Jones's wife, Hannah seems to live a mainstream (if deplorably conventional) middle-class life. She has a parlor, she honeymoons in Niagara, and she considers herself a gentlewoman. The opening scene is remarkably free of racial markers. Always aware of audience, West is beginning to craft stories that resonate interracially. Hannah could be any middle-class American woman trapped by her decision to marry for expediency; however, as the story progresses West grounds it in a black middle-class context to illuminate the lives of "sensitive, spiritless Negro women caught fast in the tentacles of awful despair," a despair intensified by the spaces they occupy. West waits until she has already established empathy before incorporating racial markers into the text. Rather than avoidance, this kind of unfolding interrogates the multiple meanings of "gentle woman" so that its association with entitlement and respectability is severed from a presumption of whiteness. The contrast between Hannah and her husband calls her own identity into question. She deploys nearly every denigrating adjective imaginable to describe him: he is savage, bestial, ignorant, brutally coarse, and illiterate. He has a flat head, a bull-like neck, and a heavy nose. In short, he is a man from which "every vestige of civilization had fled."[28] Her disappointment in life obscures and moreover racializes her view of her husband's hard work and adoration.

West's conflation of class status and respectability with skin color and her recurring concern with the apparent fragility of the black middle class create a persistent source of tension in her stories. Similar to Jessie Fauset, whose class-conscious novels map the existence and persistence of black middle-class enclaves in Philadelphia, West is intent on proving that "the Black middle class did not spring into being as the Black middle class."[29] In her interviews, she charts black social mobility along a continuum of hard work, education, and selective marriage that she traces back to slavery. The interracial relationships and children that resulted from the sexual subordination of enslaved African women by their white masters created a new people whose legal and racial status was ambiguous. Were they free or enslaved, white or black? Depending on the state in which they lived and the political climate of the time, the answer to this question could be both or neither. Some plantation owners educated their offspring (sending them to colleges like Wilberforce); they also occasionally freed and financially supported the mothers. Literary critic Xiomara Santamarina refers to this process as a kind of sexual emancipation.[30] Other fathers made no difference between the children of these consensual or nonconsensual unions and their other human property. The pseudo-scientific belief that an infusion of "white" blood "improved" blacks, as well as the tendency to employ lighter-skinned blacks as house servants, led to a social hierarchy in the African American community that persisted long after slavery had ended. The writings of turn-of-the-century authors like Pauline Hopkins, Sutton Griggs, Charles Chesnutt, and Frances Harper all explore the instability of class status based on color. During the Harlem Renaissance, novelists continued to mine themes of racial intermixing and the indeterminacy of identity; Larsen, Fauset, James Weldon Johnson, and George Schuyler are among those who recycled and/or transformed nineteenth-century literary tropes like the tragic mulatto/mulatta in their fiction.

In the oral history *Longing to Tell: Black Women Talk about Sexuality and Intimacy,* Tricia Rose identifies a critical link between class and sexuality that emerges in the women's stories about their sexual and intimate lives. As she writes in her introduction: "it struck me that the ways that class and sexual identity play out are far more complex and sometimes muddled. . . . For example, there are a few women who identify themselves as heterosexual and yet describe lesbian sexual experiences. The reverse is also true: women who identify themselves as lesbians but have had sexual experiences with men."[31] Although the oral histories in Rose's book were collected some fifty years after the Harlem Renaissance, the ways in which black subjects have had to negotiate categories of class and race in their private and public lives is surprisingly similar across time periods. The boundaries between middle and working class, between gay and straight, have long been "muddled" in the black community. Race, Rose argues, complicates class markers that we presume identify middle-class status such as home ownership, income, and job status. In the interviews, she observes, "women whose parents had what are often thought of as working-class jobs, such as firemen, postal workers, and secretaries, considered themselves middle class in the context of their mostly black communities."[32] Other women who make salaries below what mainstream society would consider middle class have jobs or education levels that their families perceive as high status.

Tricia Rose's observations about the connection between class and sexuality provide a useful framework for understanding the curious representation of sex and intimacy in West's stories as well as the questions surrounding West's own sexual orientation and private life. To fully understand

West's early developmental years as an artist in Harlem it is important to place her within a bohemian coterie that was alternatively radical, black, and bisexual.[33] The tensions between the political push for a heterosexual, patriarchal black ideology and the potential for a queer of color sensibility that allows a more fluid understanding of relationships and less strict behavioral codes becomes the subtext behind West's stories of men and women trapped in marriages, jobs, and even architecture they find stifling and destructive.[34] A brief look at West's relationship with writer/social critic Wallace Thurman, as portrayed through their published writings and private letters, provides insight into West's private life and public persona in Harlem in the twenties.

Thurman was one of two Harlem Renaissance luminaries to become fast friends with West and her cousin Helene Johnson almost as soon as they arrived in Harlem. The cousins first stayed at the 137th Street Y, but by March 1929 they are living in Zora Neale Hurston's West Sixty-sixth Street Apartment. Like Hurston, who coined the term "Niggerati" to describe the vanguard of the era in a way that both acknowledged and mocked their aspirations for political transformation through art, Wallace Thurman was known for his biting satire and irreverence. In a 1929 letter to Langston Hughes, Thurman castigates nearly every major writer from the era:

> Found [Claude McKay's] *Banjo* turgid and tiresome. *Passing* possessed of the same faults as *Quicksand*. [Walter White's] *Rope and Faggot* good for library reference. Nella Larsen can write, but oh my god she knows so little how to invest her characters with any life like possibilities. They always outrage the reader, not naturally as people have a way of doing in real life, but artificially like ill managed puppets. Claude I believe has shot his bolt. Jessie Fauset should be taken to Philadelphia and cremated. You should write a book. Countee [Cullen] should be cas-trated and taken to Persia as the Shah's eunuch. Jean Toomer should be enshrined as a genius and immortal and he should also publish his new book about which gossip is raving. Bud Fisher should stick to short stories. Zora should learn craftsmanship and surprise the world and outstrip her contemporaries as well. Bruce [Nugent] should be spanked, put in a monastery and made to concentrate on writing. Gwen-nie [Bennett] should stick to what she is doing. Aaron [Douglas] needs a change of scenery and a psychic shock. Eric [Walrond] ought to finish *The Big Ditch* or destroy it. I should commit suicide.[35]

I have quoted this rich passage in its entirety because it provides an admittedly biased, bitter snapshot of many major players in the era. Thurman's arrogance is coupled with a hard frankness that is the mark of a critic who refuses to allow artists to rest on their laurels. Note that Thurman does not mention West or

Johnson in his rant, although he was well acquainted with the cousins by 1929. In his novel *Infants of the Spring* (1932), a roman à clef about the social life and philosophical debates of the Harlem Renaissance, West and Johnson do appear as young ingénues:

> Sweetie May was accompanied by two young girls, recently emigrated from Boston. They were the latest to be hailed as incipient immortals. Their names were Doris Westmore and Hazel Jamison. Doris wrote short stories. Hazel wrote poetry. Both had become known through a literary contest fostered by one of the leading Negro magazines. Raymond liked them more than he did most of the younger recruits to the movement. For one thing, they were characterized by a freshness and naïveté which he and his cronies had lost. And, surprisingly enough for Negro prodigies, they actually gave the promise of possessing literary talent. He was most pleased to see them. He was also amused by their interest and excitement. A salon! A literary gathering! It was one of the civilized institutions they had dreamed of finding in New York, one of the things they had longed and hoped for.[36]

This thinly veiled introduction of the Boston duo to the Harlem Renaissance indicates just how powerfully the Harlem intelligentsia responded to the newcomers. They had arrived at a turning point in the movement. By the late 1920s, optimism was waning. Magazines began to eliminate contests and the artistic material they encouraged. The Great Depression loomed ahead. Thurman and his circle mentored newcomers like the cousins with the hope that they would invigorate and revitalize the movement.

Thurman's writing is especially crucial to any understanding of the sexual politics of the era. The idea of the "Gay Harlem Renaissance" is a telling misnomer. The salons and the rent parties were spaces of changeable sexual orientation, interracial exchange (of all kinds), and general bohemian *laissez faire*. Deeply entrenched politics of uplift, however, required a rigorous adherence to respectability. How else can we account for Countee Cullen's disastrously engineered marriage to Yolande Du Bois or Carl Van Vechten's amiable but platonic partnership with Fania Marinoff? In a posthumous biographical essay entitled "Elephant's Dance: A Memoir of Wallace Thurman," West attributes the failure of Thurman's marriage to the "chaste and saffron-colored" Louise Thompson, but West is reluctant to fully articulate the reasons for the marriage's failure. Instead, she addresses its potential: "Other women were marrying artists and thereby firmly entrenching themselves in Negro society by giving typical parties of the time. Thurman's wife tried it, and on all occasions came to grief through the absence of her husband or his tardy and reluctant appearance." West implies that Thurman's failure to be a good heterosexual husband was a result of his disdain for Negro society. She does not enumerate what "scandalous things were said about the disunion."[37] But Thurman's sexual orientation, as in the case of Countee Cullen, must have in part accounted for the marriage's dissolution.

Thurman's letters to West provide an intimate and revealing portrait of the young writer that attributes her conflicted representations of marriage to her own lack of sexual experience. He candidly writes: "My dear Dot I do not want you to become promiscuous nor to sacrifice your virginity purely because I ventured the opinion that it seemed to me your stories lacked passion and that your virginal state might be in some vague way responsible."[38] He also warns West not to emulate her cousin Helene, whom he views as promiscuous. Black bohemian culture appeared beset by the anxiety resulting from the sociopolitical need to affirm heterosexual relationships. Paradoxically, bisexuality was both tolerated and smothered. From reading West and Thurman one gets the sense that confusion around gender roles and questions of sexuality threaten to destabilize the personal and collective advancement of black families. The marriages featured in West's stories invalidate the black bourgeois strategy of "marrying-up" by showing the dysfunction of relationships based on false notions of beauty, culture, and entitlement.

Thurman's interest in West as a friend and a model for some of his fictional characters is most sharply defined in his characterization of Emma Lou, the heroine of his 1929 novel *The Blacker the Berry*. The novel takes up questions of color and class prejudice among African Americans in a manner that sharply resonates with West's writing life. Many critics, including West, have suggested that Emma Lou is actually meant to represent Thurman, who was by all accounts very dark-skinned. In "Elephant's Dance" West writes: "His dark-skinned heroine suffered many of the small humiliations he would not have admitted to suffering himself."[39] Like most fictional characters, Emma Lou was no doubt an amalgamation of experience and imagination; however, I see some definite parallels between Emma Lou's physical description and family background and the color dynamics of West's family background. Like West, Emma Lou finds her way to Harlem, where she attends a rent party with a light-skinned boyfriend who is so conflicted over his feelings for a dark-skinned woman that he cannot bring himself to introduce her to his upper-crust friends and instead takes her "slumming." Emma Lou comments on her complexion: "More acutely than ever before Emma began to feel that her luscious black complexion was somewhat of a liability, and that her marked color variation from the other people in her environment was a decided curse." Her explanation for her color was that: "her mother was quite fair, so was her mother's mother, and her mother's brother, and her mother's brother's son; but then none of them had had a black man for a father. Why *had* her mother married a black man? Surely there had been some eligible brown-skin men around."[40]

In West's family she was "the only dark child"; however, like many African Americans, she "was born into a family that had every color in the world, every color. They went from dark to me, from white too—I had a brown-skinned aunt and a white-skinned aunt. Half the people in my family look like white, so that therefore in my family, what my mother called 'color foolishness,' there is no color foolishness."[41] Despite her claims that there was no "color foolishness" in her family, West's particular take on this subject always seems to emphasize those family members with Anglo features. She was fond of telling interviewers "most white people think that all colored people are my color, and it's so interesting that that's what I'm writing right now, about the color."[42] In fact, West wrote obsessively about skin color for the entirety of her career. Unlike Thurman's, her critique of colorism, or intraracial prejudice based on skin color, never quite undermines associations of lighter skin with beauty and elitism. Still, *The Blacker the Berry* is an important text to keep in mind when reading West's writings about color, class, and sexuality.

If Thurman gave West both writerly and sexual advice, then it was Hurston who provided the most influential female mentorship. Novelists Jessie Fauset and Nella Larsen, though maligned by Thurman, were prolific during the period that West was writing; however, no substantive correspondence between West and the two novelists has emerged. In addition to renting her apartment to the cousins, Hurston had a close relationship with her young friends. In a November 5, 1928, letter she writes, "I trust you and Helene more than anyone else in this world. You are the fine gold in New York's show and shine. I have a lot in store for you."[43] Hurston often signed her letters to either cousin "your sister," making her part of West's increasingly expansive network of kin. From Hurston, West learned how to represent the "folk" with sensitivity. West did not write rural stories; however, her characters frequently evince a deeply nostalgic affinity for southern black culture. Some of that feeling of loss and desire for a pastoral life can be attributed to West's recollection of her mother's memories of South Carolina, but, in terms of West's aesthetic representations of the South, she could not have found a better model than Hurston.

Given that Hurston is known for her masterful use of African American vernacular and evocative representations of rural folk culture in her fiction, the similarities between her writing and West's may not seem readily apparent. Both writers, however, are concerned with intraracial class divisions and the ways in which gender and color inform the social relationships of blacks. The locales in their writing may be regionally disparate; after all, Boston's urban streets are far from the all-black, rural hamlets of Florida. Yet both writers attend carefully to how power is attained, maintained, and manipulated by men and women in intimate spheres. Several critics have pointed out the similarities between Hurston's 1924 short story "Drenched in Light," which appeared in the December 1924 issue of *Opportunity*, and *The Living Is Easy*.[44] Hurston's heroine Isis Watts, whom David Levering Lewis characterizes as an "uncontrollable hoyden," has quite a bit in common with the adolescent Cleo, the heroine of *The Living Is Easy*. In the scenes from the novel that flash back to Cleo's southern childhood, the feeling of nostalgia evokes Hurston's style. As with Hurston's iconic scene in *Their Eyes Were Watching God*, when Janie experiences a sexual awakening beneath the pear trees, Cleo's pubescent desires appear organic to her southern environment. West depicts her as a wild woman: "She streaked to the stall and flung open the barrier. The wild horse smelled her wildness. Her green eyes locked with his red-flecked glare. Their wills met, clashed, and would not yield."[45] West describes Cleo as being unable to walk "a chalkline" to please her mother;[46] similarly Isis dances "before a gaping crowd in her [Grandma's] brand new red tablecloth, reeking of lemon extract."[47] The idea of wild, hoydenish girls whose beauty and spunk must be curtailed by the relatives in anticipation of the world's discipline is a common theme in both writers' work. These girls often find their potential cut short either by grandmothers who represent old values and cower before white supremacist ideas or by mothers who have internalized a Victorian sense of propriety that they pass on to their daughters. Such belief systems produce women alienated from their own bodies and confused about their own sexuality. Their beauty becomes a tool they use only to manipulate and entrap. Their light skin symbolizes a false love for Anglo ideals, or, in the case of the Duchess (*The Living Is Easy*) and Janie, it is the visible stamp of the sexual violations visited upon an earlier generation.

Zora Neale Hurston also appears to share West's satirical view of intraracial prejudice that hinges on color. In a letter to Charlotte Osgood Mason, Hurston jokes about West's color and the company she keeps: "Well, Langston, Louise [Thompson] and a crowd of white Negroes have sailed to Russia to make a Negro movie. Only two in the crowd look anything like Negroes."[48] If we consider Hurston's comments with West's opinion of her family, then we must acknowledge that skin tone is often interpreted differently depending on the eye of the beholder. The shipboard photograph of the cast taken en route to Moscow reveals that this joke is not necessarily accurate with regard to the men, but in the black-and-white photograph West is certainly one of the darker-skinned women.

Given their close friendship, West probably would have read Hurston's aptly named play *Color Struck*, which was published in *Fire!!* in 1926, the same year as West's prizewinning story "The Typewriter." *Color Struck* takes up the issue of skin tone with aplomb. Her heroine Emma may have also inspired Thurman's Emma Lou in *The Blacker the Berry*, inspiration suggesting a triangular synergy among the three writers. Though the play was never staged, one can imagine the ease of assembling a cast from Hurston and West's multitalented circle. Louise Thompson or Dorothy Peterson could play the light-skinned vamp Effie, Countee Cullen or Langston Hughes would star as John Turner, and Hurston or West would portray the tragically color-obsessed Emmaline. I want to briefly speculate about how the visual performance of *Color Struck* may have influenced interpretations of the play. Neither Thurman nor West had seen the play performed on or off Broadway, though they may have heard informal readings of the play at literary salons, a kind of parlor play. This is significant because what is fascinating about *Color Struck* is the spectacle Hurston hoped to evoke through the stage directions of the piece's signature scene: the Cake Walk. Once one considers the cakewalk as the focal point, the overstory of intraracial color prejudice takes a backseat to Hurston's celebration of black expressive performance. Her characterization of Emma mocks that sliver of black culture holding itself aloof and refusing to celebrate what it considers low culture, out of a misguided (in Hurston's mind) desire to please or emulate "white" manners or sensibilities. The cakewalk was an elaborate couples' dance created by African Americans first as a parody of European ballroom dances to which they later added innovative elements of their own. Jayna Brown's cultural history of black variety shows explains:

> Black performers used the cakewalk as a lampoon of black middle-class social pretensions. It critiqued black bourgeois retention of the prim, well-behaved, Victorian models for civilized deportment and the black bourgeoisie's sensitivity to white approval. Dancers cadenced their versions of the cakewalk as a satirical comment on the self-conscious elitism of the black Brooklyn set and the Washington, D.C. elite. Members of the black professional classes were critical of variety stage performance. The black middle classes did not approve of the cakewalk dance's overt physicality and ostentation and publicly scorned participation in such decadent acts.[49]

Brown's description suggests why the cakewalk's popularity waned by the 1920s and 1930s—New Negro leaders criticized the dance. *Color Struck* references the dance's characteristic promenade and high kicks. While traveling on the train to the competition, the characters perform impromptu "hoochie coochies" and the "pas me las."[50] As she watches these dances, Emma becomes convinced that her partner John, with whom she is slated to dance at the competition, is in love with Effie, a light-skinned dancer who has appeared on the bus without her partner. Emma's uncontrollable jealousy drives the plot and generates much of the play's tension. Given Hurston's irreverent humor and scornful view of what she identified as the cultural repression and self-hatred of the Harlem literati, it is possible that she included the heavy dialect and hyperbolic performance scenes to make New Negro audience members squirm in their seats. The stage directions suggest that what Hurston really hoped to achieve was a play that celebrated the cakewalk with a vaudeville style performance as its crowning jewel. The storyline of Essie's "jealous love" provides the frame for Hurston's homage to black vaudeville revues like *The Creole Show* and *Clorindy, or the Origins of the Cakewalk.*

Hurston's drama marks a nostalgic invocation of the 1900s spectacle that parodies black bourgeois behavior; the play allows her to memorialize an important part of black performance culture while also poking fun at the pretensions of the middle class and their idealization of light skin. Emma and John, "the best cake-walkers in dis state," are meant to invoke famous cakewalking couples like Charles Johnson and Dora Dean (known as the Black Venus) who toured Europe in the early 1900s. The dance hall is "decorated with palmetto leaves and Spanish moss—a flag or two" to evoke an antebellum ambiance suitable for the performance. Effie and John dance to "Way Down in Georgia" while the spectators on stage (and presumably in the audience) clap and sing along until "they have reached frenzy."[51]

Color Struck also recalls Charles Chesnutt's 1901 collection *The Wife of His Youth and Other Stories of the Color Line.* In the title story a man with social aspirations abandons his dark-skinned wife only to be confronted by her years later on the eve of his marriage to a nearly white woman. The frontispiece to the 1901 edition displays an illustration of the reunited couple at the "blue vein" society ball. In *Color Struck*, Hurston seems to similarly present intraracial discrimination based on skin color as absurd, yet the excessive nature of Emma's fears compromises the integrity and authenticity of the written play on the page. Just imagine from Emma's perspective the scene where Effie and John dance the cakewalk together. The spectacle may have engendered more sympathy for Emma's anxieties from a viewing, rather than a reading, audience. Still, it is hard to empathize with a woman who accuses her lover of being enamored with her half-white daughter while the girl is on her deathbed. Like Thurman's Emma Lou and West's Hannah Byde, protagonists who sabotage their own happiness because of false notions of race and class hierarchies elicit little sympathy from readers.

Despite Zora Neale Hurston's ambivalent association with the New Negro movement and the fact that her first novel *Their Eyes Were Watching God* (1937), like West's *The Living Is Easy*, was published toward the end of the Harlem Renaissance, she remains one of the most familiar writers of the era. Her work as an anthropologist and collector of African American folklore won her the sponsorship of Charlotte Osgood Mason, a white patron of the arts who also supported Langston Hughes. Known as the infamous "Godmother," Mason demanded fidelity and maintained propriety rights over the art and research she financed. Hurston's anxiety about her relationship with Mason comes out in her letters to West. It is likely that the trust she placed in her tenants resulted in the salvaging of material she wanted to keep away from Mason. In one letter she concludes: "PLEASE DON'T LET ANYONE KNOW THAT YOU HAVE HEARD FROM ME OR SEE MY PAPERS BEFORE YOU MAIL THEM."[52]

West later shocked interviewers with her accusations that Hurston stole her fur coat. Such antipathy is comprehensible only when we understand West's competitiveness with her contemporaries. As young women in Harlem, West and her cousin no doubt looked up to Hurston even though she could be irresponsible and unpredictable. Toward the end of her life, with her legacy to cultivate, West may have been uneasy with the revival and recovery of Hurston's work following Alice Walker's article in *Ms.* magazine. Hurston's novels are now widely read and regularly taught in high schools and universities while only a select cadre of scholars and students know West's writings. Interestingly enough, Halle Berry starred in the Oprah-produced miniseries of *Their Eyes Were Watching God.* When Hurston opened her home to the young West, neither writer could have imagined that one day the same actress would play both their heroines on the small screen. Hurston may now have the lion's share of well-earned acclaim, but at least West lived to enjoy her revival and the publication of her final novel. Unlike Hurston, who died penniless in Florida without a headstone, West continued writing and publishing her articles on Martha's Vineyard for the duration of her lifetime.

West's experiences among the vanguard of New Negroes as a young writer in Harlem in the twenties and later as a welfare representative working among the urban poor, are critical to understanding the direction of her career as a short story writer, magazine editor, novelist, and newspaper columnist. Hurston's focus on insular, black enclaves and her experiments with so-called "white novels," like the understudied *Seraph on the Sewanee* (1948), no doubt helped West hone the intraracial class critique and regional distinctiveness that manifest in the short fiction she produced for the New York Federal Writers' Project of the Works Progress Administration (WPA) and her popular, "aracial" short stories in the *New York Daily News.* One wonders if her characterization of the "New Yorkers" as unrestrained immoderates in the lost beach stories derives from her experiences in Harlem. Chapters 3 and 4 seek to answer the question of why West's early sensitivity toward the disenfranchised and laboring classes, as evidenced in her early stories, does not develop into a fully realized radicalism similar to that of fellow New Englander Ann Petry, author of *The Street.* Instead, the demons of her childhood—"color foolishness" and class anxiety—ultimately determine the location and subject matter of her writing.

4

To Russia with Love

Here we come from a country where everything is denied us–work, protection of life and property, freedom to go where we will and to live where we will–where we are despised and humiliated at every turn. And here we are [in the U.S.S.R.], accorded every courtesy–free to go where we will and eagerly welcomed–given every opportunity to enjoy ourselves and to travel–free to pursue any work we choose.

–Louise Thompson (quoted in *Defying Dixie,* by Glenda Gilmore)

That year in Russia was the most carefree year of my life.

–Dorothy West (Deborah E. McDowell, "Conversations with Dorothy West")

A 1932 photograph of Dorothy West and Langston Hughes taken aboard the *S.S. Europa* reveals a smiling, sleeveless Dorothy leaning against the strikingly handsome bad boy of the Harlem Renaissance. His arm is draped possessively, fraternally around her shoulders. This photograph reveals their unveiled affection as mutual and spontaneous. The nature of that affection remains opaque, complicated by unanswered questions about their sexuality that surface from the duo's private letters. This image best captures West's optimistic perspective at the start of her "adventure in Moscow" as one of twenty-two African Americans enlisted to star in the infamous, ill-fated film production of *Black and White.*

What motivates West to travel to Moscow with relatively little assurance of her reception, compensation, or purpose? Is she motivated by personal, professional, or political aims? Perhaps she is merely bored with Harlem rent parties and sees the trip as a fabulous lark? Whatever the case, West's Russian sojourn would have a profound effect on her private life and creative endeavors.

Understanding West's experience in Russia requires me to establish an intricate tapestry of stories, voices, and histories from both sides of the Atlantic during the course of two centuries. Many scholars have written about the *Black and White* expedition. It remains a rich event within the historiographies of black radicalism and American communism precisely because of its spectacular failure as a project and the multinational politics behind the film's genesis and ultimate suppression. Various examinations of the trip by biographers, literary critics, and film historians reveal a complex narrative of encounters between East and West, black, white, and, of course, red. The diverse cast of characters and the fascinating terrain they traverse resist easy summarizing of the trip and require a broad understanding of the African diasporic subject in Imperial Russia and the former U.S.S.R.

My goal is neither to conclusively confirm West's politics as either "red" or "pink" nor to construct her as a closet revolutionary. Rather, I seek to understand why the trip was so meaningful to West and her fellow travelers. The Russian sojourn was a critical turning point in West's intimate and writing life. In several interviews she describes the trip as "the most carefree year of [her] life," even though the ostensible, official purpose of the trip is never realized.[1]

Uncovering a gendered, feminist view of the Russia trip is a challenge as the dominant and most comprehensive accounts of the trip are from masculine perspectives. Most historians rely on Langston Hughes's autobiography *I Wonder as I Wander* (1956). I piece together West's particular experience from a series of letters written over the course of her eleven-month stay in Russia and three publications directly based on the trip: "Room in Red Square," "An Adventure in Moscow," and "Russian Correspondence." Glenda Gilmore's *Defying Dixie: The Radical Roots of Civil Rights (1919–1950)* and Kate Baldwin's *Beyond the Color Line and the Iron Curtain: Reading Encounters between Black and Red 1922–1963* help contextualize the experience of women on the trip; both studies rely heavily on labor organizer Louise Thompson Patterson's account of the "Trip to Russia" in her unpublished autobiography.[2] As the trip's main recruiter and a true believer in the potential of communism as a viable solution to racial injustice in the United States, Thompson is attentive to the gender politics at work behind the scenes. Her perspective illuminates the relationships between the *Black and White* group and the Russians they encounter during their trip. Although Baldwin's study focuses on familiar, male perspectives and encounters within Russia, she analyzes excised portions of Langston Hughes's autobiography in a way that draws attention to his fixation with the unveiling of Uzbek women in the southern provinces. She speculates on how Hughes's writing challenges "the heteronormative bias of the black veil" by offering a "point of entry to rethink the exclusively female focus of postcolonial discussions of the veil; and it confronts the othering discourse of the Muslim veil as external to the disciplining of non-Muslim U.S. bodies in the 1930s."[3] I find the excised sections compelling; they show how Hughes manages to aestheticize the female body without sexualizing it, thus keeping the same safe distance in his writing that he also maintains in his personal interactions with those women with whom he shares various levels of intimacy. Knowing Hughes's interest and defense clarifies the peculiar, primary role he plays in West's private and public accounts of the trip as well as those remembrances of Louise Thompson Patterson.

To fully understand West's position and perspective I also draw on the travel diaries of black women sojourners to Russia both before and after West's visit. The nineteenth-century travelogues of Nancy Prince and Andrea Lee's memoir *Russian Journal* (1979), which was a National Book Award finalist, serve as discursive, contextual frames for West's experiences.[4] Filtering my particular take on the *Black and White* trip and the Russian episode in West's life primarily through the stories of Prince and Lee allows me to home in on how Russia (its geography, architecture, people, and political structure) provokes internal reflection about black class status and gender. Placing West's experiences within the frames of Prince's and Lee's Russian memoirs allows me access to what makes the Russian sojourn particularly transformative. Many other global sites could provoke similar self-reflective responses. The travelogue genre often inspires a deeper understanding about oneself as a citizen of the world. Travel memoirs by U.S. writers of color frequently evidence a more acute sense of American national identity. What makes Russia distinct from other European nations, like France, where blacks found eager reception in the interwar period? West ventures beyond what would come to be known as the iron curtain at a crucial moment. During the depression, the excitement and financing of the Harlem Renaissance began to evaporate. Hungry for revitalization, West plunges into the "Soviet experience" at a time when the rhetoric of newness that defined the New Negro conceptualization of selfhood would have resonated with the Soviet Union's attempts to redefine itself as what Francine Hirsch terms "a new type of state that looked like an empire of nationalities, but defined itself in anti-imperial terms."[5] While the *Black and White* group was in Russia, the Soviet regime was also working to define race and ethnicity in Marxist-Leninist terms. They believed sociohistorical conditions, rather than racial traits, determined human progress and development. West's early fiction demonstrated her interest in intraracial class hierarchies. West's presence in Russia at the very moment that old class and caste systems were being radically restructured necessarily had a profound effect on her future writings.[6]

"Perils by Land, and Perils by Sea":
Russia and the Black Woman Traveler

As a witness to the end of the cold war and one who grew up in fear of probable nuclear annihilation, I lack the romantic view of Russia and the U.S.S.R that captivates the writers I examine in this chapter. Unlike Andrea Lee with her "obscure attraction" to romantic childhood notions of Russia as "an infinite forest" "peopled by swan maidens, hunter princes, fabulous bears, and witches who lived in huts set on chicken legs" I am still haunted by visions of a vast Siberian plain marred by prison walls guarded by stoic men in long woolen coats.[7] The naïve optimism of *Black and White* cast members who kissed Russian soil upon arrival while a band played *L'Internationale* struck me as cinematically cliché. Moreover, I was surprised at the cavalier delight the group took in presumably bourgeois leisure activities, their distinctly Western, uncomradelike complaints about food shortages, and their eager patronization of the black market. Historian Joy Carew articulated several of my preliminary questions: "How could a country that turned a brutal and despotic face to its own people offer a hopeful visage to blacks suffering from generations of oppression and Jim Crow? How could a country whose Stalinist leadership eliminated thousands of people from all walks of life, stifling human potential and intellectual creativity, shelter and encourage growth among blacks who journeyed to its shores?"[8] The meeting of the Sixth Congress of the Comintern (Communists International) determined that blacks were a national group and that black sharecroppers in the American South constituted a potential revolutionary force. This decision motivated the film's inception; however, even before the Bolshevik revolution, Africanist subjects occupied a specialized status within Russian society even as successive regimes and governments sought to homogenize and/or eradicate religious and cultural differences across a diverse territory.[9]

In "A Room in Red Square" Dorothy West adds another complication to this paradox. Although the *Black and White* cast may have occupied a special status within Russian society, that privileged position did not necessarily commit them to socialism. Instead, what intrigues me and appeals to them is the absence of the U.S. color line and the privileges accorded to what West calls the "foreign specialist." With the exception of the truly committed communists—like Louise Thompson Patterson or Lovett Fort-Whiteman who were already converts before their arrival in Russia—few in the group sought any real solidarity with the Russian peasantry. Instead, the travelers desired an opportunity to seek their fortunes in a new system where race and class were not equivalent and class stratification had been dealt a fatal blow. Although a few settled permanently in the U.S.S.R. and married Russian women, others remained skeptical of propaganda that likened the situation of the Negro in

America to the Russian peasantry even as they recognized an opportunity for a dramatically different way of life.

African American travelers like Nancy Prince saw this potential in Russia well before the Bolshevik revolution. When Dorothy West stood on the deck of the *S.S. Europa* on what Langston Hughes would call a "fairy tale journey with amiable people," did she know that she was not the first, nor even the second black woman from New England to cross the Atlantic on a journey to Russia?[10] In 1825, Nancy Prince boarded the *Romulus* to accompany her husband, Nero Prince, a member of the Russian imperial court, to Russia, where she lived and worked for nine years. Prince's Russian sojourn is an amazing account of the perils faced and the perseverance required of black female travelers. She is a uniquely mobile agent. In her memoir, Russia functions as a utopic site from which to critique the systematic oppression she left behind in the United States. Her book challenges the narrative conventions and aims of the slave narrative, thus disputing its place as the predominant genre for antebellum African American writers. Styling herself as a pious, heroic figure and hard worker—she rescues her sister from a brothel in Boston—her adventures in Russia illuminate her own exceptional self-sufficiency.

In *A Narrative of the Life and Travels of Mrs. Nancy Prince Written by Herself* (1853) Prince portrays imperialist Russia as a haven free of American racism, where she is welcome into public and private spaces from which she would be barred in the United States. Her descriptions frequently emphasize the beauty of Russian architecture and the imperial court to draw a clear contrast between the supposedly democratic United States and the presumably oligarchy of Russia:

> As we passed through the beautiful hall, a door was opened by two colored men in official dress. The Emperor Alexander stood on his throne, in his royal apparel. The throne is circular, elevated two steps from the floor, and covered with scarlet velvet, tasseled with gold; as I entered, the Emperor [Alexander] stepped forward with great politeness and condescension; he then accompanied us to the Empress Elizabeth; she stood in her dignity, and received me in the same manner the Emperor had. They presented me with a watch, &c. It was customary in those days, when any one married, belonging to the court, to present them with gifts, according to their standard; there was no prejudice against color; there were there all castes, and the people of all nations, each in their place.[11]

To emphasize the dramatic difference between her reception in Russia and her experiences working and living in the United States, Prince frames her portrait of the imperial court with distinct, racialized images. The colored men flanking the doors that admitted her to a royal audience where she is "received" and "presented" must have made a stunning impression on her readers, particularly those who knew almost nothing of Russia. Prince and later West both overlook the cultural technologies of rule required to keep "in their place" the vastly diverse array of national, ethnic, religious, and cultural groups within the boundaries of the empire. Prince also described in lavish detail the succession of ceremonies and masquerades held at the Winter Palace as well as the "christening of the water" in which a "church is built on ice."[12] Prince appreciates the attention the empress bestows on her and her husband and does not question whether it is a result of the exotic fashionability of the African subject. She treasures the gold watch they are given as a wedding present and the patronage that allows her to establish a successful dressmaking business. While seamstresses working in Boston made only a pittance, the role of the black modiste was substantially more lucrative, if rarefied.[13] Twenty years later Elizabeth Keckley's memoir *Behind the Scenes* (1868), which chronicles her life in Abraham Lincoln's White House as Mary Lincoln's modiste, would shock black and white audiences with its revealing candor. Just as Keckley was accused of overstepping her authority, readers either misinterpreted or expressed skepticism at Prince's depiction of herself as a witness to grand political events like the Decembrist rebellion: a bloody coup in which "the bodies of the killed and mangled were cast into the river, and the snow and ice were stained with the blood of human victims."[14] Again like Keckley, Prince does style herself as heroic and extraordinarily self-sufficient in the face of catastrophe. During the great flood she rescues herself by holding on to a horse's leg, yet she credits "the providence of God" for allowing her miraculous escape from "the flood and the pit."[15]

Neglect of Prince's sensational narrative, for many years forgotten and even now understudied, speaks to suppression of, or confusion around, black women's writings that neither conformed to slave narrative genre nor actively argued against slavery. Like Maria Stewart, whose bold jeremiads admonished both blacks and whites, audiences may not have been prepared for highly mobile heroines like Nancy Prince or Mary Seacole. In the case of Seacole, the reification of Florence Nightingale as a path-breaking nurse overshadowed Seacole's fascinating role as a medic in the Crimean war, although recent recovery work has styled Seacole ironically as the "Black Nightingale." If African Diaspora studies and genre studies of travel writing privilege the mobile male adventurer or the genteel lady traveler, it is not surprising that these women fall through the gaps. While Seacole's *Wonderful Adventures of Mrs. Seacole in Many Lands* (1857) recounts her fascinating career as a "yellow doctress," I find particularly interesting, in the midst of the Crimean War, her establishment of a "British Hotel" where she serves tea and provides medical treatment. This image of Seacole, properly attired amid men of varied national and ethnic heritages, evokes the striking image of the black woman as a medical doctor, domestic diva, and globe-trotting adventuress. "Ragged edge" travelers, to borrow Jennifer Steadman's term for women who traveled for work and used new modes of transportation technology "without the benefit of chaperones, first-class accommodations or guided tours," like Seacole and Prince, had to create very complex personas.[16] For their own safety, they performed proper middle-class femininity (a category that normally excluded black women) as they moved about the globe while simultaneously maintaining within their business ventures a proper emphasis on benevolence and philanthropy. That Prince could run a successful business in which she trained employees in her charge provides clear evidence that, however rigid the caste system was in Russia, either it did not circumscribe individuals based on skin color or Prince fell into a loophole of exceptionalism, which she did not scrutinize.[17]

For example, Prince does not see much connection between Russia's system of serfdom and American slavery. At one point when describing the Russian countryside, she observes: "the village houses are built of logs corked with oakum, where the peasants reside. This class of people till the land, most of them are slaves and are very degraded. The rich own the poor, but they are not suffered to separate families or sell them off the soil. All are subject to the Emperor, and no nobleman can leave with his permission."[18] Should we be shocked that Prince is not overly concerned or empathetic with the plight of the peasantry? Here and elsewhere in her memoir she is most concerned with the separation of families, which she views as American slavery's chief evil. While in Russia, she opens an orphanage to care for abandoned children, and her account of the Decembrist rebellion primarily focuses on the breaking up of families as the most tragic element of the event.

Neither Dorothy West nor Andrea Lee emulates Prince's selective appreciation of Russian cultural practice; however, all three women seem to fit the exceptional category of "foreign specialist"—a role they occupy by virtue of their representation within Russia at a particular moment in history, from an exotic court appendage (Prince), a Negro comrade (West), or wife of an American intellectual (Lee). Their unexpected responses, class anxieties, and ambivalent politics allow me to identify illuminating points of comparison across time and space. In using Prince's and Lee's memoirs as bookends to West's Russian sojourn, I pay close attention to how each describes the accoutrements of travel, namely the ship, the hotel, and the railroad. Each of these spaces is overdetermined and embattled by its specific imperialistic connotations of progress, conquest, and tourism. Attention to how West and others move in and out of these mobile and fixed sites means taking on various social and legal practices that converge in rooms and cabins on land and sea.

The Magic Pilgrimage

Russia was a natural and appealing space for the New Negro artist because the Soviet Union's nationalist rhetoric of newness resonated strongly with the political and aesthetic goals of the New Negro movement. Langston Hughes wrote: "New times demand new people. In the Soviet Union, new people are coming into being."[19] In the 1920s and 1930s the Soviets were engaged in the process of creating and consolidating nationalities that would fall under the Soviet umbrella. The ethnic minorities of Central Asia, Uzbekistan, and the Russian Cotton Belt were of particular interest to African Americans. For American women, Soviet policy regarding marriage reform promised gender equity, still not quite achieved in the United States despite the ratification of the nineteenth amendment in 1920, and served as a precursor to the sexual revolution. Several American women, communist and non-communist, traveled to Russia, espoused the ideals of free love, and linked their radical politics to sexual awakening. For New Negro women, the situation was complicated by their position as raced as well as gendered subjects. Louise Thompson seemed particularly constrained and disturbed by behavior that went against the template for upstanding feminine, or masculine (for that matter), behavior. West's correspondence and publications produced both during and after her trip demonstrate the conflict between radical politics, burgeoning creativity, and sexual desire.

Most accounts of the *Black and White* film expedition issue from a masculine perspective. West's and Thompson's writings help piece together women's experience of the trip, while Prince's and Lee's narratives provide the contextual frame for transatlantic encounters between blacks and Russians over two centuries. Because others give much more detailed accounts of the trip, I provide only a cursory summary; elaborations emerge as they relate to West's particular experience. In 1932, Meschrabpom film, an international company with headquarters in Berlin, announced a plan to make in Russia a film about the black experience in the United States. Such an effort solidified Russian affinity with the experience of their black brethren who labored under the sharecropping system in the South, which they saw (even if Nancy Prince did not) as analogous to their situation prior to the Bolshevik revolution. Indeed, the University of California at Berkeley–educated Louise Thompson became radicalized after a sojourn in the Jim Crow South and a student uprising at Hampton Institute. Thompson's experiences at Hampton convinced her that racial uplift was "an unfeasible path to racial equality";[20] she sought an alternative solution and found it in the Hampton library. There she discovered in *Das Kapital* "an entire vocabulary linking capitalism to slavery and economic oppression, an explanation, she thought, for the persistent oppression of African Americans in the South, and a context and rudimentary blueprint for black resistance to white domination."[21] Indeed, although she did not join the American Communist Party until she returned from Russia, by 1934 the *Crisis* was calling her "the leading colored woman in the Communist movement in this country."[22]

Several accounts of the trip, including West's, downplay Thompson's role, but in fact she was charged with assembling the group. West says she was recruited by her current beau, journalist Henry Lee Moon, and Hughes—"They [Hughes and Henry Lee Moon] asked me to come along because they liked me. I liked the idea because I liked them."[23] Of the twenty-two people who traveled to Russia, few had any acting experience, and only one was a certified communist. Sylvia Garner was a singer, and West had performed in *Porgy and Bess*. On the whole, they were politically, professionally, and visually not the ideal subjects for making a film on the black southern worker. Moreover, with their varied skin tone—Zora Neale Hurston quipped, "Only two in the crowd look anything like Negroes"[24]—and northern educations they simply did not fit Russians' romanticized stereotype of the oppressed black sharecropper.

Who were these *metisi* (mixed bloods) as the Russians called them? Most were "young, well under thirty and some hardly out of their teens."[25] Owing to the fact that they needed to finance their own transatlantic passage in the midst of the depression, several of the group came from well-educated and/or white-collar backgrounds. Communist Pauli Murray, whose poem "Song" appeared in the inaugural issue of the *Challenge*, could not go because she was in her last year in college and remembered the Moscow trip as a missed lifetime opportunity.[26] As such, their transitory experiences in Russia are diverse and distinct from those of American blacks like Lovett Fort-Whiteman, Maud White, or even Paul Robeson, who were well-schooled and deeply invested in socialism as a viable political system. The traveling group included Langston Hughes, Louise Thompson, Mildred Jones (an art student), Loren Miller, Henry Lee Moon, Theodore Poston (all writers/journalists), Neil Homer Smith (a postal clerk working his way through journalism school), Lawrence Alberga, Matthew Crawford (an insurance clerk), Lloyd Patterson (a house painter expelled from Hampton for participating in the student strike), Dorothy West, Frank Montero, Sylvia Garner (a singer), Wayland Rudd (an actor), Alan McKenzie (a member of the Communist Party and a salesman, possibly white), Thurston McNairy Lewis (an actor), Juanita Lewis, Mollie Lewis (West's friend), Taylor Gordon (a graduate student), Constance White, Leonard Hill, Katherine Jenkins, and George Sample (Jenkins's fiancée).

As Hughes, Thompson, and others recounted, Meschrabpom lived up to its side of the bargain by paying 400 rubles per month, a generous salary in the middle of the depression, and being excellent hosts. The script for *Black and White* unfortunately exhibited irreconcilable problems. For one thing, the script attempted what West called a "Russian version of American life."[27] Hughes, Thompson, and West all refer to a scene in which "a black maid would enter and the young scion would be dancing around with her" as ludicrous and inauthentic. "That would never happen in America," West observed.[28] While the problems with the film were being worked out, the cast spent most of their time indulging in leisure activities. In Thompson's opinion the cast was "living like royalty used to be entertained in Tsarist Russia."[29] A highlight was the cast trip to Odessa. Now located in Ukraine, Odessa was a deluxe "resort for Soviet higher-echelon workers." The cast stayed in a "charming hotel near the sea, where an electric fountain fell in vari-colored spray at dinner on an open-air patio."[30] Hughes describes their adventure:

We were completely on our own, and did as we pleased, so most of the day we spent in the warm sun at the beaches with crowds of Russians. . . .
In spite of the pleas of our group leader, that summer thousands of astonished citizens from all over the Soviet Union, dressed in their best bathing suits, would suddenly see streaking down the Odessa sand a dark amazon pursued by two or three of the darkest tallest and most giraffe-like males they had ever seen—all as naked as birds and as frolicsome as Virginia hounds, diving like porpoises into the surf, or playing leapfrog nude all over the place.[31]

Hughes documents a delightfully shameless disregard for propriety and racial representation. Given Thompson's distaste for the male behavior in Moscow, I imagine she is the pleading and ultimately disregarded leader of the group. Was West, one of the few darker-skinned women in the group, the pursued "amazon"? Probably not, considering her diminutive stature and the fact that she makes only one brief reference to this trip in "Russian Correspondence." The only image of the beach trip I found features a group of men and women relaxing on the beach. Several of the women are topless and sunbathing; it is ironic that one of these women resembles, but may not be, Thompson. This image encapsulates the feeling expressed by nearly all the participants: here was a freedom unheard of at home.

Given the segregation of public beaches and the inaccessibility of private ones throughout the United States, such an experience would have been a first for most of the participants, though not, of course, for Dorothy West, who was used to visiting the beaches in Oak Bluffs. Perhaps that is why the Odessa trip does not merit note in her memory even though the notoriety of the nude bathing incident repeatedly surfaces in both friendly and hostile accounts of the trip. Additionally, because West stays on in Moscow after most of the group had returned to the United States, the Odessa excursion does not represent the climax of the trip for her as it does for her peers. Hughes's depiction of the Odessa beach is meant to shock, but when the trip is understood within a catalogue of the group's activities it does more than reinforce deep-seated beliefs about deviant black sexuality. Hughes's portrait of the "White Sands of Odessa" is fascinating in the way he captures the utter freedom these New Negroes must have felt. It is difficult to articulate what it meant for African Americans, who, because of their education and class status, knew quite well what bourgeois indulgences were barred to them solely on the basis of color, to go on a "pleasure cruise of the Black Sea," not as porters or stevedores, but as passengers.[32] These experiences prompted a profound shift in consciousness. Cast member Matthew Crawford wrote to his wife:

Unconsciously I have lost that depressing subconsciousness of being a Negro. The ever-present thought that my dark skin must circumscribe my activities at all times. I was a bit surprised at how absolutely normal my moving about the Russian people has become. All of the antagonism which I have always felt among ofeys at home has left me. I can understand why the masses of Russian people are willing to endure any sort of hardship during this transitional period from capitalism and slavery to socialism and freedom.[33]

The interlude in Odessa is abruptly cut short when Henry Lee Moon arrives with the news that the film is off. He reportedly tells the vacationers: "Comrades, we've been screwed."[34] They return to Moscow to find that their accommodations have been changed from the Grand Hotel to the decidedly less grand Minninskaya—a small hostel near the Kremlin, Saint Basil's Church, and Lenin's tomb.

The reasons for the dissolution of the project were myriad. Many accused the Russian government of "selling out" their "Negro comrades" to obtain the Dnieperstroy dam, under construction by an American colonel named Hugh Cooper. West explains, "The Russians had to have the dam and they chose the dam."[35] Indeed, this was partially correct. Cooper met with Soviet officials and said if the film went ahead he would refuse to aid the U.S.S.R. in getting recognition from the United States. The Politburo met on August 8 while the cast was in Odessa and recommended ending the production.[36]

West's Russian Correspondence

The story that I trace through the histories and letters chronicles the intimate relationships that went on behind the scenes of the political front and within the leisure sites that opened when the color line disappeared. In Russia West found herself at the center of two intersecting triangular relationships: one included Hughes, West, and Thompson, and the other Hughes, West, and Mildred Jones. It is telling that Langston's posture in the shipboard image with West is mirrored in the photograph he takes with Louise Thompson Patterson. Thompson worked in Harlem as Hughes's secretary, and to her he cables, "HOLD THAT BOAT CAUSE ITS AN ARK TO ME."[37] The excerpts I have read from Thompson's unpublished memoir do not reveal any unresolved feelings about Hughes. Thompson blamed the failure of their marriage on Thurman's refusal to come out of the closet so it is not likely she would have entered into anything beyond a platonic friendship with another writer harboring ambivalent feelings about his sexual orientation. Thompson described her marriage to Thurman as fairly platonic: "he would never admit he was a homosexual."[38] If Wallace Thurman was a key figure when West first arrived in Harlem, his estranged former wife Louise Thompson should have figured more prominently in her correspondence. Perhaps Thompson's bitterness toward her former husband influenced her interactions with West? Given West's close friendship with "Wally," it is not surprising that there is little congress between West and Thompson. West did not care for Thompson; she stated bluntly that "[Thompson] was married to Wally and nobody liked her."[39] To be fair, Thompson also earned the ire of Zora Neale Hurston when she worked as secretary to Hurston and Hughes. In West's posthumous memoir "Elephant's Dance," she cites irreconcilable class differences as the cause of the Thompson/Thurman separation and makes no mention of his sexual orientation. West's apparent dislike for Thompson may have led her to downplay Thompson's role in organizing the group. Instead, she credits a chance decision to volunteer in place of her cousin Helene at the Society for Reconciliation and Peace and the persuasiveness of then-beau Henry Moon for recruiting her.[40]

Besides the alluring invitation of her male admirers, West maintains that her interest in the trip was primarily artistic. Russia was the birthplace of Fyodor Dostoyevsky, whom she considered a literary genius. She did not believe that communism was the "solution to man's dilemma, but having learned from the Russian writers that salvation lay in the soul, [she] was glad to leave New York for a time to re-examine [her] soul."[41] For West, Russia allowed her to play out on the written page her struggles with sexuality. A comparison of her letters to family and friends with her stories—"Adventure in Moscow," "A Room in Red Square," and "Russian Correspondence"—reveals the challenge of her desires for romance, motherhood, and a writing career. Her letters to and about Langston are a treasure-trove. To read West's letters from Russia is to pry into the deepest recesses of her heart. Even more than in her published, recorded, and live interviews, her letters reveal her state of mind and touching vulnerability. Her letters are contradictory, fantasy-filled, shocking expressions of her emotional state during that "carefree year" of creative and sexual exploration. By turns, she is a lovesick schoolgirl or a magnanimous lover with multiple romantic options. Reading the letters against her publications, necessary to achieve a fuller understanding of her experience in Russia, illuminates the subtext hidden within the fragmentary narratives of "Russia Correspondence" and the composite sketch "Adventure in Moscow."

West publishes "Russian Correspondence" and "A Room in Red Square" under the pseudonym Mary Christopher. As is typical when one studies West, the reasons for this are not entirely clear. Joy Carew suggested that West used the pseudonyms for her Russian pieces as a protective measure against the coming red scare, but in an interview Deborah McDowell says that West changed her name because as the editor of the *Challenge* she did not want to appear as if she had written too many of the articles that appeared in each issue. She proceeds to tell McDowell a peculiar story, which I am not persuaded is completely true, though it appears in other interviews:

> The story goes that the day I was born, my father touched my hand and said, "Little Mary," the name of his mother. My father's middle name was "Christopher," hence "Mary Christopher," my pseudonym. My mother didn't want me named "Mary." Well, I was born at home, and, in those days, you had two weeks to name any baby that had not been born in the hospital. My mother couldn't decide on a name; she couldn't make up her mind. Well, the census man came to our house shortly before the two-week period was up and asked my mother what she was going to name me. She had just finished reading a novel called Lady Dorothy of Haddon Hall. I don't know where the name "Elsie" came from, but she asked the census man, "What name do you like best, 'Dorothy' or 'Elsie'?" Because he didn't care, he just said, arbitrarily, "Dorothy." So that's where I got my name; the census man named me.[42]

Given the portrait West paints of her mother as the matriarch of the family, it is hard to believe she would allow the census taker to name her only daughter. Rachel was not an indecisive woman, but she was prone to a kind of arbitrariness that West found irritating and irrational. Still, even in the Russia letters, the candor with which she expresses her deepest desires to her mother gives us a sense of the closeness of their relationship.

The *Challenge* published "A Room in Red Square" under the name Mary Christopher, who is described in the contributor's notes as "a young woman who went to Russia a year ago with an acting company. If she has written other things, we hope she will send us more of her manuscripts."[43] Of all West's writing, this piece from the perspective of what West calls the foreign specialist as well as native Russians anticipates the early chapters of Andrea Lee's *Russian Journal* in its catalogue of the everyday challenges of acquiring food. The room is a space that holds "very much of my happiness, and some passing sadness and wild hysteria in infrequent hours."[44] West explains that the so-called "revolutionary tourist,"[45] who hopes to find in Russia a "paradise of the underprivileged," will be sadly disappointed.[46] Instead, the foreign specialist occupies an exemplary status that makes Russia a "veritable utopia for the foreigner with something to offer."[47] The strategy of exceptionalism recurs in West's fiction as a way to circumvent the color line and the boundaries of race in the United States. It emerges here as a way of explaining the privileged experience of the *Black and White* cohort.

West shrewdly notes that socialism has not destroyed, simply reorganized, class boundaries. She admits that she has "no specialty to offer Russia." In "Room" she deemphasizes her value by attributing her presence to the "grace of face and figure." Her cousin Helene Johnson offers encouragement in her December 8, 1932, letter: "Dot baby, just imagine, you're a part of that great new economic laboratory, part of a splendid experiment, and I think before long that other countries will be following Russia's example; it's the only way out, oh Dot I can't help but envy you so much."[48] Johnson's reflections on the Soviet experiment show that some African Americans, even those who were not members of the Communist Party or union advocates, saw the Russian revolution as a precursor to a worldwide worker's revolution. Perhaps Johnson, like Hughes, draped herself in "communist accessories."[49] The radical Left was chic. For Harlemites who intermingled in the interracial political discussions taking place in Greenwich Village, calling each other comrade was a way to show their Left leanings without fully committing themselves to the party. Thus, West felt it was important to critique the romantic appeal of the new Russia without undermining the real social change sweeping the nation.

"Room" provides *Challenge* readers with a fairly enlightening and detailed account of how class lines have been redrawn, but not eliminated, under the Soviet system. West describes the new system based not on birth but on "brains": "There is a distinct higher class in Moscow made up, not of the monied nor the socially select, but of Russia's brains. There is the House of Government, a most modern apartment building, where live the government heads and their households. There are sometimes six rooms for a man and his wife. The ordinary couple live in one with the use of a community kitchen."⁵⁰ The reorganization of domestic space is an important feature of the new Soviet Union. Andrea Lee's *Russian Journal* also opens with a detailed description of her living space, called a *blok*, and its measurements: "a minute suite consisting of two rooms about six feet by ten feet each, a tiny entryway, and a pair of cubicles containing, between them, a toilet, a shower and washstand, and several, large, indolent cockroaches."⁵¹ West's article also devotes a seemingly inordinate amount of space to food, its cost, appearance, taste, and, above all, its acquisition. In fact, Russia experienced a severe famine in 1932–1934, and West recollects seeing Russian children begging for bread.⁵² Of course, later in the twentieth century the bread line became the iconic image of life in the U.S.S.R. Sugar was also scarce. West devotes several paragraphs to her attempts to guard her sugar from a guest who "invariably, and with a glad shout, ferrets" it out.⁵³ Despite her dwelling on the mundane matters of domestic life, she concludes, somewhat incomprehensibly, that she "will have a nostalgia for Moscow as long as I live. There is my lost youth and all things lovely. There is my bright adventure."⁵⁴

West maintains that spiritual reasons motivate her "nostalgia for Moscow" and her desire to return to the room overlooking Red Square, but her first travel essay does little to unlock the Russian spirit. Moreover, her letters home suggest that her primary delights are material indulgences and romantic dalliances. Even before she arrives in Russia, the trip takes on the sheen of a fairy tale. In one of her first letters to her mother, she describes a buggy ride with Langston Hughes and Mildred Jones in Helsingfors, Finland: "Langston and I rode for an hour, and stopped at an inn and had tea and pastries, and when I came back to the hotel, I went riding again with Mildred Jones."⁵⁵ Such excursions resemble the grand tours taken by upper-class socialites prior to their marriages more than the "ragged edge" travel described by her nineteenth-century predecessors.⁵⁶ West and roommate Mildred Jones stayed "a block from the Kremlin, in the heart of the capital." Their "enormous" room was lavishly decorated "with huge pre-tzarist beds, heavy drapes at the windows with deep rugs on the floor."⁵⁷ In the hotel that West tells her mother really is "Grand," Jones and West ate caviar and drank champagne, often purchased by Hughes. West finds Mildred "intelligent and very fine"⁵⁸ and a more amiable companion than Mollie Lewis, who roomed with Louise Thompson.⁵⁹ In her letters, West refers to her roommate affectionately as "Mil." There are no photos of West and Jones in the poses she strikes with Hughes, but in the often-circulated shipboard photograph of the group Mildred is certainly one of the most striking figures. Hughes frankly names the "chic, bob-haired and peach colored" Mildred as "one of the prettiest girls in our motion-picture-brigade."⁶⁰ One's gaze is drawn to her reclining position and the difficult-to-read expression on her face. She appears both aloof and serene, a visage that by comparison makes the other women in the photograph look dowdy and West and Thompson, seated cross-legged at her feet, look girlish and immature.

West's "Russian Correspondence" provides a more meditative consideration of the Russian sojourn. Like many epistolary texts, it is full of strategic omissions. Read in conjunction with West's letters, the short vignette proves revealing. I consider neither source to be authoritative; rather, the points of intersection and divergence help to achieve a fuller understanding of the magic pilgrimage. Beta, the protagonist, is a lovesick invalid trapped in her Moscow hotel. She continually sends desperate missives to her wandering lover, clearly modeled on Langston Hughes. After the film's suspension, the government sent several of the *Black and White* troupe on a tour of the southern provinces of Central Asia, which Hughes recounts in detail in *I Wonder*.[61] During this time, West is late to join the group; when she finally catches up, she finds that they have left Langston behind: "I didn't get your card until the twenty-third, because I joined the group in Baku the thirteenth. Lang, it was too awful lying there missing you all, and thinking very straight. . . . I wanted terribly to see Mil and you, and I did not know whom I wanted to see most."[62] Such vacillation of affection is a common theme in her letters. Mildred is nearby and apparently emotionally available, although she too has her side affairs.[63] But the flirtatious Hughes is always just out of reach.

The wistful, melancholic Beta in "Russian Correspondence" captures West's ambivalence and paints Hughes as a vibrant, heroic adventurer named "Tack." Several times throughout the vignette he is described as a "wild boy" upon a camel, in "brave boots" wearing a red shirt. Images of the turbaned Hughes riding a horse in Turkmenistan (1932) corroborate Beta's image of the adventurer she imagines from her sickbed "in Odessa, and on the Black Sea and in Berlin, and on the Baltic."[64] In *The Big Sea* Hughes notes that unlike "the Jim Crow experience of train travel at home," where he could not "eat in the diner and was segregated in a single coach," "on Moscow-Tashkent express, we had the run of the train."[65] Beta apparently understands how much her "brave boy" needs freedom, mobility, and independence. She unselfishly encourages him: she tells him "Russia is your salvation" and advises him to "grow and expand here. Live without women for two years. Live selfishly and succeed."[66]

Beta replicates the antiquated, Victorian trope of the patient, understanding woman left behind while the highly mobile male sets out for parts unknown. Unlike the speaker in "Room in Red Square," who provides lively examinations of Russian life, Beta is feverish and suffocating. Although desperate to join the group, she is paralyzed by a mysterious, stereotypically feminine illness. Even though Beta expresses some hope of their reunion, when she tells her lover that "your writing should be your first love, your greatest passion" she seems resigned to the impossibility of their union. When she finally boards a train and leaves her devoted friend Peg (possibly Mildred?), even the landscape is opaque and cloudy: "The sky is the color of smoke, and the mist almost veils the mountains."[67] Her traveling experience is much more ethereal than the boisterous train ride described by Hughes, where the passengers mix with Russian travelers and share food, music, and conversation. In contrast, Beta's travel seems highly circumscribed. Rather than a site of transcontinental cultural exchange, the train is confining, and Beta is by turns frustrated, bitter, and finally, accepting.

In her "nonfictional" recounting of the group's tour of Central Asia, West is completely uninterested in Russia's ethnic minorities. In contrast, Louise Thompson and Langston Hughes observe, recount, and critique the treatment of ethnic minorities, especially in Central Asia. While Thompson appreciates the delicious food on which the group dines in the Uzbek, she offers a passionate critique of the paranja (horsehair veil):

> The "jah" or "paranja" was a monstrous veil imposed on the women. Many of us in the West had thought of women in veils as romantic and exotic—the images that we saw in Hollywood movies—cute little veils over their faces revealing only coquettish eyes. But when I saw the kind of paraphernalia that women had to wear, I was astounded. The paranja was a long, thick "veil" of horse hair which covered women from head to toes, the entire form of the body with a cape that went over it. To see you had to peer through that horse hair. The cape was wide enough to cover your body, and it went all the way to the ground, hiding arms, sleeves, hands, everything. Now a woman dressed like that could never work in a factory or anywhere else, for that matter. And every Moslem girl over the age of 12 had to wear that "veil" whenever she left the house and was seen in public. So the campaign for women's freedom quickly became identified with removing the paranja.[68]

Although Thompson's observations are neither as philosophical nor as metaphoric as Hughes's musings on gender and veiling in the context of Du Boisian theories of double consciousness, the complete absence of or interest in these issues in West's writing or extant letters is striking. Additionally, although Thompson confirms Beta's itinerary in "Russian Correspondence," writing that "Dorothy West was ill when we left and did not join us until Baku," beyond appreciating West's arrival with mail from home, she has nothing to say about her.[69] It is hard to imagine that both West and Thompson spent equal amounts of time with Hughes without frequently encountering each other.

Beta's characterization may reflect West's state of mind just after she returned to New York. "Russian Correspondence" was published in 1934 in the *Challenge*, but it is so similar to her October 27, 1932, letter to Hughes that you imagine she might have been drafting the piece while she was still in Moscow. In "Russian Correspondence" West alludes to the "end of a day in which we had loved each other very much."[70] According to Arnold Rampersad, West and Hughes were never intimate. He names biracial dancer Sylvia Chen as Hughes's primary love interest during the Russia trip. Upon reading the letters one cannot help but wonder if Hughes reciprocated West's feelings? Hughes was preoccupied with his own contemplations of race and sexuality. In addition to Chen, he also had an affair with a Russian woman named Natasha. West may or may not have known about Chen. The overall of tone of "Russian Correspondence" suggests a missed opportunity. In a letter to her mother West briefly mentions and describes Chen's somewhat Negroid features and "beautiful" hair but does not seem to consider Chen a rival, though West does complain that Chen "shows off a little."[71] Because West accompanies Hughes to see Chen at the Metropole—a swanky hotel that the film group often visited—it seems unlikely that she could be unaware of their relationship. Incidentally, Chen acknowledges: "Langston was the first man I was ever intimate with." Hughes names her as "the girl I was in love with that winter." But given how freely he and West seem to throw around the word "love," especially in his sporadic letters to Chen, it is hard to gauge the sincerity of his attachment to either woman. Chen eventually marries a Euro-American from Dayton, Ohio, named Jay Leyda and tells Hughes: "Yes, I got tired of waiting on you to propose so got myself a consort."[72]

West dreamed of conceiving a child with Hughes and living a bohemian life that would allow them to pursue their individual artistic aims. She tells him in no uncertain terms, "Lang, I love you." After insisting that they are "both in full vigor" and that she is ready to bear him "a dark son" or "brown daughter," she imagines their life together: "Must we be sensible about money? I have no dowry. I am sure you have very little in the bank. Does it matter? I shall write very much. You will write very much. You have a fine fearless brain to give a baby. I have an unusually strong body. That's sufficient heritage."[73] This May 26, 1933, letter is the most personally revealing missive in West's entire archive. Although West seems convinced of her sincere love for Langston, the fact that we have no evidence that he reciprocated her feelings calls into question her repeated proposals that they conceive a child. Her father's death while she is in Russia clearly marks a turning point for her. Once she receives this news she tells her mother: "Life can give me nothing now except a child. I am ready to settle down."[74]

A union between West and Hughes would not have been a New Negro match made in heaven. Consider the orchestrated marriage between Yolande Du Bois and Countee Cullen or a relationship with which West would have been even more familiar—the ill-fated union of Louise Thompson and Wallace Thurman. Given these precedents, how realistic is the life she proposes to Hughes? Moreover, in the postscript to this letter she wonders: "Lang, I've not thought of this! After all I may have been fooled. Perhaps your feelings don't coincide with mine. If so, let me forever think you never received this letter, and let me go on cherishing my lost love."[75] Some lingering doubt must have been in the back of her mind all along.

Caught up in the free love atmosphere of the New Russia and liberated from the constraints of New Negro womanhood and New England restraint West felt free to explore her sexuality in a way she never had before. Still, what does it mean that she carries on her affair with Jones while claiming to Hughes that she wanted to "be mother to your four children"?[76] Although there is written evidence of her feelings for Langston, I sense that her interest in Hughes may have been performative, not unlike Hughes's back-and-forth flirtation with Chen. "Russian Correspondence" coyly references "that night at the New Moscow" as a missed opportunity to conceive a love child on Russian soil. Given how entrenched West's views about marriage and family were, this would have been a really radical act for a woman raised among Boston's black middle class. Such an act would have been unthinkable to the women who populate West's fiction; most of her social-climbing men and women are totally invested in doing only the right things to get ahead. Rarely did West feature a successful relationship based on mutual feeling and sexual attraction in her writing. The passionate and expressive language in West's letters about Hughes and Mildred Jones is absent from both her earlier and later fictional rendering of relationships, and the wistful regret of roads not taken for fear of going against socially acceptable norms remains.

Without her letters, we would have little insight into West's intimate activities in Russia, and without Hughes's memoirs the more sensational elements would elude us as well. Her last publication, "An Adventure in Moscow," was published in 1985 in the *Vineyard Gazette*. The piece portrays West as a shy, introverted young woman afraid to dance when asked by renowned filmmaker and revolutionary film director and theorist Sergei Eisenstein after a performance of the Bolshoi Ballet. His most famous film was the propaganda-filled *Battleship Potemkin*, which premiered in New York in 1926. In fact, Hughes recognizes the "famous white steps to the sea" from the film's most memorable scene not far from their hotel in Odessa.[77] "Adventure" is a far more spare account than either of her previous publications. It offers little insight on the Soviet system and provides only an extremely truncated summary of the *Black and White* expedition. By 1985, West may have wanted to downplay the political aspects of the trip. The piece reads like a contained anecdote written from the perspective of an older woman looking back on her girlhood. At the party, "every dancer of the ballet asked me to dance with him. I never sat down once. I felt as light as a feather. My pride in myself was monumental."[78] That West chooses to recount this event, and none of the other more sensational aspects of the trip, is curious. She makes no mention, for instance, of a female cast member's attempted suicide. Distressed because her beloved from Harlem had taken up with a Russian girl, she mistook a red bottle of potassium formaldehyde for red wine. Fortunately, when it began to burn she screamed "so loud that everybody in the hotel came running to see what was the matter." According to Hughes, the other women in the trip declared that she had "disgraced the race."[79] The idea that the men could womanize with impunity but that this woman's careless, impetuous act could disgrace the race illustrates the double standard to which women were held. According to Thompson, Henry Moon, Ted Poston, and Thurston Lewis spent too much time doing "all the things which Americans say about Negro men and white women."[80]

The cast's newfound sexual freedom across the color line and across the heterosexual line would have been tolerated in the 1920s, but by 1932 social and sexual practices, called *byt* (lifestyles), were being analyzed to determine if they conformed to communist ideology. Sylvia Garner's love affair with a Russian woman who worked as a translator for the group resulted in that woman's deportation to Siberia. Other women, including Mildred Jones, had flirtations with Russian men. A man whom West calls "Boris Bilynak" (most likely a pseudonym) proposed to Mildred. West explained to her mother "he likes Mildred because she's beautiful I guess" and then goes on to observe that "Russians are like colored folks, slightly crazy."[81]

Intimate Encounters: Gender and the Veil

Comparisons between Russian and black emotional states also appear in Andrea Lee's *Russian Journal*. Upon attending a concert where B. B. King performed, Lee was surprised to see a relaxed, uninhibited Soviet audience that whistled and "hooted with delight" as King played.[82] At the end of the performance, Soviet hippies threw flowers and attempted to get on stage while the guards, fearing a riot, quickly dispersed the crowd. For their part, the Russians were equally moved. An older man in attendance remarks to Lee that "[King] poured his whole heart and soul out there on the stage. Such feeling is very Russian—we believe in emotion, in the soul. I never thought that an American could feel that way."[83]

The notion of a spiritual connection between Russians and African Americans heightens the sense of Russians as somehow ethnically distinct from Anglo-Europeans. Their idea of empire had long advocated unity in multiplicity. This ideology underlay their policies toward the culturally, ethnically, and visually diverse peoples that inhabited the Soviet Union. Kate Baldwin argues that Russia was for many years distinct from Europe. In fact, many credit Alexander Pushkin, who was proud of his descent from a union with the aristocratic Pushkins and Peter the Great's black general, with the promotion of a national Russian literature comparable to the British and French literary traditions. Poet Claude McKay relays an anecdote told to him by a Russian informant named Chukovsky that draws attention to Russia's provisional access to the category of European whiteness. Chukovsky was staying at a London hotel when a white American family protested the presence of a black American preacher, also a guest at the hotel. The unhappy Chukovksy was asked to explain the situation to the black guest and the following dialogue ensued:

> "The white guests have the right to object to me," he explained, antici- pating Garvey, "they belong to a superior race."
>
> "But," said Chukovsky, "I do not object to you, I don't feel any differ- ence; we don't understand color prejudice in Russia."
>
> "Well," philosophized the preacher, "you are very kind, but taking the scriptures as authority, I don't consider the Russians to be white people."[84]

Do Russians lose their white status in the eyes of the black observer because of their so-called lack of color prejudice? In the racial logic of the United States, white status is by no means always concrete. The multiple social and legal challenges to the color line before and after the landmark *Plessy v. Ferguson* case demonstrate that whiteness can be won or lost based on economic status, genealogy, politics, education, and social behavior. As Hughes and the others traveled South, Russia became less white: "the people of Central Asia looked like some of us. They were brown, many of them dark brown." Moreover, Hughes's narrative of his trip through Central Asia is full of comparisons between the American South and the Russian landscape, denoted by such confusing titles as "Dixie Christmas USSR." Conversely, members of the *Black and White* group become less black: "In my photographs of Langston in Central Asia he looks [as] though he is among his own people."[85] When Thompson and Hughes were "traveling alone" in Moscow, she writes, "I think people thought we were Uzbeks or from one of the other southeastern Soviet Republics. No lines would melt away and we'd have to cram onto the trams like everyone else. Several times I was asked for directions by Russians who assumed I spoke the language and knew my way around."[86] The *metisi*, or mixed blood, appellation assigned to the group reflected both Russian understanding of the multiple ethnic origins within their own nation and their narrow understanding of American blacks. These perceptions were reinforced by the impressions of Russian travelers in the United States. The 1935 photo essay book *Ilf and Petrov's American Road Trip* includes images of sharecroppers' cabins; they write, "We saw the shameful poverty of the villages of the black South. Comrade, a church mouse is a rich landowner in comparison to the Louisianan or Carolinian Negro."[87]

Lee's depiction of the B. B. King concert also stands out because she does not disclose her own identity as an African American until two-thirds into the memoir. When Lee encounters Ibrahim, an Eritrean student at Patrice Lumumba University, she describes him with the same aesthetic specificity she gives to all her subjects. He has "the beautiful linear features of the saints in ancient Ethiopian church frescoes." Then she arbitrarily discloses that "toward me he showed the absolute lack of interest with which many Africans greet American blacks." Readers infer from Lee's comments that she has had similar encounters with other Africans in Russia. Lee uses Ibrahim's story to explain the fraught conditions that African male students experience. The unrelenting stares are hostile: "the masses call us black devils and spit at us in the street."[88] This reception is a far cry from the shouts of "Negro Comrade" that greet West and her crew as they parade through the city.

By the time of Andrea Lee's Russia, the Soviet experiment is nearing its end and rapidly dissolving, especially at the edges of the empire where racial others are most prevalent. There are many reasons why African and/or Black diasporic subjects received increasingly more hostile receptions in Russia over the years. At first, blacks were exotic objects of interest, foreign bodies whose racial identity had no corollary within the indigenous and varied ethnic groups under the Russian empire. Later, they were romanticized "Negro comrades," who comprised a separate black nation of serfs in the United States with whom the Bolsheviks were in solidarity. Anti-racism and solidarity with black Americans was part of the patriotism of the Soviet Union's ideology even as gender equality and the so-called nationalization of women formed part of the new nation's rhetoric. In *Russian Journal*, a congenial acquaintance, whom Lee suspects is also a KGB informant, offers the party stance on racism:

> [Grigorii] straightened his shoulders, blinked, and said, "Very nice, but what about the racism and unemployment in the United States?" It always floors him that Tom and I agree freely with much of his criticism of America. He never admits that there are any problems in Soviet life. "There's no racism," he told me once, studiously ignoring the fact that we'd just heard a Russian woman cursing a "filthy" African on a crowded bus.[89]

Lee is neither a committed revolutionary nor a casual tourist; she is a newly married writer accompanying her academic husband on his research. In her lush prose, evoking the drama of Russia, she describes with utter awe Russia's architectural marvels: Red Square, the Kremlin, and Saint Basil, which she describes as a "sublime fantasy in cartoon color and buoyant plaster."[90] True believers and cynics people her circle.

In her introduction to a new edition of her *Russian Journal*, Lee addresses a common criticism of the book: she provided too few details about herself and "mentioned only in passing and well into the book that [she was] African American." Lee maintains that it was not a conscious decision but reflected her youth. She also makes the point that "because my skin is not dark, my ethnic background was not much of a social issue for the Russians I met. Except for an occasional facetious inquiry as to whether I was a Cuban comrade, my new friends and acquaintances made much more of the fact that I was Western, capitalist and American."[91] She explains that her complicated background (typical of many Americans of African descent) includes "west African, Danish, English, Irish, and native American" and that her suburban middle-class parents sent her to integrated schools at the height of the civil rights struggle. Yet she began writing *Sarah Phillips*, her first, autobiographical novel, in the Lenin library. Perhaps for Lee, as for West and others, being free of the constraints and the atmosphere of American racial politics allows for a clear-eyed vision that promotes or provokes artistic expression. Lee reflects on her time in the library: "*Sarah Phillips*—conceived at the same time—represents the background not expressed in *Russian Journal*; the exploration of the familiar as opposed to the foreign."[92] Similarly, just after she returns from Russia West writes her first of many short stories featuring Judy, who became a major character in West's autobiographical novel *The Living Is Easy*.

Because Lee never describes her own appearance, we are left to understand that she believes that her Americanness, and perhaps her status as the wife of a Euro-American man, insulates her from assaults. She is not excluded, however, from the "stare":

> It was in the subway that night that I first endured the unblinking stare of the Russian populace, a stare already described to me by Tom and by friends who had been in the Soviet Union before. "You will never not be stared at." . . . They all looked us up and down with undisguised fascination and whispered comments to their neighbors. So we sat, practically riddled with stares, in the dim light of the rocking subway car, breathing an atmosphere heavy with odors of sharp tobacco, sausage, and perspiring human flesh.

Andrea Lee refuses to provide the reader with a visual image of herself, yet she turns her gaze sharply on the bodies of Russian women, particularly in her description of the women in the banya. Just as Lee is captivated by the coexistence of incongruous styles of Russian architecture like "Stalin Gothic," she finds the indulgent, sanctioned luxury of the bathhouse to be emblematic of the contradictions of Russian life. She immediately draws on orientalist language to describe the opulent décor and the bathing women as odalisques. The banya is a "vicious place" that reminds her of "a seraglio or Victorian brothel":93

> With their bulging naked bodies and homemade knitted bathing caps, the splashing women looked a little incongruous in this setting of neoclassical elegance. There was a magical feeling of freedom in the air: the unhindered freedom of women in a place from which men are excluded. I have felt this intoxicating sense of liberty in similar situations at home in America, but for Russian women the feeling must be even more intense. It is fairly well known, I suppose, that most Russian women with families have two jobs: an official, often physically exhausting one, and the exceedingly difficult one of keeping a family groomed and fed—a task that few Russian husbands lend a hand with.94

Lee's invocation of the harem resonates with Langston Hughes's voyeuristic obsession with the unveiling of the Uzbek women during his trips to southern Russia. Interestingly enough, *The Big Sea* omits Hughes's "In an Emir's Harem" and "Boy Dancers of Uzbekistan"—essays on Uzbek women that appeared in *Travel* and *Ladies' Home Companion*. Certainly the homophobic undercurrents of the red scare may have prompted him to remove anything suspicious from his autobiography.95 The removal of the veil became a symbol of female emancipation under the Soviet regime, and the unveiled Uzbek women allow Hughes to reflect on the metaphor of the veil in the context of W.E.B. Du Bois's articulation of double consciousness. According to Hughes, the closeted "lovely houris" in the bath have been replaced by the emancipated women of Tashkent: "gathering in a public tea house, unveiled, drinking tea!"96 In Lee's banya, the old gender roles coexist and compete with the new. Lee unveils Russia's women to reveal the façade of gender equality enjoyed by Soviet women. Like Hughes, she also uses these opportunities to deflect attention from her own nonwhite body in these spaces. Here, she is the one who controls the gaze.

Given her desire to control the direction of the gaze, it is not surprising that she omits the following incident in order to direct readers' attention away from her body and how it may be raced and gendered in Russia:

> We felt immortal. We sought out risky situations, ending up in some places that never made it into the chaste annals of *Russian Journal*. Such as when, on a tour of Soviet Armenia, we were warned against a

certain Yerevan nightclub said to be a gangsters' hangout. Tom and I couldn't get there fast enough, and sure enough we ended up making the acquaintance of a local crime lord who not only invited us back to his ritzy apartment for a drinking bout, but also offered the services of two small, very pretty Armenian prostitutes to Tom in return for a night with me. (We declined, but at least we'd learned the exchange rate.)[97]

Although Lee includes the story of the embattled and tragic Ibrahim, she omits the above story that describes her and her husband's risky exploits in Russia. Instead, wrapped in the respectability of her role as the wife of an American academic, she keeps her memoir chaste and deflects her own exoticism. The inclusion of this tongue-in-cheek episode would have revealed Lee as a sexual commodity whose worth on the black market, so to speak, is equal to that of two Armenian prostitutes. Lee does not indicate whether her physical beauty, her racial fluidity, or her citizenship makes her an appealing commodity. Nor do we know why her husband is offered not one but two women. There is also no analysis given of how the Soviet policies enable the exploitation of ethnic minority women. Lee seems only to consider the risk involved in venturing into an uncertain world as a reflection of their naïveté as young, besotted American travelers who feel themselves inviolable or, to use her words, immortal. Lee's complexion is similar if not identical to Louise Thompson's coloring. If Thompson's body could be read as Uzbek, it is possible that Lee needs to emphasize her Americanness to avoid situations where she might be understood as equivalent to an "Armenian prostitute" or one of many so-called "diaspora nationalities" in the Soviet Union.[98] This episode and its omission from the first edition of *Russian Journal* underline the complex position in which the black American woman traveler may find herself and the tricky national, class-based maneuvers necessary to preserve herself from the "perils of land and sea."[99]

Unlike Hughes or Lee, West only mentions one encounter with an American-born African American in Russia. She meets, but is singularly unimpressed with Emma Harris, the so-called "Mammy of Moscow." Hughes devotes an entire chapter to Harris's complex expatriate status in Russia, but West mentions her only in passing: "What I intend to say about her is that she does our laundry so I keep as clean here as I do in America with much less bother."[100] A former actress, Harris had lived in Russia for more than thirty years. She greeted the *Black and White* cast upon arrival and took part in demonstrations for the Scottsboro boys. Harris was rather ambivalent about Russia and was what you might call an "accidental" communist. A colorful hostess, she knew the black market and could procure delights like apple pie. Harris was known to "make a fiery speech in Russian, denouncing American lynch law, then come off the platform and sigh, 'I wish I was back home.'"[101]

That West considered her little more than a laundress reveals that she still maintains the judgmental selfishness of youth and a little of the bourgeois attitude of her Brahmin clan.

Like West, neither Andrea Lee nor Nancy Prince settled permanently in Russia; however, their sojourns allowed them to gain valuable insight into their place in the world. In their travel writings, Russia, tsarist or Soviet, is first and foremost a space free of American racial politics and policies, Russia's own ethnic conflicts notwithstanding. It functions as what Andrea Lee calls a "mysterious counterweight to the known world of America."[102] In the case of Nancy Prince, her Russian documents protect her from possible enslavement when her boat docks unexpectedly in New Orleans. For West, when she inexplicably receives $300 severance from the Meschrabpom Film company (everyone else receives rubles), she uses that money to start the literary journal *Challenge*. She returns with the confidence and the capital to start a magazine that will interest itself in the cause of the working class. She writes to Langston Hughes: "I could not go through that Russian experience without having some leaning toward communism. But I cannot reconcile myself to taking an equal interest in the white worker, or any interest in the white worker. . . . I want to be solely concerned with the black race."[103] West returns spiritually and artistically galvanized but not particularly convinced of a global, interracial workers movement as a practical solution to the race problem in the United States. She also commences a long-term relationship with a woman, her *Challenge* coeditor, Marian Minus. West's Russian sojourn represents the end of her childhood. She returns to the United States not as the privileged daughter of Isaac West with hopes for a conventional marriage but as an independent woman with a strong perspective on how class lines and capitalism influence the position of blacks in the United States and a sense of the kind of writing she wants to pursue. She writes Hughes without regret: "Lang, the long months in Moscow when life was good in the Minninskaya did not do for me and to me what my job as Home relief investigator is. Lang, I have seen so much and learned so much. I have a head full of tragic stories. Sometimes I cannot bear it. . . . I will never be aggressive. And I am not a leader. And I shall always write stories rather than searching articles."[104]

The frame stories included here demonstrate that black women's perspectives on their various Russian sojourns are highly attentive to the social reception of their bodies within that space, the luxurious and bourgeois indulgence that their specialized status allows, and the contrast between their treatment in Russia and their lives behind the veil of American race relations. They also demonstrate that travel writing is by its very nature impressionistic and irrevocably informed by the personal. For truly committed radicals like Louise Thompson the Soviet sojourn galvanized her dedication to social justice and the possibility of a new society based on Marxist principles. After she returns, she joins the party and ultimately earns the moniker "Madam Moscow." West is not persuaded to advocate for the communist experiment at home, but she does develop a sophisticated critique of capitalism, a comparative understanding of the rigidity of class stratification and how performing or attaining exceptional status might create an approximate, if not actual, paradise.

5

New Challenges

We who were the New Negroes challenge them to better our achievements. For we did not altogether live up to our fine promise.

–Dorothy West, "Dear Reader," *Challenge*, March 1934

West returns from Russia neither a mother nor a communist, but with the
$300 she mysteriously received from the Meschrabpom Corporation she was
determined to start a progressive magazine that would extend the literary
life of the Harlem Renaissance.[1] Her good friend "Wally" Thurman launched
the journal *Fire!!* in 1926 in an attempt to make a bold statement highlighting
the new voices of the era. In *Fire!!*, Aaron Douglas's provocative, modernist
art illustrated fiction from the bohemian coterie of Harlem writers, including
Thurman, Zora Neale Hurston, Gwendolyn Bennett, and Bruce Nugent. But
Thurman published only one issue, and West had higher hopes for her little
magazine. As the depression gained momentum, financial support and interest
in African American art and culture were swiftly evaporating. The literary
contests that had drawn West and her cousin Helene to Harlem were no longer
plentiful, and West was unable to get other black periodicals to finance a
literary section.[2] Instead of being discouraged, West decided to start her own
little magazine.

This chapter traces West's role as the editor of *Challenge* and coeditor
of its successor the *New Challenge*. West proclaimed the end of the Harlem
Renaissance with the death of Wallace Thurman in 1934—a sentiment echoed
by early historiographers from Nathan Huggins (*Harlem Renaissance*) to David
Levering Lewis (*When Harlem Was in Vogue*). Reading *Challenge* allows one to
trace the regional and class differences that marked a significant shift in black
literary consciousness. Between the pages of the two incarnations of *Challenge*
debates about aesthetics, art, and politics proliferated and then came to a
head with the publication of Richard Wright's "Blueprint for Negro Writing"
(1937). The *New Challenge* documents the writers and activists coming out of
Chicago who sought to define their movement—the Chicago Renaissance—in
contrast to the Harlem Renaissance, which they perceived as a less radical

movement crippled by its dependence on white patronage. West was excited to publish her literary cousins in the Midwest, but ultimately aesthetic, political, and personal differences led to the demise of the *New Challenge* as well. This period in West's life provides an interesting snapshot of the losses and enduring attributes of both global and local black arts movements of the 1920s and 1930s. Though she briefly sidelined her fictional endeavors during her editorial stint, the short fiction produced while working for the Works Progress Administration contains some of her most sophisticated renderings of intraracial class tensions. West also confronted the aesthetic challenge of writing stories that appealed to popular, interracial audiences. Finally, also during this period in her life she entered into a long-term partnership with fellow writer and *New Challenge* coeditor Marian Minus. Could she find personal and professional happiness at last? Although these were challenging years, they may represent the most fulfilling time in West's private life.

It is impossible to discuss the *Challenge* without understanding the motivations and the aesthetics behind its predecessor *Fire!!: A Quarterly Devoted to the Younger Negro Artists*. Wallace Thurman launched the magazine as a quarterly with the help of an illustrious board of directors, including Carl Van Vechten, and in association with Zora Neale Hurston, Bruce Nugent, Langston Hughes, and Gwendolyn Bennett, all of whom contributed to the premier and only issue. Although we can lament *Fire!!*'s ephemeral nature, short print runs are part and parcel of the little magazine tradition:

> Little magazines are by definition magazines that do not make money; they are trying to promote new ideas or forms of art, rather than sales. They are usually funded by a small group of supporters, and a few paying subscribers, and are created to provide an outlet for work that would not appear otherwise. The little magazine is always in an adversarial position with regard to the dominant culture, and when it loses that adversarial edge, or the enthusiasm of its backers, it dies. Thus most little magazines have a very short run.[3]

Although some very important works appear in West's *Challenge*, Thurman's *Fire!!* was a far more provocative and aesthetically diverse publication. In her study of New Negro periodicals and Harlem Renaissance print culture, Anne Carroll argues that *Fire!!*'s visual elements, bold color motif, and sexualized subject matter link it to the white avant-garde, but "its attention to race as an important aspect of identity means that, in effect, *Fire!!* claims a place between the two poles of the New Negro movement and the white avant-garde."[4] In its design and material *Fire!!* embraces and even defines the African American avant-garde. *Challenge* by comparison seems constrained in both design and sparse contributions.

Initially intended to be a monthly, by the second issue *Challenge* had become a quarterly. Mildred Jones, West's roommate and probable lover during her Russian sojourn, designed a graphic, modern layout for the cover, but it is surprising that West did not continue to solicit Mildred or her childhood friend, visual artist Lois Mailou Jones, to contribute more artwork to the project. In contrast, the visual art in *Fire!!* is entirely integrated into the composition of the journal. Aaron Douglas's contributions are listed under "Incidental Art Decoration" and "Three Drawings," but they are far more than incidental. The illustrations give *Fire!!* its avant-garde air of sophistication and distinctiveness as well as its experimental, hybrid aesthetic. Images like the nude, black cutout that accompanies Thurman's opening story "Cordelia the Crude: A Harlem Sketch" boldly answers Winold Reiss's conservative portraits of New Negro leaders included in Alain Locke's *The New Negro: An Interpretation* (1923). A comparison of illustrations alone marks *Fire!!* as aesthetically divergent from the more staid and conservative art that appeared in *The New Negro* or even periodicals like *The Crisis*.

Writers such as Jean Toomer and Claude McKay had already begun to challenge the expectations that New Negro art serve the ideological demands of the NAACP and/or Alain Locke. Carroll suggests that: "Rather than linking the arts to social change, the creators of *Fire!!* used the arts to expand what was shown about African Americans."[5] That is, the publication's project was presenting black art as a diverse endeavor in which neither censorship nor the advocacy of "genteel negro culture" would hamper original artistic expression.

West and her cousin Helene Johnson had just arrived in New York when *Fire!!* appeared. In fact, *Fire!!* published Johnson's "A Southern Road," but West is not a contributor. Is this because of the journal's inflammatory nature or simply a question of timing? Given Hurston's influence on West's nascent folk aesthetic, which she developed in her short stories, West would surely have read Zora Neale Hurston's play *Color Struck* in *Fire!!* The precise imagery, open lines, and meditative tone make Helene Johnson's "A Southern Road" an exceptional poem. Stylistically, it foreshadows the poetry of the Black Arts Movement and homonymically evokes, perhaps even inspires, the title of Sterling Brown's debut poetry collection *Southern Road*. Sterling Brown's "Southern Road," the title poem of the collection, embodies the blues aesthetic that defines his Afro-modernist poetics. Where Johnson uses metaphor rather than voice, Brown incorporates the cadence and syntax of the chain gang to structure and shape his poem. It is perhaps no coincidence that West publishes Sterling Brown's poem "Old Lem" in the *New Challenge*.

Fire!! pairs Johnson's "Southern Road" with Countee Cullen's "From the Dark Tower," a poem famous for its haunting refrain: "We were not made entirely to weep." Johnson's poem, however, with its concise diction, alliteration, and assonance, is simply superior. It is worth citing the poem in its entirety:

A SOUTHERN ROAD

Yolk-colored tongue
Parched beneath a burning sky,
A lazy little tune
Hummed up the crest of some
Soft sloping hill.
One streaming line of beauty
Flowing by a forest
Pregnant with tears.
A hidden nest for beauty
Idly flung by God
In one lonely lingering hour
Before the Sabbath.
A blue-fruited black gum,
Like a tall predella,
Bears a dangling figure,—
Sacrificial dower to the raff,
Swinging alone,
A solemn, tortured shadow in the air.[6]

The line breaks evoke a swaying body swinging from a tree, and the diction emphasizes the incongruous juxtaposition of a nostalgic southern Sunday with the violence of the landscape. The poem presages Billie Holiday's immortal rendition of the song "Strange Fruit" and calls to mind the feeling behind Toni Morrison's imagistic rendering of the magnolia trees at Sweet Home. In contrast, Johnson's poetic contributions to the inaugural issue of *Challenge*, "Let Me Sing My Song" and "A Widow with a Moral Obligation" lack the impact of "Southern Road." Johnson was as promising a poet as West was a promising fiction writer. Hughes wrote to West, "Somebody ought to bring out a book of hers."[7] *Fire!!*'s inclusion of "Southern Road" indicates the potential of new writers carrying on the promise of the Harlem Renaissance even though others had begun to dismiss the movement.

West hoped that *Challenge* would reinvigorate the Harlem Renaissance, but she took to heart Thurman's inability to sustain his publication. In her first issue she reflects, "We who were the New Negroes challenge them to better our achievements. For we did not altogether live up to our fine promise."[8] Her words echo the sentiments expressed by James Weldon Johnson in his foreword to the inaugural issue. He applauded West's desire to foster the work of young writers but urged hard work and industry over talent:"But these younger writers must not be mere dilettantes: they have serious work to do. They can bring to bear a tremendous force for breaking down and wearing away the stereotyped ideas about the Negro, and for creating a higher and more enlightened opinion about the race. To do this they need not be propagandists; they need only be sincere artists, disdaining all cheap applause and remaining always true to themselves."[9]

Johnson's foreword disputes the notion that art must be propagandistic to spur either social or political change. West appealed to Johnson as "the dean of Negro letters" in a 1933 letter asking him to write an introductory editorial to what she still had not quite decided would be her own magazine. She expressed her heartfelt desire to continue the promise of the New Negro movement: "It occurred to me that I could make up from much I have wasted by some way finding a space for young dark throats to sing heard songs."[10] In fact, the very first issue of *Challenge* would include a section entitled "Heard Songs." The heading indicates West's appreciation for African American oral culture.[11] Of the many contradictions that make it difficult to confirm the *New Challenge* as radically divergent from the original *Challenge* is the former's exchange of "Heard Songs" for the more conventional category of "Poetry," despite Richard Wright's championing of black folk culture and the oral tradition.

In choosing James Weldon Johnson (*Autobiography of An Ex-Colored Man*, *Lift Every Voice and Sing*), an artist whose fictional and musical contributions sparked many imitations in terms of form, style, and content, to foreground the rigor and quality of the art West allows him to set the tone for the premier issue. Rather than writing a foreword or afterword, she instead offers supportive commentary from established New Negro writers. Her first "Dear Reader" column ends with the invocation that *Challenge* be "primarily an organ for the new voices," but she misses the opportunity to set down a definitive structure, preface, and ideology of her own. What informs West's reticence? On one level she is energized and opinionated about the mission of her magazine, but on another she defers to and depends upon the charismatic male poets who were her close friends and mentors—namely Hughes, Cullen, and Arna Bontemps. They all praise West's "brave new project."[12] This reticence might be a function of the self-denigrating attitude that women writers sometimes evince; it is similar to the self-effacing modesty that characterized the prefaces of nineteenth-century black and white women writers who felt they had to apologize for their presumptuous intrusions into the public sphere. Yet, her reluctance to establish definitive parameters for her journal also suggests a refreshing openness to new ideas and new directions. Over the course of the journal's brief print run, we can discern West's ambiguous "Blueprint" through her evolving commentary in the "Dear Reader" section. Tracing the evolution

Dorothy West with her writing desk on the porch of her house in Oak Bluffs.
Photograph by Judith Sedwick. Courtesy of Schlesinger Library,
Radcliffe Institute, Harvard University.

Dorothy West Avenue.
Photograph by the author.

Dorothy West's house, Oak Bluffs, Martha's Vineyard.

Photograph by the author.

Highland Beach, circa 1950s.
East Chop Beach Club.

Highland Beach, 2008.
Photograph by the author.

Rachel Benson West
as a young woman.

Courtesy of
Schlesinger Library,
Radcliffe Institute,
Harvard University.

Black and White cast, June 1932. Dorothy West sits to the right of the life preserver. Louise Thompson sits to the left of the life preserver. Mildred Jones reclines in the chair on the far left, and Langston Hughes appears standing in the second row, third from the right.

Yale Collection of American Literature, Beinecke Rare Book and Manuscript Library.

Dorothy West and
Langston Hughes, 1932.

Yale Collection of
American Literature,
Beinecke Rare Book and
Manuscript Library.

Langston Hughes and
Louise Thompson, 1932.

Yale Collection of American
Literature, Beinecke Rare Book
and Manuscript Library.

Lois Mailou Jones, *Flying Horses*, 1944. Original oil painting.

FRIDAY, SEPTEMBER 5, 1969 — VINEYARD GAZETTE, MARTHA'S VINEYARD

COTTAGERS' CORNER

By Dorothy West

The Oak Bluffs Tennis Club played out its annual tournament at the town tennis courts over a week-end of clear weather that made these matches a daily attraction for many spectators. The gallery itself was an excitement to see. There were people of every color and facial cast. Some of the exotic combinations of coloring, features and texture of hair—a dark face with delicate features and silken hair, a golden face framed in a halo of tight red-gold curls, the color from one ancestral source, the woolly texture from another—are often extraordinary in the beauty they achieve.

Some of the Afros are wonderfully attractive when the wearer knows the cut of his face and how much halo it can stand. Some of the Afros are absurd. If they were once the badge of militancy, they are now a peculiar form of snobbery.

Ball boys for the elimination series were Sonny Funn, Brian Freeman, Wayne Elliot and Julie Anderson.

Joy and Karen Anderson, young and enterprising daughters of Dr. and Mrs. Julian Anderson, sold sodas and cakes, and made deliveries from Nick's Lighthouse to those of heartier appetites. Young Michael and Marcene Mitchell, and Rhonda Johnson sold hot dogs. These children, who made their own cupcakes, and cooked their own hot dogs, did a very brisk business.

In this year's matches the seeded players were Robert Shaw, Quentin Vaughan, Lewis Downing, Tony Santio, Jean Burnett, Laura Hayling, Dr. Bill Hayling, Doris Mitchell, Hilton Davis and Mrs. Robert Shaw.

Men's singles was won by Robert Shaw of New Jersey over Jackie Robinson, businessman of Boston. Mr. Shaw was last year's winner of men's singles.

In women's singles Jean Burnett, who won last year, won this year in her defeat of Jan Cable.

In men's doubles Tony Santio of Boston and Bob Shaw upset the favored team of Quentin Vaughan, Boston lawyer with the federal Department of Commerce, and Dr. Frederick Jones of New York.

In the women's doubles Jean Burnett and Laura Hayling defeated Ann Funn and Jan Cable. Laura is office manager for her doctor husband, Bill Hayling, whose extensive practice is in Newark. Ann Funn is counselor in a New York high school. Jan Cable is also in the New York school system.

In the mixed doubles Jean and Winston Burnett upset Hilton Davis and Doris Mitchell. Winston Burnett is head of the Winston Burnett Construction Company, one of the 100 largest general contracting companies in the country. Hilton Davis, a lawyer, is director of the Committee Against Discrimination in Housing and Education in Newark. Doris Mitchell is associate dean of residence and assistant director of admissions at Radcliffe.

In the singles for boys 14 and under Leland Pope defeated Joey Mitchell 3rd.

In singles for boys 18 and under Joey Mitchell upset Evan Margetson. Evan, like Joey, is a second generation tennis player. His father, Desmond Margetson, is an engineer, who is on the courts as often as his busy schedule allows. His mother Ann is an artist.

In singles for girls 14 and under Pam Hall, daughter of Dr. and Mrs. William Hall of Baltimore, defeated Deidre Davis, daughter of Mr. and Mrs. Hilton Davis.

In singles for girls 18 and under Laurie Guild of Boston defeated Suzanne Slaughter of New Jersey.

In boys' doubles for 14 and under Leland Pope and Joey Mitchell defeated Cliff Anderson of New York and Leslie Hayling of New Jersey. Leslie is the son of Dr. and Mrs. Leslie Hayling, new cottage owners in Oak Bluffs, and nephew of Bill and Laura Hayling.

In the girls' doubles for under 14 the sisters Pam and Pat Hall defeated Deidre Davis and Lisa Johnson, daughter of Dr. and Mrs. Randolph Johnson.

The tennis club held its final meeting and its farewell party at Cottagers Corner. Officers re-elected for the coming year are Dr. Bill Hayling, president, Juanita Johnson, secretary-treasurer, and Dr. Randolph Johnson, tournament chairman.

Mrs. Henry Hill, a new Vineyard Haven cottage owner, has been a houseguest of her aunt, Mrs. Edward Brooke Sr., and her cousin, Sen. Edward W. Brooke, for the past several days while seeing to the final details of building a house from the bottom up.

For the past several years Adelaide Hill, whose scholastic title is doctor, has been research associate in the department of African Studies at Boston University. Last year she was acting director.

This July she was appointed director of the new Afro-American studies department. It is a challenging post and she has a zest for proving her capacities.

The department of African studies did not grant degrees. The upper graduates enrolled in its course were candidates for degrees in their own discipline. They were students, black and white, with a career interest in Africa or African affairs in such fields as foreign service, government service, business and education.

The Afro-American courses will be open to graduate students only and a master's degree will be offered.

The Humanities Press in this country will soon release a book published by Frank Cass of London, edited by Mrs. Hill and Martin Kilson, professor of Government at Harvard. The book, Apropos of Africa, dealing with the period from the 1800s to 1950, documents the true character of the concern on the part of black leaders in this country with Africa and Africans.

The Exodus Was On

Extra Ferry Trips Are Made for Orderly Departures

The Island's summer population, or certainly a sector of impressive significance, folded its tents like the Arabs and perhaps not in actual silence, but certainly with smoothness and absence of confusion, stole away, this in the period between Tuesday of last week and Tuesday of this week.

It might not be wholly correct to say that this exodus exceeded predictions, but the promise of the Steamship Authority to clean up everything each day was pretty well carried out as far as could be determined, but it required unusual diligence on the part of the company personnel, both ashore and afloat, to accomplish it.

The regular schedule, with both the Islander and Uncatena, was maintained on three days out of the week mentioned, with everything in the way of car reservations sold out to and including Tuesday of this week, but the promise was made that those who had failed to make reservations might appear on a

Silver Presented at Annual Prize Night

Edgartown Yacht Club Skippers Gather for Racing Awards of the Summer Season

By Edith Blake

It took considerable clanging of cymbals in the orchestra to get the excited audience to quiet down, but eventually Comm. James A. Farrell Jr. could be heard, and the Edgartown Yacht Club's Prize Night was in progress.

"This is the finest hour of any Commodore," said the Commodore, "to thank all those who have sailed so well. This is the end of my prepared speech so I will turn this meeting over to the chairman of the race committee."

Comm. Robert P. Brown began by saying, "School is just around the corner," and followed with some happy and unhappy banter on the subject. He went on to explain that the duties of the race committee had been complicated this past season by the uncooperative southeast winds which made it difficult to work out windward starts. Also there had been a rash of broken masts which had set an all time record. He mentioned also, as a hint of things to come, that all the top-rated crews had worn life preservers on blowy days, and that next year the code flags E - G would mean that preservers should be worn.

Many More Starters

For the series races this past summer there were 865 starters which was over 100 more than the summer before. Depending on the number who qualified first, second and third prizes were awarded. For July, Comm. Hugh Bullock's Shields, True took first, and Rev. James R. Whittemore's Missile placed first in the Solings. Captain Whittemore said when he accepted the award, that it had been won by Jeff Storer and Mike Sands, who, "really did it in July".

The second Soling was Rickie Bartram's Vanski, and when he accepted the prize he also made an announcement and said that the boat pronounced was not Van-ski but Vonsk. Third place went to Commodore Farrell's Springbok which was sailed by Neddy Brooks, who did not make an announcement simply because he was not there to receive the award.

David T. Guernsey Jr.'s Pieces of Eight was first in the Smyras and Dennis Dixon's Cachalot second. N. Dudley Johnson's Alliance third. Commodore Farrell at this point began handing out white cards instead of silver, and Commodore Brown explained that some of the prizes were late getting back from the engravers which was sort of disappointing to the young, but that the older people could take it.

In the Wood Pussies Francis Johnson Jr. took first with Arpege and there weren't enough skunks-er Woodpussys to award the other two prizes.

Posie Bass took first in her Beach Boat, Millet, with William Ambrose Jr. second in Misty Miss, and Martin Begien Jr. third in Golden Arrow.

In the August Series

In the August series races, Commodore Hugh Bullock again took first place while Vanski made first in the Solings. This time Commodore Brown hesitated before he pronounced it, and when he got it right the audience applauded, and Rickie Bartram looked pleased.

In the Smyras Dennis Dixon won first place and Commodore Brown, just to be on the safe side, asked Smyras and William Ambrose Jr. in the Beach Boats.

In Boats it was won by William Ambrose Jr.

In the Commodores' Cup Series the Commodore's Cup was won by Brandon Harrison in his Soling Saint's Quest, and the Vice Commodore's cup went to Jeff Storer in Sassafras.

Hugh Bullock in True won the Shields Commodore's cup and others were not awarded.

In the Smyras, the Commodore's Cup went to Hateful Hatsey Potter while Dennis Dixon took the Vice Commodore's and Dennis Dixon took the Rear Commodore's cup.

The Beach Boats

William Ambrose Jr. won in the Beach Boats followed by "that sea lawyer" Martin Begien.

Mrs. Polly Vietor Sheehan won in her Wood Pussy Acorn with the only perfect score, and Francis Johnson Jr. was second.

William Nelson then rose and presented a prize to the Beach Boat crew member in the boat with the best combined score, and the winner was Baird Jones aboard Misty Miss.

Commodore Brown said that it was always difficult to remember to look at who was making the best starts in the Beach Boat class when boats "were hitting each other", and other confusions were raining on the crowded line.

"And after all this watching and scoring," he continued, "this year we have a tie." Gordon Walsh Jr. and Cary Dixon drew for the single trophy and Cary won, which was fair since Gordon was already carrying off a truck full of loot.

In the All Day Race, which windwise looked like a complete failure but got better, the prizes for all classes were donated by H. Williamson Ghriskey. On combined time for the morning and afternoon races, Townsend and Martin Morey in Checkmate took first in the cruising class. The following day they were another among that rash of dismastings and put out of commission for the rest of the season. Winners in the other classes were: Soling, Vanski; Smyra, Saint's Quest; Wood Pussy Acorn, sailed by Louise Vietor Oliver, and Beach Boat, Willet.

The Carl L. Vietor Memorial Trophy presented by Alexander O. Vietor to the Beach Boat with the highest combined score for July and August was won by William Ambrose Jr., and the Smyra with the highest combined score was sailed by Dennis Dixon.

The prizes for the Easter Atlantic Coast Soling Championship races donated by Commodore Farrell had been presented after the races. Another new trophy is the Paul M. Runyon Memorial Trophy presented to the Edgartown Soling with the best percentage score for the season's racing. It was won by Brandon Harrison, who was not there to receive it.

"He's probably already in school," commented Commodore Brown. The Walsh Trophy donated by Robert G. Potter, awarded to the Vineyard Sound Soling Association boat with the best score in August, also went to Captain Harrison.

Another new Soling trophy given of Mr. Radley is the John J. Radley Jr. Trophy awarded to the yacht with the best score of the season, regardless of its being an Edgartown boat, and this was won by Rev. James R. Whittemore's Missile.

The Shipshape and "Bristol Fashion" prizes awarded after sneak inspection-attacks on the racing fleet, donated by Vice Comm. Camden McVey, went to Lee Whitney, first, Gordon Walsh Jr., second, and Wendy Walsh, third.

"Cottagers' Corner."

Vineyard Gazette, 5 September 1969.

The Seahorse,
Oak Bluffs,
Massachusetts.

Photograph by author.

Halle Berry with Eric
Stahl and Carl Lumbly in
"Oprah Winfrey Presents
The Wedding," 1998.

Everett Collection.

of her role as an editor and contributor also provides insight about how the *New Challenge* emerged from the *Challenge*.

After *Fire!!*: West's Blueprint

Taken collectively, West's "Dear Reader" columns reveal a complex portrait of her aesthetic beliefs and artistic claims. They are a mini-manifesto that evolves over the course of the journal(s) and her writing life. We presume that a writer's work will develop and change over the years rather than remain stagnant. In the case of Dorothy West, certain inconsistencies make it difficult to chart a linear path of aesthetic development. However tempting it may be to claim West as a closet radical, her "Dear Reader" commentaries make it difficult for that label to stick. In January 1936 issue West writes: "Somebody asked us why *Challenge* was for the most part so pale pink. We said because the few red articles we did receive were not literature. We care a lot about style. And we think a message doubly effective when written effectively without bombast or bad spelling."[13] This is perhaps West's strongest statement in defense of her aesthetic. It is ironic that she was often compelled to publish work that did not quite live up to her high standards. She acknowledges this in the "Voices" section of the same issue: "Juanita C. DeShield sent us her story some time ago. At first we didn't dream that we'd ever print it. But here it is, a diamond in the rough, very rough but a diamond."[14] West wanted to encourage raw talent, but she was frustrated by writers' lack of attention to elements of style and language precision in favor of political impact. The idea of *Challenge* as "pink" rather than "red" accurately describes West's politics, a perspective she took to Russia as one who wore communist accessories without subscribing fully to either its ideology or its idealism. West sent Langston Hughes a copy of *Challenge* in exchange for an edition of *New Masses* that he sent her. After cheekily suggesting he might want to respond to the "article on Russia" included in the issue, she writes that she could not have gone "through that Russian experience without having some leaning toward communism." West insists that she wants the "magazine to be one of diverse opinions," but she is primarily "concerned with the black race."[15]

   In the June 1936 issue of *Challenge* West prints a scathing letter to the editor from a subscriber who is frustrated with the unevenness of the contributions. He tellingly contrasts *Fire!!*'s poetry with *Challenge*'s lackluster poems:

> Most disappointing are those who, young once, showed promise surpassing even you latest young'uns. I'm thinking of Waring Cuney's "Song of a Song," Mae V. Cowdery's two "poems" in your third issue, and Helene Johnson's "Let me Sing my Song." Look in FIRE (remember it?) and you'll see that same poetry but refreshing then in that they were new

and showed promise. (That Waring at this date should come up with a song to the masses! Your title and cover must have fooled him.)

The letter writer, identified only by the initials C.C.G., continues to trash Richard Bruce Nugent's contributions to the *Challenge* by citing the superior, "exquisite" "Smoke, Lilies and Jade," which also appeared in *Fire!!*. West's commitment to include interracial material does distinguish *Challenge* from *Fire!!*. She is "glad to note that not all of the voices are Negro" (45). In this same issue West publishes Alfred Mendes, who has a novel published in England, and a rather disturbing, erotically surreal story from a convict at Leesburg Farms, New Jersey, named Russell Garner, and a foreign correspondent writing from Denmark.

West's editorial endeavors place her in the company of several black women who struggled to balance their shepherding of emerging literary talent with their own desire to produce creative, distinctive art. Pauline Hopkins at the *Colored American Magazine* and Jessie Redmon Fauset at the *Crisis* played similar editorial roles. Likewise, each also faced conflicts with male editors that led to their resignations. Additionally, all three published fiction under pseudonyms to disguise the amount of material that they, as editors, were including in the magazine. Like West, Fauset and Hopkins sought to include high quality literature and art. In particular, Fauset sought black female artists, like Laura Wheeler, as illustrators and cover artists for the *Crisis*. After Fauset left the *Crisis* in 1926, following a dispute with W.E.B. Du Bois, the literary quality dramatically diminished. It is no coincidence that the emergence of *Fire!!* coincides with Fauset's retirement as the *Crisis*'s literary editor. Pauline Hopkins had no qualms about linking the politics of uplift to her personal aesthetic. From its inception the *Colored American Magazine* (*CAM*) advocated what Hopkins's biographer Lois Brown calls "race romance."[16] Hopkins did not shy away from the violence facing blacks during Reconstruction, but she also included biographical series like "Famous Men of the Negro Race" (November 1900–1901) in *CAM*. The fusion of race romance and current political material made *CAM* a highly successful periodical. The success, not to mention the quality of the contributions and number of subscribers and agents, plummeted when the magazine moved from Boston to New York and came under the control of agents of Booker T. Washington, who immediately ousted Hopkins.

How much did West know about the challenges that Fauset and Hopkins faced as female editors and writers? The struggle to both mentor new authors and produce one's own art can be overwhelming, especially when subject to the takeover by aggressive, male editors. When she had free rein, Hopkins's editorial role seemed to fuel her fiction; she was incredibly prolific during her tenure at *CAM*. Like West, she used at least two known pseudonyms.[17] The same company that published *CAM*—the Colored Co-Operative Publishing Company—also published Hopkins's novel *Contending Forces* (1900). After Hopkins and Fauset vacated their respective editorial posts, the material in both periodicals changed for the worse: "More and better fiction and poetry was published by the *Colored American Magazine* during the years Pauline Hopkins was editor than at any other time in history."[18] Prior to her resignation, Hopkins received the following letter from white publisher and music critic John Freund: "Either Miss Hopkins will follow our suggestion in this matter and put live matter into the magazine, eliminating anything which may create offence; Stop talking about wrongs and a proscribed race, or you must count me out absolutely from this day forth."[19] It turns out that Freund was backed by Booker T. Washington, who supported his plans to transfer the magazine to New York and place it under the editorship of Fred Moore.

There was a critical difference between Hopkins's ouster and West's editorial quandary: rather than allow the magazine she founded to be coopted by Richard Wright and reduced to a vehicle for the South Side Writers Group, West ended the publication: "But the Chicago students decided they were going to take over the magazine. Therefore they wrote this article. I don't know what they thought of me—I was just a woman, I guess. But the minute they decided they were gonna take over the magazine, I stopped it, and that was the end of that. I had no choice."[20] Later Wright bullied West into turning over the copyright for "Blueprint." However, West's willingness to have the journal fail rather than allow a complete takeover demonstrates how strongly she believed in the journal's original aesthetics and runs counter to how some historians and Richard Wright's biographers have understood this episode. Like Fauset and Hopkins, West perceived how the matrix of gender and power would work to supplant her voice in the publication she founded; this "hostile" takeover occurred despite the fact that Marian Minus was coeditor of the *New Challenge* and Margaret Walker evidently worked hard behind the scenes to amass the South Side Writers contributions.

To augment the fictional contributions in *Challenge*, in addition to her Russia pieces, West published two stories in the journal under pseudonyms: "Cook" under Jane Isaac and "The Five Dollar Bill" under Mary Christopher. The appearance of the character Judy in the "The Five Dollar Bill" foreshadows the young protagonist whose point of view infuses *The Living Is Easy*. Later, West said she wrote the novel quickly, in six months, but clearly the seeds, characters, and relationships were explored in her early fiction. The "Five Dollar Bill" is reminiscent of Henry James's novel *What Maisie Knew* in that it deals with a child's reflection on the manipulations of adult life. In this story of betrayal an unfaithful wife forces her daughter, who loses her innocence, to side with her against her father. The text is overlaid with the complex emotions that West—an only child—felt for her parents. Little Judy clearly worships "the father" but maintains an unshakeable loyalty to "the mother." The story provides a sketch for the fully developed narrative that became West's first novel. It does not take up the folk elements that West incorporated into *The Living Is Easy*, nor does it contain specifically identifiable African American content. The mother uses the ever-important class distinctions, primarily based on higher education, to convince Judy to keep her mother's lover, a college boy, a secret from the father.

West demonstrates her uncanny ability to poignantly render the inner life of working-class characters in her short story "Cook." In this story, penned under the pseudonym Jane Isaac, she presents the story of Lavinia Williams, a woman who works as a domestic in Boston to support her sister and her family's life in Harlem society. Her employers have no idea of the "double life" that she leads: "They didn't like Negroes, particularly, and had no interest in cook's inner life."[21] The reader follows Williams on a train away from the hypocrisy of Boston to Striver's Row—the heart of the black Harlem elite. There a black maid greets Cook with a joyful "Welcome home, Miss Williams." In this space, Cook has a name and an identity. She is unfortunately still treated like a servant in her own house, even though her labor supports the upper-class façade of her dependent relatives: a vapid, social-climbing sister and her struggling doctor husband. Although Cook sees through the hollowness of her sister's world, she is protective of her idealistic brother-in-law and innocent niece Lestra, who is a piano prodigy. She enjoys being able to endow their dreams: a new party dress for her sister Dell, a European tour for Lestra, and a hospital for Neil. As Cook reflects on her life—what her labor has enabled for others and what she has not claimed for herself, namely a husband and child—she becomes a nostalgic martyr.

West's final "Dear Reader" in April 1937 cites a lack of "fair material" rather than financing as the reason for the *Challenge's* demise. She challenges African American youth to become socially engaged: "Our special hope is for the young Negro to grow to complete awareness of his heritage, his position as a member of a minority group, and his duty to take some active part in social reform. He must not escape, through his university training, to a consideration of himself as an entity apart. He must know the South, whose centre is not the campus. He must know the North, whose main stem is not Sugar Hill."[22]

In her goodbye to the *Challenge* West acknowledges the Chicago group, citing the appearance of Marian Minus's contribution as indicative of the promise of the South Side Writers Group. West throws down the gauntlet: "We have retaliated by offering them a special section in a forthcoming issue, that they may show us what we have not done by showing us what they can do."[23] In fall 1937, the *New Challenge* appears to take up West's challenge; West and Minus serve as coeditors, and the charismatic, enigmatic Wright becomes an associate editor.

New Aesthetics and a *New Challenge*

What does the publication history of the two *Challenges* tell us about aesthetic and class conflicts in this period between the two Renaissances? The Chicago group wanted to define itself in opposition to the Harlem Renaissance by critiquing what they saw as the limitations of uplift ideology and the aesthetic and political compromises fostered by white patronage. Despite the Rosenwald underwriting and the influence of the University of Chicago, especially the department of sociology, it was important for the Chicago Renaissance to appear as if it were primarily promoted, fueled, administered, and produced by African Americans in the city. West wished to extend the Chicago Renaissance while emphasizing the quality of the writing rather than its subject matter or politics.

There is little agreement about Richard Wright's arrival at the *Challenge*. Marian Minus was clearly the main connection between West and the Chicago group. Minus (1913–1972) was a graduate of Fisk University and held a Rosenwald scholarship at the University of Chicago. Considering that the "we" at the *Challenge* included Minus and West, it is likely that Wright was motivated to assume the editorship of the *Challenge* for political as well as personal reasons. Why does the *Challenge* fail? Political disagreements? A love affair turned sour? According to Michel Fabre, who draws on correspondence between Wright and Margaret Walker, Wright played a central role in radically reorienting the vision of the *New Challenge* and "did most of the work for the publication and made almost all the editorial decisions."[24] Fabre cites disagreements between Marian Minus and Dorothy West as generative of the magazine's failure.

Because West and Minus's relationship endures long after the journal's last issue, it is unlikely that a rift between the two women provoked the magazine's demise, as Michel Fabre presumes. I am also not entirely persuaded by Margaret Walker's version of the story:

It was strange, therefore, to hear him declare himself naïve about Marian Minus. He was too sophisticated not to understand that Marian Minus had a lesbian lifestyle, although he said he had fallen in love with her before he discovered it. She was a student at the University of Chicago and occasionally came to the South Side Writer's Group—one of the few women who persisted. Marian dressed mannishly, but I doubt she and Wright may have had anything but a casual friendship. She was the link between the South Side Writer's Group and the *New Challenge* Magazine. I was complete mystified and shocked to read years later in Harold Cruse's book *The Crisis of the Negro Intellectual* that the Communist party sponsored the magazine and that Wright left Chicago to become the editor. That was certainly not his only reason for leaving; however, it was my understanding that Dorothy West was already the editor and would remain so. This misunderstanding evidently caused the break between Wright and the two women.[25]

The *New Challenge*'s masthead clearly lists Dorothy West and Marian Minus as coeditors of the magazine and Wright as associate editor. In the *Amsterdam News* an article announced: "New Challenge Now on Stands" with the subheading "Dorothy West and Marian Minus Magazine's Editors." Surprisingly, the brief article lists Richard Wright as one of several contributors—not as an editor.[26] Most critics eschew West's editorial role in favor of considering the *New Challenge* as a vehicle for Wright and the South Side Writers Group. The notion that Wright took over the majority of the editorial duties while radically reorienting the magazine to his own interests seems unlikely. Instead, the articles chosen present a productive tension that foreshadows the aesthetic debates about black writing that occurred during the second Black Arts Movement of the 1960s and 1970s. The premier issue heavily features the Chicago group, but this is no surprise given West's encouragement of and interest in publishing emergent writers. In the April 1937 "Dear Reader" she reached out directly to the Chicagoans:

> Yet we are not entirely discouraged, for we have become greatly interested in a young Chicago group, one of whose members appears in this issue. These young Chicagoans hold meetings regularly, where their work is read for open discussion. The meetings, we are told, are lively and well attended. CHALLENGE has come in for considerable dispraise, but we have never resented honest opinions.[27]

Writing as the editorial "we" West is gracious, open, and welcoming of criticism. Her intent with the *Challenge* was to showcase and discover writers of promise and encourage the kind of literary exchange she found so critical in her own experiences as a fledgling writer. Local writing groups like Eugene Gordon's Saturday Evening Quill Club in Boston encouraged West's early fiction, and some of her first publications appeared in Gordon's journal. In addition, Marian Minus "emigrated" from the South Side Writers Group: she is the "member who appears" in the final issue. West had no problems holding her own among the "radicals." Whether in Russia or Harlem or Chicago, she spoke her mind, but kept it open.

Rather than representing a clean break from the New Negro of the Harlem Renaissance, Richard Wright's carefully executed argument in "Blueprint" reveals, the continuity between the two groups. In her literary history of the Chicago group Michelle Gordon points out that Wright fails to acknowledge the evolving aesthetics and radical proclivities of Langston Hughes, Claude McKay, and Arna Bontemps—all writers who straddle both Renaissances:

> What emerges [in "Blueprint"] is more of a transition between the Harlem Renaissance and the Chicago Renaissance than the clear break Wright proclaims in "Blueprint": the period's sharp Left-ward turn in black writing was propelled by not only the creative dialogues, grassroots work, and artistic productions of the SSWG, but also by earlier Marxist-inflected radical writing and cultural organizing centered in Harlem in the 1920s and early 1930s.[28]

Wright's "Blueprint" was a call for black writers to develop a proletarian-centered, Marxist aesthetic that would illuminate what he felt was the most authentic subject of African American culture: the working class. He begins by dismissing black literary tradition as "confined to humble novels, poems, and plays, prim and decorous ambassadors who went a-begging to white America." He proceeds to directly attack the writers, ideologues, and architects of the Harlem Renaissance as a "liaison between inferiority-complexed Negro 'geniuses' and burnt-out white Bohemians with money."[29] Though he includes no names, his targets are unambiguous. For Wright, the white patronage of philanthropists and Negrophiles like Carl Van Vechten and Charlotte Osgood Mason was contaminating and nurtured accommodationist art. To make a clean break from the interracialism of the Harlem Renaissance, he argues for blacks to adopt a proletarian aesthetic. Marxism is a first step. He argues that "through a Marxist conception of reality and society . . . the maximum degree of freedom in thought and feeling can be gained for the Negro writer."[30] Although the ten-point essay is replete with references to Lenin and the proletariat, it also contains useful, if narrowly defined, directives. For instance, "a Negro writer must learn to view the life of a Negro living in New York's Harlem or Chicago's South side with the consciousness that one-sixth of the earth's surface belongs to the working class."[31] This directive is obviously compatible with the folk aesthetic argued for by Langston Hughes's "The Negro Artist and the Racial Mountain." Yet Wright does not seem to be in conversation with Hughes's essay or George Schuyler's "Negro Art Hokum." He also eschews earlier articulations of the black writer's charge written by journalists like Victoria Earle Matthews, who in "The Value of Race Literature" called for a distinctive African American literature exemplified by the writings and editorial perspectives of authors like Pauline Hopkins and Ida B. Wells-Barnett. These activist authors wrote for interracial audiences without sugar-coating their arguments against lynching and sexual violence.

Despite Wright's rather narrow conception of the black literary tradition, it is hard to read the "Blueprint" without being persuaded by his impassioned rhetoric. One cannot forget the significance of this essay's appearance in the *New Challenge*—arguably the last publication of the Harlem Renaissance. The *New Challenge* heralds the direction in which black writing will proceed until the Black Arts Movement—an interim era dominated by Wright, Ralph Ellison, and, eventually, James Baldwin.

While several pieces included in the *New Challenge* exemplify "Blueprints"'s aesthetics, others reflect West's ideals, which the collectively written note that opens the journal communicates: "We envisage the *New Challenge* as an organ designed to meet the needs of writers and people interested in literature which cannot be met by those Negro magazines which are *sponsored by organizations* and which, therefore, cannot be purely literary" (emphasis mine). West felt strongly that a publication connected to an organization, while well supported, could not be independent of that organization's ideology. The magazine reiterates West's inclusive interracialism by adding the sentence: "while our emphasis is upon Negro writers and the particular difficulties which they must meet, we are not limiting our contributors to Negroes alone."[32]

How did West feel about Wright's "Blueprint"? What affect did it have on her writing? She certainly disagreed with Wright's assessment of Zora Neale Hurston, who was the first to influence West's representation of intraracial dynamics between the folk and the black bourgeoisie. West published Hurston's short story "Fire and Cloud" in the second issue of *Challenge* even though she may have been a little disappointed with the quality of the story: a folksy vignette about a conversation between Moses and a lizard. Hurston actually offered to pull the story. She wrote to West: "If you do not like this un-Negro story, why not go to 'Story' Magazine . . . and get permission to re-publish 'The Gilded Six-Bits'?"[33] West's support of Hurston prompted her to include a laudatory review of *Their Eyes Were Watching God* penned by Marian Minus in the *New Challenge*. This early review contradicts the common critical presumption that Hurston's novel was poorly received among her fellow artists and intellectuals. Minus praises Hurston's ability to capture African American idiom, which is evident in "the poetry and imagery of the dialect." Moreover, she writes that Hurston's superb execution renders scenes like the hurricane and mad dog episode poignant and compelling rather than fantastic or absurd.[34] She adds that it is hard to see how Hurston does not exemplify the "complex simplicity," the skillful elevation of folk culture that Wright calls for. In his conclusion, Wright states that: "writers faced with such tasks can have no possible time for malice or jealousy."[35] Yet competitiveness certainly propels him to describe Hurston's prose as "cloaked in that facile sensuality that has dogged Negro expression since the days of Phillis Wheatley."[36] Despite their public posturing, Wright and Hurston were more aesthetically similar than divergent. In *New Negro, Old Left*, William Maxwell aptly describes their attempts to harness "folk ideology to provide a symbolic countermeasure to a Great Migration that threatened to empty the population and cultural power of a southern Black Belt" as a "harmonic convergence."[37]

Although the Left praised the *New Challenge*, the Communist Party did not financially support the venture, and some attribute its demise to this failure of sponsorship. West gives her side of the story to Dalsgård:

> Richard Wright was a communist. All of a sudden he got tired of being a communist because he wanted to be free to write what he wanted to write. The magazine had already started. Then he came to New York. I did not know him before. Marian Minus had known him. She was at the University of Chicago. Richard Wright—I've always had a little problem with Richard Wright—used to come on campus. He was a beginning writer, and he was forever bitter because the students at the University of Chicago did not pay any attention to him. They did not know him. Marian was the kind of person who was always willing to help others. She corrected his papers and stories. In fairness to him he wanted to marry her. She did quite a bit, so he knew her well. When he came to New York—I dare say because he knew Marian—he got involved with the magazine. . . . *The New Yorker* magazine . . . said of me, "Dorothy West is a communist." They got everything all mixed up. The young people at the University of Chicago were leftists. I never was, because I was too independent to be anything.[38]

West's interview with Deborah McDowell corroborates much of what she told Dalsgård.[39] Her knowledge of the South Side Writers Group came from Minus.

According to Mitchell and Davis, West met Minus in New York in the early 1930s. Mattie Marian Minus was a graduate of Fisk University and pursued graduate work at the University of Chicago where she became involved with the South Side Writers Group. In 1936, Minus wrote West from Chicago:

> Someone just rushed to tell me that Dick Wright is a Trotskyite. If only you could have seen the horror in her face! . . . The Party is, of course, embittered because Dick was the Communist flag[?] in literature as far as Negroes are concerned. Now he will write because writing is his life. He will always have a message because he has always been a proletarian. But thank heaven he won't be forced to type[?] out shibboleths just because he is a Communist. They should have seen long ago that he was beyond that stage and was crying to be allowed to let his mature work be born. They are so stupid.[40]

With its illustrious contributors and aesthetic manifesto the single issue of *New Challenge* has drawn more attention than the entire run of *Challenge*. Owen Dodson, Frank Marshall Davis, and Margaret Walker contribute poetry, and a review of "These Low Grounds" from soon-to-be famous Ralph Ellison appears as well. But the final issue of the *Challenge* under Dorothy West's full editorial control merits serious consideration. For one, it features Marian Minus's "Present Trends of Negro Literature." In many ways, Minus's piece anticipates Wright's "Blueprint." For one, they both came out of the South Side Writers Group. Her biographical note, describing her as one of the "vanguard of the Chicago group," distinguishes her among the other contributors, yet she is one of the least known members. She begins her essay by taking on questions of universality. She writes: "no literature can approach greatness if it is not the integrated reflection of the heritage from which it springs."[41] Her observation is in concert with Langston Hughes's "Free Within Ourselves": Hughes insists that black writers must mine their culture without regard for either the prescriptive suggestions of uplift or white patrons. Like Hughes, she advocates that an emphasis on folk culture provides the most authentic rendering of the "remnants of [black] heritage." Minus felt that an authentic novel successfully rendering the black experience had not yet been written, although she pointed to Arna Bontemps's novel *Black Thunder* (1936) as the best effort thus far.

Ultimately, neither incarnation of the *Challenge* was sustainable, but this is neither surprising nor even disastrous. To collapse for lack of funds, management, or subscribers was the fate of many little magazines. What is surprising is how long West managed to keep her *Challenge* afloat when both of Thurman's editorial endeavors had no more than one issue. West also struggled to acquire publishable material. As the depression persisted, would-be writers, plentiful in the early years, seem to have put down their pens and returned to work. Even the talented Jessie Fauset returned to teaching, a job she felt would completely overshadow her creative production, which it did—the 1933 novel *Comedy: American Style* was her last. Still, West found some gemstones in the rough, and a few pieces stand out for their freshness. Frank Yerby, the author of "Drought" and "Seagull" (May 1935), continued to publish until his death in 1991.

The *Challenge* and the *New Challenge* extended the Harlem Renaissance into the late 1930s. This unique venue showcased emergent talent who continued to assume the mantle through the 1940s and 1950s. Wright's "Blueprint" remains one of the most influential artistic manifestos of the twentieth century, but it should not be separated from the context in which it was published. In fact, Michelle Gordon contends that it should be read as a collective piece reflecting the ideals and directives of the South Side Writers Group. Of the contributors and contributing editors of *New Challenge*, writers like Margaret Walker fostered the Chicago Renaissance after Wright relocated to New York. In her long poem "For my people" she rendered the aesthetics of the "Blueprint" with startling accuracy. Sterling Brown's contribution "Old Lem," capturing the voice of the southern sharecropper and the bluesman, found its way into *The Collected Poems of Sterling Brown* (1980).

The story of the *Challenge/New Challenge* does mark the end of the Harlem Renaissance's little magazines. As the torch was passed from one generation of writers to the next, it was ironic that West's writing career was just beginning to mature. After 1937, she and Marian Minus lived together on and off for more than a decade as they shared a life and work and an agent. During the next decade, until she left New York for good, West continued to hone her aesthetic by writing stories for the *Daily News* and the Works Progress Administration (WPA), the federal relief agency for many unemployed writers and artists.

A Proletarian Story

To support her consideration of Dorothy West as a "closet revolutionary," literary critic Sharon Jones points to several stories that demonstrate West's "folk, bourgeois and proletarian aesthetic." Several of these stories, namely "Mammy" (1940) and "The Penny" (1941), were published in *Opportunity* and the *Daily News*, respectively, after the *New Challenge* had failed and while West was working for the Works Progress Administration. At the WPA, West was in good company. Zora Neale Hurston, Langston Hughes, Ralph Ellison, Claude McKay, and Richard Wright were just a few of the writers who also worked at the WPA.

West's post-*Challenge* stories offer a glimpse into Harlem during the mid- to late thirties viewed through the window of a working writer. West cultivated a reflective, psychologically complex narrator whose voice gave an indelible flair to her Harlem stories. Lionel Bascom, who published some of West's unpublished and selected stories from the *Daily News* in *The Last Leaf of Harlem*, singles out "Pluto" as one of his favorites. In "Pluto," a knock at the door disturbs a young writer at work. A mother and her son have come to ask for money. Immediately, the writer offers excuses, until she is struck by the child's interest in a wooden toy: Pluto. The child wants to play with Pluto. He is inexorably drawn to the lackluster toy in the way that a child who rarely has time for extended play can stretch his yearning across a room. Throughout the story the writer returns to his face and his desire for Pluto. At one point, she reflects that they "had interrupted me in the middle of an excellent story. It was about poor people, too; a good proletarian short story."[42] The self-reflective voice in "Pluto" stands out, but what makes it sparkle is its empathetic seeking to capture the point of view of an impoverished child while simultaneously revealing the elitist perspective of the writer who hopes to portray an authentic portrait of poverty.

West found her work with the WPA more radicalizing than her trip to Russia. She wrote to Hughes: "Lang, the long months in Moscow when life was good in the Minninskaya did not do for me and to me what my job as Home Relief investigator is. Lang, I have seen so much and learned so much. I have first hand knowledge of hunger and sickness and despair. I have a head full of tragic stories. Sometimes I cannot bear it."[43] The four Harlem stories that appear in *The Last Leaf of Harlem* (2008) capture the depth and vibrancy of the locale; they anticipate Ann Petry's Harlem stories and of course her great novel *The Street* (1948). The stories that appeared to such acclaim in the 1920s as indicative of the promise she showed as a young writer ironically pale in comparison to the sparse tightness of the WPA stories. From the storefront congregation of Daddy Grace, where an "oily tongue[d]" preacher squeezes his flock for every cent, to a Harlem rent party with a pretentious hostess to an amateur night in the Apollo, West paints a vibrant portrait of the immensely diverse population that lived and moved in and out of Harlem in the thirties.[44] These stories show a mature self-reflection that served her well as she began work on *The Living Is Easy*. With the demise of the *Challenge/New Challenge* and the turn of other black periodicals away from fiction, there were few forums for black short fiction. Thus West, who was clearly becoming an expert at the short story, a form she used for the entirety of her writing life, found few outlets for her work.

Two stories published within a year of each other reflect West's interest in representing both the urban poor and those African Americans who find themselves caught in untenable situations as they attempt to straddle the color line. "Mammy" begins with a young African American welfare investigator charged with a "collateral" visit to an employer to verify the eligibility of an applicant for relief. Visiting the white employers of domestic workers requires the caseworker, who occupies an ambiguous space, to venture into places where class and color lines run parallel. Although she is a state employee and not in domestic service, her skin color renders that authority invisible to those who view her as fundamentally inferior. As she arrives at the Manhattan apartment to conduct her investigations, the white doorman eyes her with a "sense of outrage," and the black elevator operator rudely attempts to prevent her from using the elevator for the benefit of a white female occupant. After the stress of asserting her right to enter through the front door of the building and use the elevator the young woman is left "feeling sick" and "trembling": "Her contact with Negroes was confined to frightened relief folks who did everything possible to stay in her good graces, and the members of her own set, among whom she was a favorite because of her two degrees and her civil service appointment. She had almost never run into Negroes who did not treat her with respect."[45] Her education and employment set her apart from working-class blacks; she inhabits a position of privilege that is not challenged until she ventures out of the safe space of her office to conduct casework. The investigator's preoccupation with her own class anxiety blinds her to the fractures in a collateral visit she perceives as perfunctory. The stress of keeping up her hard-won authority, which she wears wearily, prevents her from understanding Mrs. Mason's, "Mammy's," unusual position within the Coleman household.

The offensive endearment of "Mammy" contains the self-deceiving belief of white southerners in the mutual devotion and loyalty of their servants. The "odious title sent a little flicker of dislike across the investigator's face."[46] The case worker is so convinced of the script that Mammy has simply left her job impulsively owing to a misunderstanding that she fails to read the clear signs that something is very wrong in the Coleman house. For instance, how does the doorman know that she wants the Coleman's residence? Most important, she fails to read accurately the anguish of the daughter of the house who has presumably given birth to a stillborn child: "A pale young girl lay on the edge of a big tossed bed. One hand was in her tangled hair, the other clutched an empty bassinet. The wheels rolled down and back, down and back. The girl glanced briefly and without interest at her mother and the investigator, then turned her face away."[47] It is inferred that Mammy left because the baby's death "unsettled" her mind. Later, when the investigator returns to confront Mammy, the text suggests that the Colemans practice infanticide, a charge confirmed by the investigator's discovery that "Mammy" is actually Mrs. Coleman's mother. Instead of a woman "clearly disoriented in her Northern transplanting," Mammy becomes the authenticating repository of the Colemans' blackness. This revelation transforms the story into a narrative of passing that continues to be suppressed because of the investigator's unwillingness to deviate from the directives of her position. Even after she discovers the Colemans' secret she reiterates that "her job was to give or withhold relief. That was all."[48]

"Mammy" joins several other stories that illustrate how desire for material wealth and status warps relationships between husbands and wives and parents and children. While "Mammy" offers another incisive critique of intraracial class anxiety, stories like "The Penny" and the "The Roomer," published in the *Daily News*, reveal the flawed and exploitative perceptions that circulate among all classes. Both stories are stripped of obvious racial markers. The subject matter of "The Roomer," which features a wife who squirrels away additional rent money to buy herself a new coat and luxurious food, becomes a part of the story line of *The Living Is Easy*. In "The Penny" a miserly woman who views poverty as a condition of the lazy and shiftless bribes a little boy into accusing his father of child abuse. The pleasure at having her misperception of the situation confirmed sends her "afloat in the clouds."[49]

While the selected short stories in *The Richer, the Poorer* (1995) represent some of West's most polished short fiction and conveniently echo the themes in her novels, the *Daily News* stories are harder to classify. Penned for a popular audience, they are stylistically uneven. Some are mere vignettes; others are poignant self-reflective meditations. West's agent, George Bye, secured the gig writing stories for the *Daily News*. At the same time, Marian Minus was also writing stories that defied the color line. Between 1945 and 1952 she wrote stories about middle-class Anglo Americans for *Woman's Day* and also published fiction about African Americans in black periodicals. Minus also typed West's stories. West wrote longhand on yellow sheets of paper. One day as she was typing Minus was so struck by one of West's sentences that she stopped typing and stared out of the window for a moment. "I did it right," West tells Dalsgård, expressing pleasure at Minus's response to her "simple sentence."[50] Lionel Bascom assembles many of West's *Daily News* stories chronologically in his anthology *The Last Leaf of Harlem*. They defy thematic grouping, but read collectively they embody West's flexible aesthetic: she is as comfortable writing aracial stories about middle-class families on the Vineyard as she is about writing politically aware and socially conscious considerations of intraracial class issues among the middle class.

West's *Daily News* stories enabled her to develop a type of writing she had experimented with in earlier stories like "Hannah Byde" and "The Five Dollar Bill," stories in which at first racial identity was either ambiguous, deliberately disguised, or universally presumed to be white. In many of the *Daily News* stories the protagonist could be any race. This important strategy kept West in print but removed her from studies of black writers that classified texts based on subject matter traditionally identified with urban black culture. As she progressively became more interested in writing about black middle-class life, West found it harder to be published. In fact, she tells Deborah McDowell that she began to write aracial stories because, although they often praised her writing, "magazines didn't buy the stories that were about Black people."[51]

Once West's entire oeuvre, the scope of her career, is taken into consideration, it is clear that it exceeds the confines of "the last surviving" classification. West emerges as an important, consistent, American short story writer. When the *Daily News* stories are added to her publication tally we see just how prolific she was throughout her lifetime. West's status as a minor writer is predominantly a result of critical periodization that positions her as the last of the Harlem Renaissance writers. Although West continued writing stories that she considered "potboilers" for the *Daily News*, *The Living Is Easy*, which dealt with the black middle class in Boston, was not published until 1948, after she had abandoned the urban and artistic enclaves she inhabited in her youth.

6

The Living Is Easy

I don't know which is more interesting, whether fiction or life . . .

—Dorothy West (Linsey Lee, "Interview with Dorothy West")

West had been writing for more than twenty years when her first novel was published. Without the publication of *The Living Is Easy*, the novel that solidified her place as an influential and important American writer, I would not be writing this biography. While conducting dissertation research for what would ultimately become my first book, *Portraits of the New Negro Woman*, I came across a box in the James Weldon Johnson/Carl Van Vechten collection of Yale University's Beinecke Library. As is so often the case with the papers of women writers, this collection was confusingly filed under "Mildred Wirt," a pseudonym that has been attributed to West but one that she denies.[1] I discovered the final, handwritten draft of *The Living Is Easy*. I could barely contain my excitement. I held in my hands an original draft penned by the author of a novel I had recently read and loved. That tactile experience spurred my interest in West, and I eventually published an article on the novel.[2]

At the top of her handwritten manuscript West wrote: "If this ain't it, it'll have to do. This is my last go around. I need not add that I'm sure you're damned of it if it isn't yours."[3] Presumably these words are addressed to West's agent George Bye. Originally, West had hoped that *Ladies' Home Journal* would serialize her novel. This aspiration was in line with her desire for a larger interracial audience and the commercial success of more popular fiction writers. Other African American women novelists had similar hopes for their fiction. Jessie Fauset's 1931 novel *The Chinaberry Tree*, published by Frederick A. Stokes, included a foreword by Zona Gale, a middlebrow modern who courted mainstream success and modernist aesthetics. Susan Tomlinson observed that Gale's foreword "foregrounds the exceptionality of the novel's depicted community and barely alludes to the novel's themes, so that the text is made to resemble a sociological study rather than a work of fiction."[4] Tomlinson notes that Gale's introduction downplays the literary aspects of *The Chinaberry*

Tree by arguing for Fauset's qualifications to write an account of the black bourgeoisie; moreover, such assertions are in line with the promotion of Edith Wharton's *The Custom of the Country* (1913), which was serialized in *Scribner's* magazine before being published in its entirety. Also, Nella Larsen, anticipating that her novels might be read outside the sphere of the Harlem Renaissance, purportedly undertook the writing of a "white novel" during her Guggenheim fellowship; no such manuscript is extant to corroborate this assertion.

The editors of *Ladies' Home Journal*, presumably concerned that advertisers would withdraw their financial support if they serialized a novel about black middle-class life, declined to publish the novel. West told interviewer Deborah McDowell: "The magazine was very enthusiastic about serializing the novel, but when their board of editors met—Blackwell's; they were power people—they decided against it. I have always felt that they feared the loss of advertising revenues by serializing a novel by a Black woman about Black people."[5] If *The Living Is Easy* had been serialized in *Ladies' Home Journal*, then the novel might have enjoyed a longer life in print. West was perfectly suited to be a "cross-over" writer, to use a contemporary term, because she had already published several short stories in the *Daily News* in which the racial identity of the characters was either ambiguous or silent. In fact, a columnist announcing the book release party for *The Living Is Easy*, which was hosted by Marian Minus and Harold Jackman at Frances Reckling's 125th Street Studio, writes: "You've been enjoying [West's] short stories for years in New York's largest daily, but probably didn't realize she was a Negro."[6]

Houghton Mifflin published her manuscript as a novel in 1948, and *The Living Is Easy* was reviewed widely in both national and local papers from the *New York Times* and *Los Angeles Times* to the *Chicago Defender* and the *Atlanta Daily World*. The interracial reception of the novel suggests that the fears of *Ladies' Home Journal*, who believed that the novel would be poorly received and offend advertisers, were unfounded. Critics universally praised her writing as promising. They especially highlighted her aptitude for satire, an aspect some wished she had emphasized more. Readers were captivated by the ingenuity of "social climber" Cleo Judson. Contemporaneous reviewers saw the novel as an ethnographical treatment of Boston's black elite, just as Gale's preface to Fauset's *The Chinaberry Tree* considers it to be a sociological study of the insular "Red Brook," a fictional community in New Jersey. West's illumination of the social spheres of the "bluebloods of dark skin in Boston at the turn of the century" struck her reviewers as a new perspective.[7] Unlike later reviewers, who considered the novel as primarily autobiographical, earlier readers saw West's geographical background as the credential for uncovering the customs and behavior of the brown Bostonians in a way that captured the specificity of Boston and its inhabitants. In Henry Moon's review for the *Crisis* he wrote "Boston, we've been told repeatedly is more a state of mind than a geographic location."[8] As a "proper Bostonian" herself, West was seen as an authentic and qualified ethnographer of her milieu, much as Edith Wharton's novels were seen as ethnographic studies of the "tribes" of Manhattan. Although reviewers do not mention Wharton directly (they do reference her counterpart Henry James), one review sets up West's comparative study by listing the storied names of Anglo Brahmins: "Members of Boston's most elite Negro families are as exclusive as the aristocratic Cabots, Lodges and Lowells."[9] Additionally, heroine Cleo Judson, described by one reviewer as a "yellow Scarlett O'Hara," is comparable to Wharton's relentless Undine Spragg, the unscrupulous social climber of *The Custom of the Country.*

Reviews affirmed her skill as a writer, but the real value of the novel, especially for African American periodicals, was the way it highlighted the distinctiveness of African Americans as individuals. In fact, West appeared on a WMEX radio talk show called "This Is Brown Boston," whose major purpose, director J. Riche Coleman indicated, was "to show our white listeners that it is inaccurate to think of all Negroes as Uncle Toms or buffoon-comedian types. We hope to show that it is as IMPOSSIBLE TO LUMP ALL NEGROES TOGETHER AS A GROUP AS IT IS WHITE PEOPLE."[10] A cluster of reviews argued that West's novel "enlarged the canvas of Negro fiction" by treating her characters as "individual human beings."[11] Edward Wagenknecht writes: "They are not 'Negroes,' indeed, any more than the characters in a novel by a white novelist are 'whites.' They are themselves. And for that all Negroes—and all interested in the art of fiction—should be grateful."[12] Finally, one review saw West's gender and subject matter as separate from its racial content. *New York Times* reviewer Seymour Krim characterized it as "an indoor novel" in which the "woman part is central." This reader clearly perceived Cleo's power struggles with the confines of "kitchen and the parlor," rather than the marketplace in which her husband reigned.[13]

In 1982, the Feminist Press reissued the novel with a new cover featuring Richmond Barthe's 1931 (*Portrait of a Woman) A'Lelia Walker.* A'Lelia Walker was the daughter of Madame C. J. Walker, the CEO of a black hair empire and the first black millionaire. During the Harlem Renaissance, A'Lelia threw lavish parties at her home, Villa Lewaro. The choice to include her image on the cover of the new edition of *The Living Is Easy* situates West as a Harlem Renaissance author, despite the novel's late publication date; West, however, disliked the choice of A'Lelia for the cover. She tells Dalsgård:

If you have read the book, you know that the woman character is light skinned. So when I got the book and looked at its cover, I didn't like it. The picture of A'lelia Walker was not well chosen. It had nothing to do with her being brown. It's just that the period was wrong. I can tell by the head costume that the period was wrong, and then of course because she did not look like the light-skinned woman I had described in the book.[14]

Dalsgård does not follow up on the discussion about the cover in the published interview; instead, she changes the subject abruptly and asks about West's relationship with Claude McKay. As an interview subject, West was difficult to direct and frequently returned to her favorite topics of conversation: color and class hierarchies among blacks and her family history. Her commentary is full of contradictions. First, West suggests that her problem with the cover is the style of clothing worn by A'lelia, but in fact twice in the paragraph she states that A'lelia bears no resemblance to the characters in the text. Why would the Feminist Press choose Walker's image to grace the new cover?

Given the popularity of black women's novels featuring darker-skinned heroines, perhaps the publisher did not want to alienate readers who might feel validated by the portrait of a strong brown-skinned woman, especially an heiress to a fortune? I do not want to read too much into the cover, but it is important to note how often West emphasized issues of color and the primacy of complexion in her writing. Of the novel's three major female characters—Cleo, the Duchess, and Althea Binney—all are extremely light-skinned or white-skinned. The one exception is young Judy. Perhaps a painting of a young dark-skinned little girl, holding her light-skinned mother's hand—the introductory image of the novel—would have presented a more thematic cover image, but it also may have unfairly emphasized the autobiographical aspects of the novel.

The original cover, most likely referencing Cleo, features a light-skinned, but still identifiably African American, woman with a stylish updo and glamorous, almost-too-flashy gold jewelry. More important, her three-quarter profile is superimposed upon the grand doorway of a home, which immediately evokes the architecture of a Boston brownstone. This profile could not belong to Althea Binney (Thea is light enough that the Harvard youths who accost her brother mistake her for white) or the ash-blond Duchess. The figure's lowered eyelids convey an emotion wholly in line with Cleo's aspirations and the attitude she hoped to cultivate in her daughter: "a proper Bostonian never showed any emotion but hauteur."[15]

Most treat *The Living Is Easy* as an autobiographical novel, but the lines between fact and fiction in West's writing are often difficult to demarcate. To most readers the title obviously references the aria "Summertime" from the 1935 opera *Porgy and Bess*, composed by George Gershwin with lyrics by DuBose Heyward. The phrase is the opening line of the folk opera's most famous song: "Summertime and the living is easy." Through her friend Edna Thomas, West secured a role as a "supernumerary," an extra, in the London cast of *Porgy*, so the song, in addition to its popularity, may also have had a particular relevance to her.[16] West comments, "As far as *The Living* is concerned, I remember walking with a friend, we were talking about my mother, and I said, 'To her the living was easy.' That's that. That was the end of that. But that stuck in the back of my mind. . . ."[17] Like all writers, West disguised and may have even lied about the origins of her characters. She apparently based one character on a beautiful brown-skinned woman from New York known as the Duchess, but in the book she made that character "a blue-eyed woman with light hair and very fair skin."[18] According to West, many misidentified her fictional Duchess as actress and Boston socialite Edna Thomas.

West readily admits that she "did write about her mother" in *The Living Is Easy* but that if she had the opportunity to rewrite her first novel she would write it differently.[19] Several pieces of the novel surface in her early fiction. In the 1929 short story "Prologue to a Life," the main characters, Lily and Bart, also meet through a bicycle accident; however, "Prologue" is not so much of a "prototype" of *The Living Is Easy* as it is a reimagining of her parents' early lives a subject to which West returned repeatedly throughout her career. In addition, although West may have regretted using her mother as a template for the seemingly ruthless Cleo, Cleo is nowhere near as unsympathetic as the color-struck matriarch of Fauset's *Comedy: American Style*, with whom she is often compared. Unlike that of Fauset's self-hating Olivia, Cleo's selfishness has its limits. For example, Cleo encourages her sister to take the job as a cook and leave the house that has become her prison, and she also petitions Simeon to get his dying wife a priest so she can make her final confession. These acts of benevolence show that, unlike Olivia, Cleo has the capacity for self-reflection, even if it is too late to undo the damage she has wrought. West's childhood (and early fiction) may have provided the blueprint for her first novel, but the scope of *The Living Is Easy* with its richly textured narrative and characters exceeds the category of autobiographical fiction.

Unlike contemporaneous reviews that saw that novel as primarily northern with the southern scenes included only to situate and distinguish Bart and Cleo from the other black migrants in Boston, recent criticism has highlighted the dichotomy between North and South. In her reading of West as closet revolutionary Sharon Jones privileges the southern aspects of the novel over the northern, whereby she situates West's proletarian sympathies with the southern migrants. Farrah Griffin also includes a discussion of the novel in her study of the African American migration narrative *"Who Set You Flowin'?"* as an alternative to Richard Wright's version of the migration novel and notes that *The Living Is Easy* is "so strikingly different from any ever written by Wright that it is of no surprise that there were tensions between the two at the *New Challenge*."[20] Critical interest in the southern flashbacks of the novel reflects the momentum in studies of black modernism and the Harlem Renaissance that wish to decenter Harlem, or urban space in general, as the primary site of the modern in black writing. This is not to say that the crisis Cleo faces has nothing to do with her position as a southern migrant. Lawrence Rodgers observes, "to be accepted as part of [black Boston] society, she must outwardly cut all social and psychological ties to her Southern roots, 'disclaim' her past, even though she inwardly needs to be fortified by her recollections of its effects on her."[21] West's satirical interrogation of how class performance and division interact with geography (northern or southern) makes the novel such a rich text for readers—past, present, and future.

The "It-Girl" of the Black Brahmins

The August 2000 issue of *Vanity Fair* revived the concept of the "it girl" by citing Gwyneth Paltrow as the embodiment of "it" for the twenty-first century among a retrospective parade of former "it girls." The "it girl" became a part of American cultural grammar during the 1920s: This term identified a woman who embodied the spirit of her age. *Vanity Fair*'s 2000 spread included thirty socialites, entertainers, and businesswomen with expense accounts and trust funds that underwrote their outrageous, jet-setting behavior. All but two (Naomi Campbell and Kidada Jones) of the new face of "it" were white. A few months later, *Essence*, a popular magazine that targets black professional women, countered with its own interpretation and presentation of "it girls" in an article entitled "Working It." Although *Essence*'s assemblage of "it girls" presented many fabulous black women, its list did not challenge the foundation of exclusivity, privilege, and color prerequisites without which an "it girl" could not rebel. *Vanity Fair* presumes that individual achievement determines admission to the cult of "it," while *Essence* emphasizes the importance of specifically defining "it" for black women, thereby expanding the definition to include women who would otherwise be excluded. Neither magazine challenges the social structures that make "it" possible. The majority of the "it girls" featured in *Vanity Fair* are supported by generations of wealth, subsidized by corporations like US Steel or fashion empires like Estée Lauder. *Essence*'s "it girls" possess a different sort of wealth; dependent on their celebrity status, these are almost exclusively entertainers or entertainers' daughters, for the most part light-skinned or biracial. It is ironic that both magazines situate the "it girl" as an empowering model for feminist and racial progress; however, the very concept of the "it girl" actually disempowers and excludes. The twenty-first century "it girl" remains a decorative accoutrement dependent upon and enabled by the masculine authority of father or husband: she is the princess who can never be king.

The reappearance of the "it girl" ideal in popular culture frames my discussion of Dorothy West's *The Living Is Easy* (1948); "it" draws attention to the way in which social institutions, like heteronormative marriage, and cultural productions, like mainstream newspapers, establish and maintain bourgeois class structures through a symbolic, specifically gendered figure of success. West's novel explores the issues of belonging, authenticity, and entitlement implicated in *Essence*'s attempt to apply the terms of "it" to African American society. The "it girl" persona underscores what is valued in the public sphere for women—namely wealth, beauty, and social status. As such, "it" signals a pathway by which women may acquire limited power in spaces presumably dominated by masculinity and capitalism. Yet precisely by blurring the boundaries between private and public, domestic and commercial spaces, West's protagonist Cleo Judson achieves a measure of socioeconomic power. Through Cleo's quest for social mobility, self-determination, and self-aggrandizement, West weaves together intersecting social geographies into a feminist interrogation of heterosexual marriage and black bourgeois society. Her novel offers a scathing critique of the most subtle, and not so subtle, forms of intraracial oppression along class and color lines within the African American community of Boston in 1910.

While discourses of authenticity have been crucial in establishing literary traditions in minority communities vis-à-vis mainstream aesthetic concerns, the work of women writers like Dorothy West, Marita Bonner, Helene Johnson, and Ann Petry, who wrote at the edges of African American literary periods such as the Harlem Renaissance and the Black Arts movement, resists the stylistic or thematic assumptions presumed by periodization and other authenticating moves.[22] As the Harlem Renaissance era closed, artists sought alternative ideologies to maintain the spirit of artistic activism heralded by the New Negro era. Periodicals like *The Messenger* carried a strong radical/socialist message, while Dorothy West's editorial endeavor, *The Challenge*, was known as a "pink publication."[23] During an interview, West tells Deborah McDowell that in spite of her trip to Russia and her editorship of *The Challenge*, which published several black Marxist writers including Richard Wright, "they tried and failed to make a communist out of me."[24] Some critics assume that West wholeheartedly advocated W.E.B. Du Bois's theory of the Talented Tenth because of her privileged upbringing among the Boston's black middle class, but others branded her an ardent socialist based on her tour of Russia in 1932. Neither appellation really captures the complexity with which West engages the function of marriage, space (social, domestic, and commercial), and black participation in the capitalist system. Since she was frequently dismissed by her peers as a "pink" writer, contemporary scholarship often fails to take West seriously. They treat *The Living Is Easy* as merely an autobiographical sketch of early twentieth-century black life in Boston and consider West a representative of a bygone era, significant only in her ability to relate firsthand interactions with Harlem Renaissance luminaries Claude McKay and Langston Hughes. While West critiques the stratification of the black middle class, she maintains an abiding respect for those crafty enough to assimilate into a system not of their own making. Her consideration of class, labor, and capitalism reveals an astute understanding of the possibilities and limits of black social and economic advancement in the United States.

My spatially inflected reading of The Living Is Easy is attentive to ways in which social and urban geography informs race, gender, and class conflicts. A preponderance of African American literature deals with the complications of traversing and regulating space. The train motif, for instance, is a common cultural metaphor for socioeconomic mobility. Literature that dramatizes the Middle Passage, the Great Migration, Jim Crow, and the antebellum hierarchies of the field and the house frames West's portrayal of how spatial politics govern social life and racial progress. Although a New York Times review classified The Living Is Easy as an "indoor novel," her fiction complicates the dichotomy of the nineteenth-century doctrine of "separate spheres" that situates the private sphere as a white, female, upper-class space, and the public sphere as a white, heterosexual, masculine space.[25] Cleo Judson's progressive transformation into a matriarch, whose social, economic, and interpersonal machinations manipulate the public and private spheres of urban American culture during the early part of the twentieth century, constitutes an amalgam of race, gender, and class struggles for equality and opportunity in urban America's social economy. The power struggle within Cleo's marriage parallels her attempts to establish her position as a guardian of upper-middle-class society through accumulation of property and an irreproachable performance of bourgeois mores. In short, Cleo aspires to the symbolic stature of an "it girl" without comprehending the role's inherent contradictions.

Unlike the African American social satires of the previous decade, such as Jessie Fauset's Comedy: American Style (1933) or Wallace Thurman's The Blacker the Berry (1929), The Living Is Easy diverges from the passing narrative genre popularized during the Harlem Renaissance by introducing a new type of African American heroine. She is not the solitary introspective protagonist of Nella Larsen's Quicksand (1928), nor does she exhibit the conflict between art and romance faced by the women in Jessie Fauset's subversive sentimental novels. Cleo Judson is a young, vibrant woman whose family revolves around her. As a child, she blooms in the South Carolina woods, and, similar to Janie in Zora Neale Hurston's Their Eyes Were Watching God (1937), Cleo is so full of life and mischief that her mother, in an attempt to protect her from the dangers that young black women inevitably face in the South, sends her North. Cleo is exiled from her three sisters but exposed to the social stratification that informs Boston's peculiar combination of philanthropy and elitism; her wild ways are refined through conventional education. For Cleo, northern drawing rooms unfortunately prove as dangerous as southern parlors. When the son of her white benefactress begins to covet the light-skinned, green-eyed Cleo, she impulsively marries Bart Judson (a wealthy, older black man known as the "Black Banana King") to avoid a probable rape. Once married, Cleo engages in a battle of wills with her husband and then with her only child, Judy.

At the start of the novel, Cleo is in the midst of moving her family to Brookline, where they will be the first black family to reside in the exclusive Boston neighborhood. As Cleo and her daughter traverse the city to view their new residence, the description of their expedition illustrates Cleo's desire to be associated with the upper echelons of Boston society: "The trolley rattled across Huntington Avenue, past the fine granite face of Symphony Hall, and continued up Massachusetts Avenue, where a cross-street gave a fair and fleeting glimpse of the Back Bay Fens, and another cross-street showed the huge dome of the magnificent mother church of Christian Science."[26] The reverent language and detailed naming of specific landmarks in this passage reference Boston's history of abolitionism and intellectualism; the diction suggests Boston as a space where African Americans should be able to achieve social and economic parity. Although this vision of Boston indicates Cleo's admiration of the city, it is peculiarly counterposed by her idyllic memories of her southern childhood: "All of her backward looks were toward the spellbinding South. The rich remembering threw a veil of lovely illusion over her childhood." Her belief that she can recreate the South of her childhood in a northern space motivates her to bring her sisters to Boston: "Her sisters, with their look of Mama, would help her keep that illusion alive. She could no longer live without them. They were the veins and sinews of her heart."[27] Cleo's veiled memory of the South drives her perception of motherhood and womanhood. As soon as she convinces her husband to move into a new house far too large for her immediate family, she plans a reunion of her sisters. To reconstruct her southern childhood within Boston, Cleo must convince her sisters to leave their husbands and relocate with their children to live with her. She also intends to show her husband that she can rule a domestic kingdom as well as he can manage a commercial business. Through Cleo's quest to improve the social standing of her family and assert her own agency, West explores the tension caused by intraracial class discrimination among the upper- and working-class black communities of early twentieth-century Boston.

The Living Is Easy demonstrates the precarious instability of social, geographic boundaries and the mutability of time and space by "conjuring" the South in a northern locale.[28] This narrative maneuver allows Cleo to manipulate time and space to reconstruct the pecking order of her childhood through her sisters' transplanted bodies. Despite Cleo's valorization of her southern experiences, she is careful to distinguish her familial past from the violence and poverty of black experience in the South of the novel's present.

Her memories of the South are intimate and insulated; however, her South is not the South that accompanies the majority of southern migrants to Boston.[29] For Simeon Binney, editor of a radical black newspaper modeled after William Monroe Trotter's *The Guardian*, the southern-born residents of the South End fully represent "the colored population of Boston."[30] In *The Clarion*, Simeon conscientiously reports the disenfranchisement and other racialized atrocities plaguing the Deep South and forcing the black Brahmins to confront realities of the national crises from which they believe themselves to be insulated. According to Simeon, racial unity should transcend the social barricades of convention. During the Harlem Renaissance, periodicals used article series such as the *Messenger*'s "These Colored United States" to reveal newspapers' potential to provide illuminating investigation of national identity and racial geography. Such periodicals urged the southern masses to "Go North."

Black-owned publications also read the black public sphere as a space that maintained, to borrow from Houston Baker's application of Jürgen Habermas's formulation of the public sphere, "a nostalgic, purely aestheticized fascination with the narrative of a beautiful time-past."[31] For instance, the black Brahmins tolerate Simeon's newspaper only because he is a member of the Binney Clan. As such, the radical underpinnings of *The Clarion* are subsumed beneath a black conservative nostalgia based on an erasure that celebrates individual enterprise and suppresses any challenges to the hermetically sealed world of the black Brahmins. We see this ideology at work in Cleo's spatial rearticulation that neatly dissociates her family from the undesirable occupants of the South End of Boston: "The South End was no longer the colored population at all. All the nice people were moving away along with the whites. Soon it would be solid black." In Cleo's mind, southern migrants are as unrelated to her as "poor darkies" are different from "respectable coloreds."[32] Fixing a place with a specific static identity, an authenticity, as it were, is one means by which social boundaries are erected and maintained. The irony underlying West's critique of bourgeois mores is most apparent in her presentation of the black Brahmins. Although the Brahmins have little control over Boston's geography, they police their social boundaries and rally against southern emigrants, with the exception of a select few whose money and/or light skin gains them a grudging admittance to their privileged circles.

The social and urban geography of Boston provides the battlefield for Cleo's private and public power plays. Much as it is today, turn-of-the-century Boston was a city marked by ethnic and economic boundaries. The mid-1890s black Boston society was divided into the "West End Set" and the "South End Set." The limits of Cleo's domestic power reflect the boundaries of African American political and economic influence from the turn of the century into the 1930s and 1940s. Exclusion and divisiveness based on color, education, economics, and neighborhood mark Cleo's society; these factors determine where one falls in the hierarchy of what W.E.B. Du Bois identified as the Talented Tenth, based on his theory that the elite of a minority group would lift up the whole through exemplary behavior, higher education, and financial success. West's novel reveals the theory as an attractive facade of black capitalism. After a meeting with the Duchess, a notorious West End gambling hostess, Cleo questions what she perceives as the black bourgeoisie's ridiculous distinctions: "What is this business of belonging? A tailor and a stable-owner were the leaders of society?" Cleo does not understand why the Duchess, a black woman with ash-blond hair and imperial blue eyes who "could have crossed the color line and bought her way into any worldly circle, preferred to yearn for a counterfeit of the Brahmin cult." The black Brahmins formed a select community of African Americans whose lives "were narrowly confined to a daily desperate effort to ignore their racial status." Their position had been established by "Boston birth and genteel breeding and they acknowledged no more than a hundred best families" in the Northeast. Although the children of these valets, chauffeurs, and butlers who set the behavioral standards exceed their parents' expectations by attending Harvard, their sons' degrees do not endow them with the keys to the city but ironically serve to further segregate the burgeoning black population from "true," white, Brahmins. Instead of welcoming black doctors into research laboratories, white doctors counsel their black counterparts to cater only to black patients, sparing the white doctors the pain of having to work in the "poor ward of the hospital."[33]

West's Cleo perceives that the "counterfeit" world she seeks to infiltrate is built on untenable notions of racial superiority; however, instead of working to dismantle these false distinctions of class and color, she manipulates the social hierarchies of the black elite to serve her own selfish needs. Both her constant derision of her husband's thrift and her nickname for him, "Mr. Nigger," speak to the tendency within the black bourgeoisie to self-segregate according to color, class, and education. Cleo's sisters' husbands also recognize her color prejudice. After Cleo convinces Lily that her dark-skinned husband is out to kill her, he refers to them as "two goddamned color-struck hussies."[34] Boston was known for having the chilliest clique of the black aristocracy, and Lily's husband is scornful of what Willard Gatewood in *Aristocrats of Color* terms "blue veinism"—a system of social stratification that excludes those whose skin is not pale enough to let their blue veins show through.[35]

Cleo's attempt to relocate her immediate family across town and her extended family from South to North, a move which ironically sets in motion the ultimate dissolution of her power and income, underlines the elusiveness of social mobility as determined by geographical location. Her obsession with belonging and entitlement prompts her to overcompensate for attributes she lacks. For instance, despite her disappointment with her daughter Judy's dark skin, facial features, and timid nature, Cleo believes that by molding her daughter into a lady she might access the belonging and entitlement of a true Bostonian. As such, Judy's welfare is a partial motivation for the move: "The prospect of Judy entering school in Brookline filled her with awe." To reinforce the illusion that she and her family are part of the select black Brahmin society, Cleo employs Thea Binney to teach her daughter proper deportment, even though her husband believes Thea's tutelage is reiterative since "two expensive doctors of Cleo's uncompromising choosing could bear witness to [Judy's] tranquil Boston birth."[36] In spite of Thea's financial ruin, she is the "it girl" of the black Boston elite by virtue of "being born a Binney." Together with her husband's family, the Hartnetts, the Binneys are one of the city's first families. Although Thea's husband, a struggling doctor, is poor, "as a Hartnett he belonged to a family even older than the Binneys." Furthermore, "the Hartnetts had been freemen for five generations, and no one of them in those hundred years had been born or schooled outside of Boston." Even more telling is the story of Cole Hartnett's father: When "Mr. Hartnett failed in business, and blew his brains out just like a white man," all of black Boston "was a little proud of his suicide."[37] The black elite's valorization of Mr. Hartnett's suicide as a mark of prestige is characteristic of their grotesque investment in the appearance of wealth and the emulation of white Bostonians.

As the black Brahmins carefully distinguish themselves from the undesirables of their race, white Bostonians, the "real" Brahmins, actively reconfigure urban space to maintain racial and ethnic segregation. According to Gillian Rose, any dominant claim to public space must contend with repeated challenges; bodies must be policed to ensure that they conform to set spatial restrictions.[38] If we place Rose's hypothesis in the context of West's novel, then we observe that the violence applied can be meted out without regard for the tenuous class standing that the black bourgeoisie believe affords them security. Consider a case in point: The racially motivated beating of Thea's brother Simeon, editor of The Clarion, indicates the insidious nature of such policing. A group of white freshmen accost the dark-skinned Simeon as he escorts his light-skinned sister Thea across Harvard yard; they threaten: "Watch your step, nigger. Let go that white girl."[39] Thea runs quickly home while Simeon eagerly engages the fight, which results in his imprisonment. This incident illustrates that in spite of their abolitionist roots, when it becomes "necessary," white Bostonians do not hesitate to resort to violence to reinforce racial boundaries; the whims of the dominant society always circumscribe blacks' spatial negotiation. Although the perpetrators later bestow a "Harvard gentlemen's" apology to Simeon after they discover that Thea is his sister, it is merely a tactic to prevent him from publicizing the event. In this way, they privately enforce social restrictions against interracial dating while at the same time suppressing an incident that would illuminate the public pretense of Bostonian liberalism.

As a direct result of her acquaintance with the presently poor but still illustrious Binneys, Cleo intercepts an advertisement for a house before it is printed, a house "on a street abutting the Riverway, a boulevard which touched the storied Fens and the arteries of sacred Brookline." Although the house is advertised in the *Clarion* as a Brookline address, it is actually in Roxbury (now a predominately black neighborhood): the border of Brookline begins directly across the street. Upon discovering this misrepresentation, Cleo swallows her disappointment and continues to refer to her residence as Brookline because "several colored families were already living in Roxbury."[40] Her acquisition of a house in an affluent neighborhood from which white residents are fleeing, given the Irish influx, points to the slipperiness of societal divisions and underscores the necessary policing that maintains them. As she approaches the class status she desires, the rules and the geography continually shift and reconstitute themselves out of her reach; the house formerly advertised as a Brookline address reverts to Roxbury as soon as a black family inhabits it. Cleo abandons the South End in an effort to escape the influx of black southern migrants, which the "nicer colored people" perceive as a "plague of their own locusts."[41] This description likens black "cotton-belters" to a biblical scourge. At the same time, it implies kinship through the naming of the epidemic as "their own," suggesting that Cleo's attempted escape is undermined by a kind of unconscious racial self-sabotage. To make this case, West has Cleo convince her husband that they will be able to sustain such a large home by taking in boarders. He does not know that the boarders will be her sisters. Cleo's "scheme," the common practice of taking in recently emigrated boarders, was a primary factor that presumably reduced the value of working-class neighborhoods in Boston.[42] Thus, West mocks the paradox that the stability of race and class structures resides within their elasticity; these structures maintain their boundaries even as the borders are crossed, undermining any attempts at subversion.

While the social spheres of the black elite are for the most part insulated and separate from white Boston, in a few intersecting areas partial tolerance coexists with the tension in these border spaces. For instance, as Cleo and her daughter ride a public, integrated trolley, white passengers respond positively to their presence: "Boston whites of the better classes were never upset nor dismayed by the sight of one or two Negroes exercising equal rights. To them the minor phenomenon of a colored face was a reminder of the proud role their forebears had played in the freeing of the human spirit for aspiration beyond the badge of the house slave." Indeed, when Cleo fears that her new landlord is prejudiced against African Americans, he reminds her proudly that his father was a leader in the Underground Railroad movement and that her accusation of color prejudice is "grossly impertinent." This same landlord is relocating to the "real" Brookline, "the last stronghold of [his] generation" because of a "thundering herd of Irish immigrants that have overrun" his side of Roxbury.[43]

West's novel explores the status of various ethnic groups (particularly the Irish) that perplex the black Brahmins who hoped that "undesirable immigrants" would replace them as the underclass necessitated by capitalism. While Irish and Italian immigrants appear in fiction by Marita Bonner,[44] West's contemporary, as equally oppressed members of a multiethnic community, in West's novel the relationship between blacks and Irish is fractured:

> In contrast to other ethnic groups or immigrants, Boston blacks did not consider themselves a minority group. The Irish were a minority group, the Jews, the Italians, the Greeks, who were barred from belonging by old country memories, accents and mores. [The black Brahmins] felt that they had nothing in common except a facial resemblance. Though they scorned the Jew, they were secretly pleased when they could pass for one. Though they were contemptuous of the Latins, they were proud when they looked European.[45]

Although colorism is a significant arbiter of intraracial class division, to reduce the class stratification in the black community to light color privileging is to oversimplify. In the cited passage, West illustrates that skin color and ethnic identification can be manipulated and recapitulated to gain advantage within the competitive social and industrial economies of Boston. And despite their efforts to self-segregate, blacks and Irish continue to brush up against each other. Cleo's daughter Judy and her cousins walk to school through a largely Irish neighborhood—an adventure that results in daily battles and insult wars. "Nigger, nigger, pull the trigger," is rebuffed by "Yah, yah, yah, go wash your paddy face in the frying pan." Despite these frays, the black children realize they are financially superior. Some, like Vicky, have no innate "contempt for the Irish" neighbors; she despises them only because they taunt Judy. Others absorb an Irish dialect: "'Id liefer let them look, too,' said Penny. She had a penchant for picking up Irish expressions."[46] The children's interactions illustrate Cleo's inability to insulate them within the small sphere of acceptable Brahmins. The complex prejudicial relationship between blacks and the Irish is further complicated by the fact that while lower working-class blacks referred to their Irish neighbors as "nice white people," the upper-class blacks exploit the labor of "young untutored immigrant girls" who "held their jobs until their more sophisticated countrymen explained the insurmountable distinctions between a man who looked white and a man who was white."[47] Once granted opportunities for racialized socioeconomic advancement, Irish immigrants transitioned from outsiders to insiders by establishing their "whiteness" through political alignment with their Anglo oppressors, a shift that the black bourgeoisie are never able to effect, no matter how hard they try.

E. Franklin Frazier's landmark study of the black middle class, *Black Bourgeoisie* (1957), discredits the possibility of a separate, functional black economy under capitalism and condemns the black aristocracy for replicating white blueblood society with its inherent class hierarchy of insiders and outsiders. According to Frazier's analysis, the small financial and educational gains of the black middle class are so minuscule that they have no real effect on the American economy. From his perspective, the black bourgeoisie has no actual power. It is dependent on an ideology of intraracial exclusion, perpetuated by cultural institutions, including the black press, to maintain the fiction of the black bourgeoisie's imagined community.[48] In Frazier's words, "The Negro newspapers help to create and maintain the world of make-believe in which Negroes can realize their desires for recognition and status in a white world that regards them with contempt and amusement." Although in West's novel Simeon Binney's *The Clarion* theoretically advocates progressive politics and a radical social agenda, in practice Binney is restricted to reporting pleasant, uplifting subjects that did not remind his readers of the severe racial oppression or heightened racial violence they suffered, particularly in the South. When *The Clarion*'s reports failed to support the façade of black progress, the readership waned. From the perspective of the black elite, except his sister's social column, "nothing else in the paper met with their approval. Every other word was colored. . . . Had [the editor] used the word Negro, they would have refused to read it altogether."[49] Given the fragile distinctions by which the Brahmins separated themselves from those presumed to be lower in status, semantic debates, such as "Negro versus colored," take on a vital signification. While West's novel predates Frazier's study, her characterization of the black aristocracy resonates with Frazier's critique of the tenuous foothold that the black middle class struggles to maintain in the American economy.

Cleo's marital problems appear to dramatize another of Frazier's observations: "If the husband has risen in social status through his own efforts and married a member of an 'old' family or a 'society' woman, the husband is likely to play a pitiful role."[50] West's juxtaposition of the Judson family's marital struggles with the Binneys' provides an interesting opportunity to critique the role that heteronormative marriage plays in social stratification. Although Cleo is not born a society woman, she aspires to that status and competes with the other women in the novel to be the "it girl," relegating her husband to the compromised role suggested by Frazier. At the commencement of the novel, Thea Binney is Cleo's "model of perfection" and the "it girl" du jour:

She had been a day pupil at private school, and later a boarding student at a select academy, an institution which had taken her natural airs and graces and cast them in the same impeccable model that produced the young ladies who were to take their inherited places behind the tea-tables of Boston. These young ladies were now the young wives of wealthy businessmen with old if not illustrious names. They lived on fashionable streets and were served by butlers who were, as often as not, old friends of Thea's father.[51]

The last line of this passage undermines the apparent innocuous comparison between "she" and "they" by pointing out the irony of Thea's position as a black "it girl." Though the narrator reveals that Thea began life with the same opportunities as the other young ladies of Boston, we are reminded of the relationship between her father and her schoolfellows' butlers. This last line interrupts Thea's future; she has been groomed for a position that she cannot hope to fill because her father's newly acquired wealth is easily lost and cannot compete with generations of financial security. Despite the tenuousness of Thea's situation, Cleo's desire for Thea's coveted social status is a source of discontent between Cleo and her husband, who, unlike Cleo, is contemptuous of black elitism and strives to amass sufficient funds to secure their daughter's financial independence, rather than her social position.

Cleo intends to infiltrate the black aristocracy and then rule as the new "it girl," displacing the current reigning "it girl," her friend Thea Binney. Her only other inadvertent competitor in the "it girl" race is Lenore, an infamous gambling hostess known among the Brahmins as the Duchess. Lenore hosts a gambling den in her West End home, where the husbands of women too "civilized" to receive her regularly lose money while young black men working their way through college invariably win.[52] Each of these three women is missing a vital part of the "it girl" profile, to which they all aspire. Thea has manners, beauty, and breeding, but no money. Cleo has beauty, means, and the will to assimilate, but no elite ancestry. Lenore has money and beauty, but no aptitude for social leadership; in addition, she suffers from a tarnished childhood. Together, their calculations for happiness fail miserably because they are built on a shifting foundation fractured by class elitism, intraracial discrimination, and black valorization of white social hierarchies.

According to Ruth Randolph and Lorraine Roses, Marita Bonner's short story "On the Altar" is a precursor to the marriage conflicts in *The Living Is Easy*. In Bonner's story, a grandmother annuls the marriage of her granddaughter to an unsuitable, dark-skinned man and forces her to abort their child so that she will be free to marry a doctor. Thus, Bonner reveals the type of sinister social maneuvers necessary to maintain the exclusivity of the black aristocracy. "On the Altar" also reflects Frazier's thesis concerning the prominent role of the black press in perpetuating delusions of black material success. Through the society column of the local paper Elizabeth's rejected, dark-skinned husband discovers that his wife has left him: "Mrs. Blanche Kingsman Breastwood and her granddaughter, the lovely Elizabeth Grey, dainty blonde replica of her mother, Mrs. Louise Grey, are circling the states."[53] While the black press implies that Elizabeth is on a grand tour, in reality her grandmother sequesters her in a cabin where she is visited daily by a doctor who gives her injections to ensure that her child will be stillborn. The subsequent press release of Elizabeth's second marriage underscores Bonner's critique of the speciousness of black bourgeois society: "The society columns burst forth into a hysteria of redundancy, bad taste and worse writing. They listed the showers and the parties and the details of every gift and every garment and every scrap of food served . . . things, things, things."[54] The catalogue of items satirizes a performance of aristocracy that resonates with West's derisive portrayal of bourgeois vacuity in *The Living Is Easy*.

Similar to Bonner's tale, West's novel destabilizes the perception that an advantageous marriage is the key to social stability or personal happiness. Cleo functions simultaneously as matchmaker and marriage-dissolver: the marriages she engineers have equal potential for social progress or spiritual death. In exchange for arranging the Duchess's marriage to Simeon Binney, Cleo acquires the Duchess's "graceful Chippendale" furniture for her new home. One by one, Cleo convinces her sisters to come to Boston on a long holiday. Once they arrive, she poisons their minds against their hardworking, but certainly not rich, husbands, which leaves the sisters dependent on Cleo's generosity. Charity's transformation, for example, demonstrates Cleo's manipulation of her sisters. When she first arrives in Boston, Charity is a happy mother with a sexually fulfilling marriage. Her relationship with her husband Ben is the antithesis of Cleo's nearly celibate marriage. Unfortunately, because she overstays in Boston due to Cleo's feigned illness, Charity's husband divorces her. In response to her grief, Cleo tells her, "[All] you lost was a nigger who didn't have a dime when you married him and's got no more now." Charity responds, "You married money. I married love." As a result of her divorce, the once shapely Charity begins to eat herself into numbness until she becomes a "grotesque creature" who in "painful consciousness of her obesity no longer left the house." Bereft of her husband, Charity's passionate marriage is no longer a threat to Cleo's frigidity; instead, Charity embodies the tragic opposite of the "it girl," serving significantly as a powerless, unattractive, sacrificial (or "charitable") backdrop for her sister. Cleo is unable to look directly at the new Charity, who no longer reminds her of their mother. Her disregard for her sister's well-being as well as her myopic selfishness proves the narrator's early assessment that "her yearning for her sisters was greater than her concern for them."[55]

Ultimately, Cleo convinces each of her three sisters to leave a fulfilling marriage to live under her thumb while at the same time orchestrating Thea Binney's marriage to Cole Hartnett with disastrous results for both. Desperate to maintain Thea's standard of living, Cole uses his medical training to perform abortions on Irish immigrants. When an operation results in a fatality, he is arrested while Thea remains oblivious: "The fact that she wore furs, and could afford a maid and a child, simply meant that Cole was doing his duty by her. His disgrace simply meant that he failed that duty."[56] Thea has no qualms about how Cole privately acquires their income; she summarily abandons him to avoid the public shame and implications of interracial interaction that result when he is caught.[57] This is not the first time West has introduced the abortion theme into her work; she previously hinted at the use of abortion, and/or child murder, as the most sinister and extreme form of colorism. In "Mammy," a story ostensibly about the welfare system and the difficult position in which a young welfare worker finds herself during a straightforward case, West reveals the submerged specter of child murder as a method of preserving a passing family's identity. This theme usually appears in narratives of passing that hinge on the fearfulness of giving birth to a dark child, the magnified embodiment of otherwise invisible "one-drop."[58]

Cleo's own marriage mirrors the fateful outcomes of those she orchestrates. After she arrives in Boston as the ward of an elderly lady, her employer/benefactress's nephew buys her a new bicycle upon which Cleo "pedaled away as easily as if she had been cycling her entire life."[59] Cycling, with its enhanced individual mobility, epitomized the independence of New Womanhood. Just when she is on the brink of adulthood and anticipating an exciting career on the stage, Cleo collides with Bart Judson: "The impact sent them sprawling on either side of the path, with the shiny new bicycle rearing like a bucking horse, flinging itself against a boulder, and smashing itself to pieces." The destruction of the bicycle ends Cleo's dreams of independence and catapults her into marriage with Judson. In "rescuing" her from the clutches of Mrs. Boorem's nephew, Bart raises her social status from that of a sexually vulnerable ward to an asexual middle-class matron. Though Bart vows to replace the bicycle, he never fulfills that promise. Instead, he substitutes the security of his surname for Cleo's ability to negotiate the city on her own. Carol Allen affirms "empty marriages also help maintain segregation by channeling sexual forces (which can challenge segregation when they extend across racial and ethnic lines) into a craving for material goods and money."[60] Love does not enter into Cleo's marriage; her daughter Judy was conceived "on the one night her body's hunger broke down her controlled resistance."[61] The paradoxically chaste role of the middle-class wife diverts Cleo's sexual energy into individualist consumerism. In this respect, *The Living Is Easy* functions as a cautionary tale:

marriage can be a fatal, suffocating institution if it is undertaken purely for financial or social gain.

According to Sarah Deutsch's *Women in the City: Gender, Space, and Power in Boston 1870–1940*, in the exact time frame spanned by West's novel, just as the working-class spaces of the city became sexualized, the middle-class home was implicitly desexualized.[62] The desexualization of the middle-class matron clarifies both Cleo's reluctance to engage in recurring sexual relations with her husband and her inability to honor her sister's impoverished but sexually fulfilling marriage. It also explains her interest in preventing her sisters from finding employment. As working girls, her sisters would achieve a measure of autonomy that Cleo finds threatening to her domestic domain. She realizes too late that her machinations have ruined her sisters' lives, alienated her daughter, and destroyed her marriage: "It had never occurred to her in the ten years of her marriage that she might be his helpmate. She thought that was the same thing as being a man's slave." West intimates that Cleo's family life would have run smoother if she and her husband had formed a marriage based on an equal partnership, rather than a contest of wills in which either patriarchy or matriarchy won.

This equality is unfortunately impossible for Cleo, who remains frustrated by the lack of control allowed by the institution of marriage: "Her nature found Mr. Judson a rival. He ruled the store and all the people in it. Her sphere was one untroublesome child, who gave insufficient scope for her tremendous vitality. She would show Mr. Judson that she could take a home and be its heart. She would show him that she could bend a houseful of human souls to her will."[63] Littered with language that emphasizes Cleo's desire for control, with words like "despotic," "ruled," and "bend," this passage illustrates how spatial distinctions of power form the bedrock of Cleo's marital conflicts. She wages her battle on two fronts: The domestic space of the home and public space of the market.[64] Portraying Cleo's visit to her husband's place of business, West inscribes the protagonist's abhorrence of the market's overwhelming masculinity: "Here in the market was all the maleness of men. This was their world in appraisal of anything which they moved without the command of women. The air hung heavy with their male smell and the pungent odor of their despotic sweat. . . . As she neared them, their eyes approved and dismissed her, because they were too busy for long appraisal of anything that could not be bought and sold in the Boston Market."[65] The final wry observation emphasizes the source of Cleo's frustration and fear: she "could not be bought and sold" because she was already the property of Mr. Judson. In contrast to the masculine space of the market, where Cleo feels impotent, she competes with her husband and achieves total control over their home.

The domestic sphere provides "insufficient scope" for her ambitions and "despotic nature." Her husband's desire to amass a comfortable savings directly conflicts with her desire for luxury, and her excessive spending provokes frequent clashes that occur within or about their living space. Her resentment of her financial dependence leads her to transform their home, a private space, into a hybridized public space: a domestic corporation in which the employees are her family members. For Cleo, however, the collapse of public and private dichotomies that signify dominance does not result in liberation for either herself or her sisters; instead, Cleo is obsessed with maintaining control. According to Doreen Massey, "Power accrues to those who exercise control over the environment; similarly, power adheres to those who produce narratives that sustain and naturalize places as opaque, natural, or fixed and thus beyond contestation or negotiation."[66] Only the children in the novel perceive Cleo's vulnerability and the fragility of her chokehold on her family. Her daughter Judy observes: "Cleo was the boss of nothing but the young, the weak, the frightened. She ruled a pygmy kingdom."[67]

The spatial dimensions of Cleo's complex matriarchy are unlike any other in early modern black fiction; they serve as precursor to the mother-daughter relationship portrayed in Paule Marshall's *Brown Girl, Brown Stones* (1959). Perhaps signifying on an early review of the novel Ann duCille aptly describes Cleo in *The Coupling Convention* as the "Scarlett O'Hara of black fiction," citing Cleo's narcissism, which motivates her to lie, cheat, and steal from those she claims to love in order to remain at the center of their world.[68] Yet she is extremely vulnerable and occasionally performs small acts of kindness, though her so-called "acts of mercy" frequently have an underlying selfish objective. Short for Cleopatra, her first name invokes that scheming last ruler of Egypt, while her maiden name, Jericho, references the city destined to fall in spite of its impenetrable walls; Cleo's namesakes thus seem to foreshadow the tragic outcome of her plans. In instructing her daughter about race, she relates the history of her foremothers: A cadre of women who commit suicide in response to insults to their pride. Unlike the conventional African American matriarch whose suffering, sacrifice, and survival ensure her offspring a better future, "the old time Jericho women lived proud as long as they could. When they couldn't live proud, they preferred to die."[69]

This Is Brown Boston

Not content simply to rule her family and friends through her matchmaking endeavors, Cleo wants to be "accepted as an integral part of Boston's society." To accomplish this goal, she seizes the throne of the "it girl" with disastrous results. In West's novel, many scions of the black elite, including Cleo's husband, are on the verge of bankruptcy; however, imminent financial ruin does not deter them from hosting weddings, parties, and other social events that reinforce the semblance of exclusivity and superiority within the black aristocracy. The event that solidifies Cleo's position among the black elite is the party she gives at her "Brookline" home; the turnout of black Brahmins ensures that she now "belongs." The legitimacy of Cleo's insider status rests partially on the attendance of Thea Binney, the "it girl" of black Brahmins, who in spite of her actual impoverished status is so certain of her supposedly aristocratic bloodline that she wears an old frock to the party. Thea encapsulates *Vanity Fair*'s "it girl," given the "ability to change the chemistry of the room just by walking into it."[70] Upon arrival, she shares an embrace with Cleo that "served as public proof of the intimacy between her and Mrs. Cole Hartnett, born Binney."[71] The language that describes their relationship encodes the ease with which public and private delineations become enmeshed in black society.

Thea arrives at the party prepared to shun the infamous Duchess, only to discover that an advantageous marriage, pioneered by Cleo, has transformed her infamous new sister-in-law into the highly respectable Mrs. Simeon Binney. The Duchess agreed to marry Simeon to avenge black society's shunning of her mother's interracial liaison, while Simeon weds the Duchess out of financial necessity. West satirizes the vacuity of the society matrons through their reception of the Duchess: "They had been praying for a cheap blond with some betraying Negroid feature. They were overwhelmed with what God had given them instead. In an acute rush of color-consciousness each wondered nervously if it was she who had caused Mrs. Binney's undisguised disappointment in a gathering of the best people." Following Cleo's lead, the women in their circle accept the Duchess as one of their own. A remarkable scene of social reconstitution follows the Duchess's entrance: The society leaders abandon Thea and swarm around the Duchess. Within seconds the Duchess has become the new "it girl," but she feels no pleasure in their acceptance: "She no longer wanted the rights she had won by her marriage. She had paid too high a price for the privilege of pouring tea."[72] The "cost" of her decision to marry Simeon outside the Catholic Church results in a spiritual bankruptcy, corrupting the love that she and her husband eventually develop for each other.

What about Thea's brand of entitlement allows her to escape unscathed and preserve her "social leadership" in the midst of poverty and scandal?[73] Jennifer Wilks suggests that Thea's character exceeds the tenets of New Negro womanhood and is instead a throwback to what she calls "True Negro Womanhood": "so complete is Thea's deployment of femininity, gentility, and passivity that the character suggests another, more accurate name for the correspondence of nineteenth-century gender conventions with archetypal representations of early-twentieth-century black women."[74] Later in the novel even Cleo is struck by Thea's seeming obliviousness to the maneuverings that have maintained her position: "Cleo harbored a dark resentment that Thea still saw herself as impervious to stigma. She could have a jailbird for a husband and not falter in her quiet assumption that being born a Binney was an immunity." Like white women who tolerated the rape, degradation, and abuse of African American enslaved women upon whose backs their pedestals of true womanhood were erected, Cleo muses that "Thea should be accustomed to men killing women for her."[75] Thea's passivity and unremarkableness as a character seem to reinforce her access to the iconic category of true black womanhood. She has few skills. In fact, she has nothing to recommend her but her claim to the Binney birthright. Yet precisely her lack of distinctiveness preserves her from the fates that make vulnerable Cleo with her new money and the Duchess with her exceptional beauty and illegitimate birth. Ultimately, Thea achieves and maintains her status at "the expense of individuals" that fall outside the "purview of model modernity."[76]

Another significant move that establishes Cleo's earned preeminence is her foreclosure of the possibility of aid to Dean Galloway, the headmaster of a black college who travels to Boston to enlist the support of the black elite in an unfair court case in the South. Gatewood implies that philanthropy and uplift have always been cherished duties of the black middle class; however, West's novel disputes Gatewood's claim through Cleo's insistence that any attention she and Judson might pay to the Dean's cause would damage their acceptance into white mainstream society by drawing attention to racial difference. Furthermore, Cleo publicly threatens to withdraw her support of The Clarion should Simeon publish anything regarding the trial of the "unfortunate," but socially undesirable, southern black man. Unbeknownst to Cleo, the black defendant turns out to be her brother-in-law. Her refusal to garner communal support results in further depletion of her husband's already diminished resources. This particular plot twist illustrates that, without a coalition of pooled resources or the recognition of a shared black kinship crossing class, color, and regional boundaries, the exclusionary practices of the black middle class precipitate its own self-destruction.

Cleo's actions demonstrate the price of preserving a black middle-class "paradise," an aspiration that West revisits in The Wedding to further critique the idea of an insulated, idealized community replicating the social geographies of mainstream culture. I apply the concept of a false or decaying "paradise" as Toni Morrison uses it to underscore the mythos of the black bourgeoisie in her novel of the same name. Paradise (1998) builds on West's critique by exploring colorism, elitism, and patriarchy as structures that (de)compose the black bourgeois ideal.[77] While Morrison suggests that it is human nature to create hierarchies, to exclude, and even to oppress, she bears enormous sympathy for the "8-rock" families and inscribes respect for the innate human desire to construct safe, thriving communities. Paradise illustrates the dreadful price that a hierarchical society built on sacred and secular myths of racial and gender superiority must pay to preserve its insularity. Cleo's climactic party marks her triumph—her entry into paradise, as it were. Yet neither her husband nor her sisters attend. To maintain the appearance of entitlement and gentility, Cleo must dismiss her southern family and banish her dark-skinned husband from the party provided by the fruit of his labor. The tenuous, illusory community of the elite substitutes for a true community of family and thus signals Cleo's inevitable downfall. Cleo's light skin and eastern education, along with her husband's money, admit her to the society that "took it for granted that [she and her sisters] were the cream of the South because they were the right color," even though "their accents distressed" at least one society matron. Shortly after the party, Cleo's broken sisters abandon her, and her husband goes bankrupt as a result of her excessive spending. Cleo is no longer where "the living is easy"; she has forsaken the accoutrements of that space: power, youth, and pleasure.[78] Ann DuCille comments on Cleo's family structure, "For black women writing in the 1930s and 1940s, claiming subjectivity and female authority meant disentangling the categories of woman and man from the shackles of patriarchal ideology and restrictive gender roles, as well as from what white psycho-analytical feminist Jessica Benjamin calls 'the bonds of love'—bonds Cleo Judson fiercely resisted."[79] Even after her husband finally leaves her, she confuses financial loss with familial love.

The Living Is Easy is a fascinating exploration of class and marriage among the black bourgeoisie of the early twentieth century. Focusing on one American family, it chronicles the black middle class's attempt to create a separate social sphere beside mainstream American culture with the hopes of eventually blending seamlessly into the Brahmin fold, leaving behind those who, for lack of education, culture, color, or economics, could not convert their imagined community into a material reality. In his 2002 review of Stephen Carter's *The Emperor of Ocean Park*, Ward Just pronounced Carter the Theodore Dreiser of the African American middle class and cited the novelty of the subject matter and the incisive critical eye of the narrator.[80] In his laudatory review Just might have situated Carter's fiction in the tradition of African American novelists like Dorothy West, writers attentive to class and race clashes nearly fifty years earlier. It is vital that reviewers and multiple audiences become aware of the long tradition of socially and spatially conscious black writing in the United States and that they see Stephen Carter's cynical exposure of an affluent "darker nation" not as a (re)invention of the wheel, but as simply another link in a long chain that stretches back through the civil rights movement, the Harlem Renaissance, Reconstruction, the Civil War, slavery, the American Revolution, the Middle Passage, and across the Atlantic.

Ward Just's anointing of Stephen Carter's novel is somewhat germane in that following the publication of *The Living Is Easy* West retreats from New York and Boston (the cities of her youth and childhood) to retire to Oak Bluffs, Martha's Vineyard, not far from Carter's Ocean Park. From her cottage in the Highlands, West began a series of columns appearing primarily during the summer months in the *Vineyard Gazette* under the title "Cottager's Corner." Before Carter began drafting his first novel in his home near the park referred to in its title, he no doubt came across West's column in the local paper. For nearly thirty years, West's column recounted the history and events relevant to Oak Bluffs' community of color. "Cottager's Corner" may have provided a retreat from the highly visible artistic circles in Harlem, but the view from West's front porch would provide her with enough material to sustain her writing of both fiction and nonfiction.

7

Cottager's Corner

From far and near cities, from a variety of professions, from a range
of cultural and civic involvements that crowd their winter calendar, the
Cottagers are steadily arriving for a summer season in which much of
their time will revolve around Cottager's Corner, once the old town hall
in Oak Bluffs, now the increasingly busy center of community oriented
activities.

–Dorothy West, "Cottager's Corner"

One highlight of the summer season on the Vineyard is the Cottagers' annual
house tour. For day-trippers, summer folk, and year-round residents the tour
provides a unique opportunity to enter the private domiciles of Oak Bluffs. The
houses included on the tour often have historical value, famous occupants, and
unique renovations or design features. One year's home featured an extraordinary array of antiques; another showcased the house of now-deceased novelist
Bebe Moore Campbell. To outsiders, the house tour offers an opportunity for
lessons in cultural and architectural history. The tour indulges voyeuristic
activity that either promotes simple house envy or encourages visitors' desire
to acquire such unique homes.

One pleasure of studying a writer so firmly grounded in a specific place is
the requisite visitation of those sites that appear in her writing. In July 2005
and July 2008, I toured ten houses featured on the Cottagers' tour. In 2008,
several homes on the tour were located in Dorothy West's Highlands. West's
home was not included, but the anecdotes I acquired—some spontaneous,
others solicited—enriched my understanding of the neighborhood history
West inhabited and fostered. For instance, on the porch of the Coleman house
a member of the Cottagers told me the story of how West's editor "Jackie O"
would sit cross-legged on the floor when she came to visit because West had
her papers spread all over the house. The house tour, an annual event that
renders private sites temporarily public, provides the narrative frame that

allows me to follow the evolution of West's column and its unique role in both documenting and representing the black presence in Oak Bluffs.

"Vacation-Minded and Island-Oriented"

"Cottager's Corner," the original title of Dorothy West's column in the *Vineyard Gazette*, began in 1967 and continued until her death in 1993 under the name "Oak Bluffs." "Cottager's Corner" may have begun as an article in 1967, but by 1971, when the organization acquired the old town hall on Pequot Avenue, Cottager's Corner became and still is also the name of a building that functions as the headquarters of the women's organization. Like Dorothy West's cottage, the building is also a stop on the African American History Trail. West proudly recounts the building's pivotal focus for residents; moreover, West acknowledges that the organization's purchase of the building "gave the Cottagers and the town a vigorous measure of pride."[1]

From 1967 to 1971 "Cottager's Corner" named both a building and a newspaper column; thus, a Cottager is a person who inhabits a cottage as well as a member of a women's organization.[2] The slippage between people and property is evident in West's column and her oral histories. The mutability of the term "Cottager" reinforces the significance of place as a crucial element in understanding the unique character and composition of the black colony in Oak Bluffs. Robert Hayden subtitles his lay history *African Americans on Martha's Vineyard "A History of People, Places, and Events"*; this qualification underscores the relationships between the main subjects covered in West's aptly titled column. Reading the early installments of "Cottager's Corner" drives home the importance of location as a factor that shapes social relations and nurtures kinship ties during the more than one hundred years that blacks have lived on the island.[3] Over three decades, West expanded her focus from the local microcosm of the black colony to incorporate national and international topics—politics, ideology, the arts—and revealed how a specific local history can act and participate in the global community that comprises the African Diaspora.

Founded by twelve women in 1956, many of whom where already members of national black women's organizations and historically black sororities, the Cottagers developed a specifically local group that both emulated and diverged from the types of organizations that sparked the African American women's club movement at the end of the nineteenth century. While the main motivation of the Cottagers is altruistic, the fact that West gives primacy to their social activities reveals how the "politics of respectability" were promoted and sustained by black women's organizations, even those that kept the motto of the club movement—"lifting as we climb"—firmly in mind.

By covering the activities of the Cottagers in her *Vineyard Gazette* column,

West positioned the organization as the heart of the black community of Oak Bluffs. After 1973 the title changed to "Oak Bluffs," and the scope of her reporting broadened to include a wider variety of activities occurring in Oak Bluffs. According to West, when the *Gazette* first inquired if she would do the column she refused. Later, she agreed to take it on for a short time with the understanding that they would eventually find a replacement. After a while she realized they were not looking for anyone else: "the thing that irritates me is that somebody will say that I wrote something very good in the column. But the point is, that took a lot of time to write it good, and they don't realize that."[4]

West's contributions to the *Vineyard Gazette* document her central role in founding and promoting a women's organization of homeowners while also serving as a lay historian of the black community in Martha's Vineyard. She is explicit about her historiographical role: "This writer has been asked to identify, in so far as it is possible for her to do so, the sections of the Island occupied by the first vacationing blacks."[5] This is a history that the column reiterates each summer. The repetition serves a key purpose: It not only reminds newcomers of the history of the space they are visiting, but it also illustrates how the Cottagers are indivisible from the maintenance and origins of the black colony:

> Several of the charter members are the third and fourth generation to summer here. There was a time when those cottage owners who were black numbered less than a dozen—indeed it was a gala summer when that number was achieved. Their buying power made almost no ripple in the island's economy, and they, themselves, had no wish to make waves. But they had importance as forerunners. These early vacationists from Boston were among the first blacks anywhere to want for themselves and their children the same long summer of sun and sea air that a benevolent Island provided to others who sought it. These first blacks made later generations vacation-minded and Island-oriented.[6]

West characterizes these early settlers as inspired gatekeepers with modest desires. They sought a "benevolent Island" retreat for themselves and like-minded citizens. What better way to ensure continuity than to establish an organization that fostered and protected these ideals?

The Cottagers are an outgrowth of the types of organizations founded during the African American women's club movement, which flourished during the 1890s and eventually came under the umbrella organization of the National Association of Colored Women. West's description of "the Cottagers' priorities" shares many of the goals and philosophies of other black women's clubs:

To promote and help support worthwhile charitable and educational projects which improve the quality of living in the community; to promote interest in, and to cooperate with other agencies in programs designed for community development, and to enjoy the fellowship inherent in the friendly association of the membership.[7]

The first cottagers may not have been hardcore civil rights activists, but many were already members of African American sororities founded at historically black colleges and universities during the early 1900s, organizations that evolved out of the club movement. In fact, the Cottagers were short-handed for the 2008 house tour because many members had traveled to Washington, D.C., to celebrate the centennial anniversary of Alpha Kappa Alpha—the nation's first black sorority.

West describes the impetus of the Cottagers' club in a story she told Linsey Lee. Evidently, white islanders were critical of the well-to-do black islanders' apparent lack of altruism. West remembers eight women gathering, and they at first found it difficult to generate interest in the group:

And so then it was like pulling teeth, and I went to some friends, and they didn't want to join because it's an all-colored club and we didn't want an all-colored club on this island. And then some people said that in the summertime all they wanted to do was have fun, because they were all teachers, all had good jobs, and they did need relaxation. However, my point is, the club was formed and then it grew and grew and then suddenly, one day, I will never forget, somebody said to me, "You can't get anywhere on this island unless you're a Cottager." I laughed. And then I heard it again. And then I thought, what do they mean? . . . I used to say indignantly to people, if when we started this club I had gone up to you and said, "Will you give me $10 and become a Cottager?" You would have said, "Who are you? And of course I'm not going to give you $10." And that's the way those things start and all of sudden we're an exclusive club and we're snobbish. . . . [8]

While West emphasizes the organization's humble beginnings, present-day perception of the Cottagers as an exclusive club is documented in Jill Nelson's *Finding Martha's Vineyard*; several residents whom she interviews are members. For example, Eloise Downing Allen cites the organization's lack of political involvement as her reason for leaving the organization.[9]

Historian and Vineyard Haven resident Adelaide Cromwell, surprisingly *not* a member of the organization, does not remember West being particularly active in the group:[10]

[West would] go to parties, but she wasn't going to use her column and her pen to just tell who had the best party and how many people were there. She wasn't going to lower herself to do that. So I don't think she was active in the Cottagers, she worked with them, she helped them, because I know they got that building down where the place is now, which was a firehouse. . . . But I'm not sure that she was what you might say a card playing member of the Cottagers, although they were friends.[11]

Though Cromwell's resistance to join the organization may result from its more recent elitist connotations, it may also just be a desire for a more private life. For instance, West introduces Cromwell within her column in 1969 as a houseguest in Oak Bluffs: "Mrs. [Adelaide] Henry Hill, a new Vineyard Haven cottage owner, has been a houseguest of her aunt, Mrs. Edward Brooke Sr. and her cousin Sen. Edward W. Brooke, for the past several days while seeing to the final details of building a house from the bottom up." Cromwell ultimately decides to purchase a home in Vineyard Haven, away from the more social climate of Oak Bluffs.

West may have told Cromwell that she had no desire to cover purely social events; however, the manner in which she describes "Ham and Bean Suppers" and the fashion shows sponsored by the Cottagers blurs the lines between fundraising, social networking, and community-building endeavors. West may have modeled "Cottager's Corner" after "Oak Bluffs Breezes," a column that appeared in William Monroe Trotter's *Boston Guardian*. In the 1930s, "Oak Bluffs Breezes" covered the comings and goings of blacks who visited the island from Boston, Providence, and New Bedford. "Breezes" reported that the vacationers are made up of "the most distinguished and outstanding members of the colored race" and noted that following a meeting at Bradley Memorial Church several members of the congregation "have agreed to make Oak Bluffs their vacation home."[12] Several columns introduce newcomers by first documenting the location of their cottage and then detailing their employment, education, birthplace, and familial or local connection to the island, a practice West's columns continued.

"Cottager's Corner" also mirrored the chronicling of black social organizations in periodicals like *Half Century Magazine, The Washington Bee*, and *The Colored American Magazine*. Though West's articles were profoundly local—the article covers the summer season activities of a black women's group centered in the Highlands area of Oak Bluffs, Massachusetts—they maintained a national and even international flavor. Her subjects are uniquely mobile; they travel to Europe and Africa; they hail from Philadelphia, New Jersey, and Washington, D.C. In her study of black women's magazines, *Ladies' Pages*, Noliwe Rooks argues that black women were never portrayed in mainstream magazines as "charming, outdoorsy, or from New England."[13] Instead, such periodicals either "did not speak to African American women at all" or degraded them through stereotypical images. However, a new image of womanhood emerged in "Cottager's Corner." In fact, West primarily represented African American women as "charming," "outdoorsy," and in, if not originally from, "New England." The featured Cottagers are all beautiful, elegant, well-educated women. They are wives, mothers, daughters, teachers, actresses, and opera singers; they play tennis, garden, and fish. Whatever their origins, once they appear in West's column they are Cottagers first and foremost.

Rooks notes that fashion was an important part of early black women's magazines, but surprisingly West rarely comments on fashion in great detail; however, she pays close attention to other markers of class and ladyhood including skin color and marital status, which appear to be the most important prerequisites for acquiring property. The following excerpt typifies the manner in which West frequently introduces black socialites:

> As a last note this writer, to whom the colors of colored people are a constant excitement, was entranced one day this week to see walking towards her Jackie Brown Llewelyn, Mrs. Bruce Llewelyn, a Vineyard cottager since her early girlhood, and her young daughters, Lisa and Missy. Jackie is a stunning shade of brown. She is perfectly beautiful, her features, her carriage, her style. Her children are pale gold and golden brown, and blue eyed. They were the most striking group on the busy street, as lovely to look at as exotic flowers.[14]

This description evokes the metissage portraits of black diversity popularized in novels like Nella Larsen's *Quicksand*, where she describes a Harlem Party as a "moving mosaic":

> for the hundredth time she marveled at the gradations within this oppressed race of hers. A dozen shades slid by. There was sooty black, shiny black, taupe, mahogany, bronze, copper, gold, orange, yellow, peach, ivory, pinky white, pastry white. There was yellow hair, brown hair, black hair; straight hair, straightened hair, curly hair, crinkly hair, woolly hair. She saw black eyes in white faces, brown eyes in yellow faces, gray eyes in brown faces, blue eyes in tan faces. Africa, Europe, perhaps with a pinch of Asia.[15]

This visually evocative language is commonplace in Larsen's writing. Given that Larsen was one of the premier novelists of the Harlem Renaissance and the first black woman to win a Guggenheim, West would certainly have read Larsen's two novellas: *Quicksand* (1928) and *Passing* (1929). Perhaps Larsen inspired the painterly language West uses to describe the audience on the tennis courts of the Oak Bluffs Tennis Club, whose tournaments she routinely covered in her column. There are "people of every color and facial cast. Some of the exotic combinations of coloring, features and texture of hair—a dark face with delicate features and silken hair, a gold face framed in a halo of tight red-gold curls, the color from one ancestral source, the woolly texture from another—are often extraordinary in the beauty they achieve."[16] Such descriptions reflect West's obsession with color, but they also reflect a diverse, multiracial community. On any given day, a similar panorama might be viewed on Circuit Avenue outside Mad Martha's ice cream shop, at Inkwell beach, or on the porches of several of the homes in the Highlands and or the Gold Coast.

Just before the twenty-sixth annual house tour, I spoke with current Cottager Anita Christian, who named her two aunts as founding members of the Cottagers.[17] According to Ms. Christian, the organization began in 1956. She remembered her aunts and the other ladies playing cards and having tea while she served them. Now there are always one hundred members in the organization (rather like the national association of one hundred black men), but in the earlier days there were approximately thirty women. Like West, Christian remembers the founders numbering eight, but Cromwell puts this number closer to twelve. They included "Thelma Garland" and "Barbara Townes"—names that appear with such frequency in West's column that at times it reads like the minutes from a Cottagers' meeting. Indeed, "Cottager's Corner" could be considered the public minutes of a private organization that temporarily allows outsiders into the social sphere of the black enclave.

Cottager for a Day

If West's column imaginatively recounts the Cottager's summer activities, the annual tour allows direct interaction with Cottagers and the homes they and others in their community inhabit. My first stop on the 2008 tour was Shearer Cottage. More than any other site on the Vineyard, Shearer Cottage has been credited with popularizing Oak Bluffs as a national, as opposed to regional, vacation site for African Americans. It was a point of entry into the Highlands lifestyle. At first glance, Shearer Cottage resembles rustic lodge rather than cottage. The bunkhouse extends from its main building: a long row of cabins facing a wide expanse of lawn upon which parties, barbecues, and concerts have been regularly held since the opening of the guesthouse. Guests stay for a couple of weeks one summer, and return, quite frequently, to the same room. Eventually, they consider purchasing their own home. This pattern, which extends over the hundred-year history of black vacationers on the Vineyard, has been responsible for the settlement of the Highlands as a black colony.

Isabel Washington Powell, the former wife of Congressman Adam Clayton Powell Jr., remembers coming to Shearer on her honeymoon:

> He took me to Shearer Cottage at Oak Bluffs. Shearer is one of the island's treasures that various black professionals, artists, politicians have patronized for years, and kept as their little secret. . . . The fact that it's owned and run by blacks made me take even more pride in our visit to Shearer. Off from the main house, to one side, there was a row of barrack type rooms. Adam and I stayed in one of these studios.[18]

While improvements have been made, like converting the dining room to a lounging area for guests, Mrs. Powell's description accurately captures the "simple and elegant" guest rooms. Powell freely admits to her interloper status: "We were New Yorkers, who had to set the style, to be that example for the next one who would follow in our footsteps. Except for the mosquitoes and earwigs, I was living a fantasy."[19]

Powell's language so accurately echoes both West's and Cromwell's characterizations of "New Yorkers" as distinct from other island vacationers (see the stories about the lost beach) that the similarity suggests that Powell was well aware of how the so-called founding families might have viewed her when she first arrived. It is also striking how easily her transformation into an islander is effected when she becomes a property owner: "Bunny [Adam] had bought us a cottage of our own. I was so surprised, I screamed with delight. It was just the most darling little get away you could imagine. We named it the Bunny Cottage. It had been part of a barn and had been brought over to this lot. Later they built an addition on to the house and transformed it into a cottage."[20] From 1936 until her death in 2007 Isabel Powell was a fixture in the Highlands. On my first visit to the island she was sitting on her porch. Although she did not offer us one of her famous Bloody Marys, my young son engaged her in a conversation. I was struck by the resemblance to her sister, Fredi Washington, the renowned activist and actress known for her role as Peola in the film *Imitation of Life* (1931). A plaque commemorates the Bunny Cottage as a site on the African American History Trail.

Like Isaac West, Charles Shearer was born a slave in Virginia. To a man who himself had once been property, owning property was an important expression of freedom. The Baptist revivals held in Temple Park in Oak Bluffs drew him and his wife Henrietta to the island. The Shearers first ran a profitable laundry business before they "built a twelve-room house at Cottage City . . . and opened a summer inn."[21] Shearer Cottage was established as an inn in 1912. Not only did it draw a regionally diverse group of African Americans to the island, but it also fostered the artistic community of the island by offering art classes and staging concerts. During my tour, a docent relayed that the painter Lois

Mailou Jones taught art in what is now the family room of the cottage. Before the Cottagers acquired the town hall, they frequently held their meetings at Shearer or other locations in the Highlands, and West's column regularly recounted the events held on the grounds.

West's investment in the historiography of Shearer Cottage and Highlands is evident in her columns and her oral histories. She explains the significance of "The Highlands":

> So I'm an old-timer. I call it the Highlands. But a lot of new people just as soon call it East Chop, you know what I mean? You see. But I just like the word "The Highlands." I just like the sound of it. And that was the word that I always used. And on the old maps, well I think even now, many—none of the new—if you read the Gazette you will never see anything about the Highlands. But if you read books about the Island, nine times out of ten, they will refer to this—I mean this section is really the Highlands.[22]

Jacqueline Holland's article, "The African American Presence on Martha's Vineyard," which appeared in a special issue of the *Dukes County Intelligencer* (1997), corroborates this history. She describes how the Highlands developed as a black space: "By the start of the 20th century, there were two groups of blacks: the 'year rounders': and the 'summer visitors.' School Street in Oak Bluffs was mostly white in the early 1900s and blacks lived just off it on First Avenue and on the other unpaved streets that meshed with 'Portuguese Village,' extending to the other side of Vineyard Avenue."[23] Yet these two groups were bound together by their shared investment in a utopic community that required constant tending and a vigilant cultivation of visibility. Those early black settlers sought to communicate their proud history of entitlement while also maintaining discretion with regard to racial difference so that their skin color was considered as secondary, even incidental.

From Shearer Cottage the house tour proceeds to Coleman's Corner. The history and location of this "corner of Cottages" is fascinating. At one time owner Luella Coleman owned ten abutting lots in the island. Three cottages still remain in the family so that the area constitutes a compound of sorts. The owner of the cottage notes the significance of growing up next door to the Bunny Cottage and down the street from Dorothy West, but the proximity was not necessarily harmonious. Joyce Rickson recounts:

> The irony, the real irony, late in life, was the fact that she did not like the Colemans at all; however, Bo, he lives at Coleman Corner, Granny Coleman, who had the house and had all her grandchildren there, there were 4 girls, one passed away, and 1 boy. Bo was the boy. Bo had a child

by a woman, Lee, who ended up being her caregiver in later years until she passed away. And they had a daughter, Blithe, and Dorothy was crazy about Blithe. And so when Dorothy passed away, her estate went to Lee. The house is owned by Lee, Lee Costanza.[24]

Leonara Costanza was Dorothy West's caretaker, and she inherited West's house instead of West's cousin, Abigail McGrath, who lived next door. Versions of the name "Coleman" appear twice in West's fiction. Coleman is the name of the passing family accused of infanticide in West's short story "Mammy," and "the Coles" and their "mansion" are central to *The Wedding*. In a park across directly across from West's house is a bench dedicated to to McGrath's mother, poet Helene Johnson.

As I walk from the new Coleman house down Myrtle Avenue the entire Highlands seems crowded with venerated and familiar personae. To say this neighborhood is tight-knit is a dramatic understatement. West describes a typical event: "There are plans by those involved in last summer's benefit cocktail party to repeat the affair of the building fund. The re-useable setting, the old, turreted, balconied house called Twin Cottage, owned by Liz and Fred White, the handsome Shearer clan of Popes and Whites, and Walkers, and Jacksons who vie with each other in adding zest to a party, will welcome all who know what a mad, mod night will unfold before them."[25] Given Elizabeth White's love of the acting and the theater, Twin Cottage was the site of several dramatic performances, including a production of *Othello* which was reported in the *Gazette*: "Mrs. White staged a live production of *Othello* some years ago at Twin Cottage, her splendid sprawling house, whose porches and balconies were ideally suited to an outdoor performance."[26]

Although the Twin Cottage is the last stop on my tour, the site does not resemble in any way the fairy-tale residence described by West. The original structure is no longer extant. The "Twin Cottage" was built by a whaling captain for his daughters in either 1869 or 1872. The wings were identical. In place of the Cottage is a newly constructed colonial. The new owner has several pieces of furniture belonging to the cottage and has a plaque inscribed with one of Liz White's poems to commemorate the cottage's history. Liz White acquired the cottage in 1954. Its resemblance to the Globe Theatre made it a perfect place for staging summer theater productions. After reading about this historic landmark and viewing the amazing photographs of the doubled cottage on the hill, visiting the new home was a letdown. Yet such architectural overlaying is intrinsic to the history of Oak Bluffs. West tells Linsey Lee:

Most of these houses [in the Highlands?] came from the Campground. And sometimes I'm very aware of the creatures who used to live here.

This was all woods. You know where Our Market is, don't you? All right. When people want to know where I live, we are at Our Market. And you will look up, and you will see a lot of trees, "but," I say, "there are many houses among those trees. Because very few people know where we are. We sort of like it that way though. This is one of the oldest sections."[27]

The invisible traces of black Vineyard history are commemorated and marked by plaques, but they also exist in the oral archives and, of course, in West's columns. The original Twin Cottage exists only in West's columns and in the grainy black-and-white photograph framed on the wall of the new house that occupies its foundation.

Like the Twin Cottage, the duplex once shared by the Wests and the Joneses is no longer extant. The duplex, which originally belonged to Phoebe Ballou, one of the storied twelve West insists were the first black vacationers to come to the island, can be seen only in a black-and-white photograph in which both families pose in front of their conjoined home. It supposedly burned down during a fire caused by an errant cigarette.

The image is familiar. It could belong with the images collected by Du Bois for the Negro Exhibition in Paris to concretely visualize the progress African Americans had made from slavery through emancipation. The men and women in this photograph are stylishly dressed and dignified. They represent their success by standing in front of their property, a pose that reinforces the relationship between home ownership and social belonging. These images also defy the notion that the only blacks living on the island prior to the founding of Shearer Cottage in 1912 were domestics. According to West, whites knew of the black vacationers and yet tried to deny their presence. West recounts an incident on Circuit Avenue where some white vacationers deliberately asked a group of black vacationers dressed in their Sunday best where they might get their laundry done.[28]

At one point during my interview with Dr. Adelaide Cromwell I impulsively remarked that the large green house on Ocean Park was one of my favorites. She immediately frowned and said something along the lines of "Oh, you like that house, do you?" Owned by Peter Norton, of the Norton Anti-Virus Software, the house is evidently too large, too garish, and not authentically restored. Yet, I still find its attempt to be authentic rather striking. Even Cromwell acknowledges that he reportedly researched the historical accuracy of the home's exterior paint: an olive green with maroon trim. Perhaps to an outsider, the Norton House represents a fantasy of Vineyard life, while to an islander the expense of its transformation speaks only to a nostalgic loss, a remembrance of what is no longer there.

West's Atlas of the Highlands

Oak Bluffs primarily flourished because realtors steered prospective buyers toward the Highlands and the Gold Coast adjacent to the Inkwell and away from Edgartown. In the 1940s, white agents known as "straws" would help black families circumvent practices designed to prevent them from buying homes.[29] Although racially restricted covenants, either official or unofficial, are now unconstitutional, black homeowners still make an effort to locate African American buyers to preserve the cultural heritage of the neighborhoods. Escalating prices have made the sustaining of a summer household prohibitive, yet many families still return for a couple of weeks each summer. The questions about conservation and preservation resonate differently among residents.

Senator Edward Brooke is one of many Vineyard residents who was seduced by the natural beauty and relative freedom of the island. In his autobiography, *Bridging the Divide*, he describes his relationship to Martha's Vineyard as a love affair:

> By the time we reached the wharf in Vineyard Haven, I had fallen in love with the island. This was my first real vacation since the war ended, and I thought I had discovered heaven on earth. I fell under the spell of the island's sandy beaches, tall sea grasses and sand dunes, weather-stained wood-shingled houses, and the clay cliffs at Gay Head rising up from the beach. Soon I was house hunting, and I found one on Canonicus Avenue in Oak Bluffs. It had a view of the ocean, a fine stone fireplace, three bedrooms, two baths, and a larger living room.[30]

Other accounts echo the language Brooke used to describe the topography of Martha's Vineyard, but more than the natural beauty of the environment prompted this admiration; residents who fall under the spell of the island understood that this "heaven on earth" was accessible and affordable—in Brooke's day—to people of color with means. He purchased the house for $4,500 in the area that became known as the Gold Coast, which was integrated in the mid-1950s so Brooke was a pioneer of sorts in that neighborhood.

To cement his sense of belonging he ritualized his participation in the culture of Oak Bluffs without referencing any racial markers or barriers: "We swam with the girls [his daughters] and countless times took them to ride the Flying Horses in Oak Bluffs, the oldest merry-go-round in the United States. . . . We delighted in such pleasures as the Sunday band concerts in Ocean Park. *As fathers have done for decades,* I would carry the girls on my shoulders around the bandstand" (emphasis mine).[31] Other residents' memoirs, fiction, and interviews enumerate the activities Brooke viewed as timeless traditions. Indeed, in "Fond Memories of a Black Childhood" Dorothy West recalled meeting the afternoon boat, "band concerts," and "invitations to lemonade and cookies and whist."[32] Many of the various constituencies who still visit the island—daytrippers, summer people, and weekenders—are prompted to return by a feeling of nostalgia they articulate as the pull of the Vineyard. A desire to preserve a kind of authenticity continues to motivate current conservation and preservation efforts. In the Introduction, I referenced Shirley Thompson's observations of how the architecture of the Creole cottages in the Treme reflected the social and ethnic makeup of the Fauborg's inhabitants. The feel of a place is about more than architecture; the feel is also embedded in the particular culture of its inhabitants. Would New Orleans still be New Orleans if its culturally rich denizens were permanently displaced? How will those displaced people transform the new spaces in which they find themselves? Similarly, when residents recount routine activities such as visiting the carousel, eating Mad Martha's ice cream, or the feeling of exhilaration that overcomes them when the ferry docks in the harbor, they reveal their investment in a timelessness that they have imprinted onto the actual physical structures of the sites that reinforce their "fond memories."

One of Brooke's recollections situates him among those successive generations of fathers who have taken their children to ride "The Flying Horses." A national landmark, this oldest operating carousel in the United States was built by Charles W. F. Dare in 1876. Located at the end of Circuit Avenue across from Oak Bluffs harbor, it is a marvel enjoyed by children of all ages. If riding "The Flying Horses" is an experience that reinforces ties to the island, then it is also a concrete location that maps the black social spheres of the island. As such, it is no coincidence that Lois Mailou Jones chose to paint Turnell's Flying Horses in a way that captures the timeless quality Brooke and others invest in the carousel. Jones has painted the places and people of the Vineyard for her entire life, and the space itself is critical to her art. In fact, a conversation on Inkwell beach between the composer Harry Burleigh and the artist Meta Vaux Warwick Fuller prompted Jones to pursue her career as an artist abroad.[33] Jones did not escape the pull of the Vineyard, and she returned again and again to her home at 25 Pacific Avenue and to the island as a subject of artistic study. Reared within the cocoon of the Vineyard, she sought and created nurturing communities of color as she traveled the globe. She also gravitated toward island art, as demonstrated by her many paintings of Haiti.

The carousel that appears in Jones's painting Flying Horses is the same carousel that is there today. Children still ride it, and mothers of color, like the observing woman in the far left corner looking down at the riders, still enjoy watching their offspring strive for the brass ring. Capturing the prize ring secures the victor a free ride on the carousel, but the symbolism of the act of reaching for the ring goes far beyond the ride itself; this activity, undertaken by generations of African American children who have visited the carousel, is almost synonymous with the civil rights era and its hope that each generation would exceed the next by keeping their "eyes on the prize," which is almost an analogous expression for catching the brass ring. Of course, the timelessness evoked by this image, reinforced by its continued reference as an essential ritual in oral and written histories, could not exist if conservation efforts by the local citizens and government had not also valued the carousel and supported its preservation. This coalition of artistic production, memory, and preservation efforts illustrates how many factors go into maintaining the area's timelessness; it also indicates how a violation of a privileged space threatens more than a building.

The founders and supporters of the African American History Trail work to recover and commemorate the black presence on the island through tours and plaques. In some cases the actual site or building has vanished, and the location, as in the case of Rebecca Micheal's unknown gravesite, has to be approximated. But such historical guesswork does not prevent the installation of a plaque as an effort to conserve and create a memorial site where no physical referent exists.[34]

Such efforts make good practice in an area where cottages were often picked up and transported elsewhere. One home we visited on the house tour was heavily renovated, but architectural records reveal its development:

> The layout of the four connected cottages is as follows: Cottage one faces the park and is crossed in the rear by cottage two, whose front façade runs perpendicular to the park. That cottage became the front façade and the entrance parlor was enclosed with an open porch that wraps around the front of the house. The former front face of the next cottage now acts as a side entrance into the house. This section of the house was extended on the north side with a bay window. The third cottage to be attached was added on behind the second cottage and if its front façade was still visible it would face the street. Behind this cottage a fourth cottage is connected in the same manner as the second one.[35]

West describes this complicated practice to Lee: "if you know about the Campground at all, it was very crowded. So that therefore they bought Campground houses and moved them up here. . . . You see that this door opens? Well, this stretch was the house, and with two little bedrooms upstairs. Now you added that, you added the porch, you added a kitchen, you added a bathroom and the back bedroom and so forth." Phoebe Ballou, the matriarch of the Jones clan, also bought a "neat, white cottage (which had been moved from the campground)" and now occupies 25 Pacific Ave.[36]

How does one map the black presence on Martha's Vineyard? We expect to find the names of locations clearly marked. After all, a map's function is to tell us where we are and where to go. On Martha's Vineyard, maps are both ubiquitous and plentiful. Like the famous silhouette of The Black Dog, the outline of the island appears on bumper stickers, in antique frames, and on magnets. I have even seen the island cast as a golden charm to be worn as a necklace. Robert Hayden chose a map of the island as the cover image of his book. I own an early poster that can be dated to the mid-1800s only by using place names. On my map Oak Bluffs is still Cottage City, Vineyard Haven is still Holmes Hole, and Gay Head is not yet Aquinnah. The many maps of the Vineyard over the ages record the overlaying of names upon places as another way of tracking history.

Less concrete is the map on the back of the house tour brochure. For those unfamiliar with the area, the map presents a puzzle and a challenge to navigate the infrequently marked circular roads in the Highlands or the one-way streets extending out from Circuit Avenue. In his *Atlas of the British Novel*, Franco Moretti argues that space is not "outside of the narrative, but an internal force that shapes the narrative."[37] Moretti uses the art of cartography to show how place generates narrative. Similarly, geography and spatial relations shape all genres of West's writing. Her columns essentially provide the raw, spatially inflected data she uses to map and personify "the Highlands" as "the Oval," a ring of houses that is more than a neighborhood, in her final novel *The Wedding*.

Although the black colony might be considered an insular community (invisible to those not in the know), there is an insistence on openness in the homes that appear in West's short fiction. In the short piece of creative nonfiction "The Sun Parlor," West, acting here as a reflective narrator, critiques the kinds of barriers and boundaries erected in domestic spaces, especially if they foreclose the free movement of children. The story features a character name "Sis" based on Joyce Rickson.[38] Whether the events in the piece really happened is inconsequential. A bit of dialogue West attributed to her mother is most interesting. This scene reveals a side of Rachel West very different from the mothers who populate West's fiction. When a visitor questions the children's presence in her meticulous home, Rachel responds: "the children don't belong to the house. The house belongs to the children. No room says do not enter."[39] As the titular "Sun Parlor" becomes a space of sacred obsession for the narrator, these words echo throughout the book—a reiteration of Rachel West's policy advocating openness and expansiveness. Similarly, what Joyce Rickson remembers most about Rachel West is not her icy beauty, but her determination to claim everyone as kin. Children like Joyce whom Rachel encountered in their Boston neighborhood became transformed through their Vineyard visits into "cousins," or rendered as characters in West's fiction, like "Sis."

A 1904 article in the *Colored American Magazine* describes Boston as a "Paradise for the Negro." How does this rhetoric that claims Boston as a special place contribute to the formation of Oak Bluffs as a utopic site? Dig beneath the article's title and some revealing contradictions emerge. In one section the article declares that "there is no attempt to disenfranchise any citizen because of his color," yet the same writer admits that there is little social exchange between black and white residents: "It isn't so much the amicable living together of two races—so to speak—as the amicable living together of individual beings, some white, some black, who mind their own individual affairs."[40] This clannish spirit appears to be replicated in the formation of the black colony:

> This writer had been asked to identify, in so far as it is possible for her to do so, the sections of the Island occupied by the first vacationing blacks. There were no separate sections. There were too few black vacationists to form a colony. They were Bostonians, a broad description that included blacks from Boston proper and the surrounding suburbs. They did not live side by side in the city. And it never occurred to them to settle together here. It was not that they gave thought to it. It was that they didn't. They bought the houses they could afford, hoping to find one in a location to their liking.[41]

If *The Living is Easy* painstakingly maps the geography of Boston, then it is not surprising that West's column documents how New England spatial relations influenced the way people lived together on the Vineyard. Moreover, West emphasizes that in the early days the colony evolved through serendipity, rather than design. Later expansions seemed more purposeful as more and more were drawn to the idea of Oak Bluffs as a hidden black oasis.

On our first, brief visit in 2005, we lived in a yellow, unnamed cottage on a hill high above New York Avenue, overlooking Oak Bluffs harbor. This cottage was just across the street from the Highlands, adjacent to the School Street neighborhood near Sunset Park—the original Eastville. Inhabiting these historic locations provided an insider's perspective on the texture of the community. In 2008, we found a Victorian cottage known as "The Sea Horse." Located in the "Gold Coast," it was steps from Inkwell beach—an idyllic location, though we would come to refer to the one-hundred-twenty-year-old cottage, which had no laundry facilities, as the tent made of wood. Still, we sat on the porch every evening as the offshore breezes brought cooling air and scattered mosquitoes inland. We nodded to neighbors and passersby. We lived for two months in a close-knit neighborhood but remained strangers. At the same time, through shared sporadic conversations, impromptu dinners, and birthday parties that my inquisitive, fearless eldest son crashed, we were tentatively drawn in with the understanding that our neighbors would look forward to seeing us again, next year. Next year seemed to us too soon; after all, we were there on borrowed funds if not borrowed time. As one year turned into two, we also felt that distinct pull of the island. Brenda Williams-McDuffe explains: "What's fascinating about the Vineyard is that everyone who comes here and loves it has a feeling of history and ownership defined by their experience on the island."[42] Our children flew kites in Ocean Park, rode the Flying Horses Carousel, ate ice cream on Circuit Avenue, and swam daily in the Inkwell. My son still references Nashawena Park, which he calls "the park where I met Summer," a young girl he played with for an hour during our first week and someone he continued to seek in vain. We do not own anything on the island, but somehow, the island owns us.

The Cosmopolitan Columnist

In a column published July 12, 1968, West manages to intervene in the discourse surrounding two issues facing the global black community. She embeds her sociopolitical commentary within the structure of the social column and the format of an obituary. She writes: "Those cottagers and others who were friends of Gladys Riddle Martin were saddened to hear that she was one of the four who died in a plane crash over Biafra, Africa around July 1. Her husband, Capt. August Martin, who lost his life also, was the pilot of the plane." In this first reference to the couple's demise what leaps out is the location. A member of the Cottagers' community dies on another continent; this in itself speaks to the mobility of the summer residents. What is more striking is that the location of their death is over Biafra, Africa. The Nigeria-Biafra War (1967–1970), a civil war that tore Nigeria apart, was a precursor to postcolonial conflicts and genocides that have followed in countries like Liberia, Rwanda, and the Congo. The war was in its early stages when West penned this article and used the name of the newly formed Biafra. A few paragraphs later she explains that the plane had been chartered by the Red Cross to travel to Biafra from Lisbon "carrying medical and other supplies to the self-proclaimed republic of Biafra." She notes that Captain Martin often used his vacation time off from Seabord World Airlines to fly on humanitarian missions throughout Africa; "he and his wife had a great interest in Africa and strongly identified with its needs and aspirations."[43] In this article West establishes that members of the Oak Bluffs community directly engaged in global struggles for black freedom, an assertion that belies the notion of the community as separatist elites. She then departs from any discussion of the war, its causes, and its ambitions to discuss in detail the trajectory of Mrs. Martin's career. Gladys Riddle was an actress and performed regularly in local productions and on and off Broadway, but her near-white appearance thwarted her career. Indeed, like those of

Fredi Washington, the sister of Isabel Washington Powell, and Madame Lillian Evanti, who was a frequent visitor to Shearer Cottage, Riddle's refusal to renounce her African heritage resulted in an aborted career:

> What is important to her story and its unmeaningful end is that whatever her potential it was constantly frustrated by producers and directors who said she was too fair to be Negro, which was hard for her to buy in a society that says one drop is enough for life membership. Directors were also reluctant to cast her as white for reasons that were also never clear, since acting is just that, not real life but a reasonable facsimile.
>
>   Gladys Riddle did not want to be a black actress. She did not want to be a white actress. She just wanted to be a good enough actress for her audience to identify with the emotion she was able to portray.[44]

This article treats the interracial audience of the *Vineyard Gazette* tuning in for an update of "who's who" on the island to an understated critique of the film industry and the world's ignorance of foreign conflicts. Rather than belittle such events, West embeds them within her local reporting, which connects the small enclave to the outside world.

In another article West weaves a discussion of black power into an introduction of new island tenants. Her own thoughts on race, those not filtered through the subject of her column, appear in sporadic flashes. Rather like the insight she integrates throughout the short press run of *Challenge* in her letters from the editor she writes that "race has so often seemed irrelevant to this writer. In so many instances it has served no more useful function than to give anonymity to frightened blacks or frightened whites, who thereby escape being persons in their own right. To be afraid is a normal reaction to the enormity of living. To stay afraid is an abject surrender to self-doubt."[45]

These comments are also reflected in West's criticism of Richard Wright; she tells Deborah McDowell that he was afraid of white people—and "the New Yorkers," who in her mind could not fully reconcile themselves to the "freedom" of Oak Bluffs. It also seems that West does not see black power as a commitment to civil rights or race pride but as a fashion statement: "Some of the Afros are wonderfully attractive. . . . Some of the Afros are absurd. If they were once the badge of militancy, they are now a peculiar form of snobbery."[46]

The black community documented by West is an imagined community that exists both within the geography of Oak Bluffs and in the African Diaspora. Her attempt to provide a definition of black power does less to enlighten the *Gazette*'s interracial audience who seeks to understand the movement than it does to explain the need for a black retreat that is both separate and integrated. Residents like the Martins, or Dr. Pinderhughes, live and work on the front lines of a racially divided United States. They are professionals—teachers, legislators, doctors, lawyers, electricians, all who navigate the battlefield off island. In the same article where she announces Dr. and Mrs. Pinderhughes's purchase of a new cottage "on Samoset Avenue in Oak Bluffs of a size to accommodate their five children," she quotes from a speech he gave on racial bias at Tufts University that expresses the "real purpose of black power": "to unify black people to protect themselves . . . and participate more actively in determining a constructive course for their lives" and not as "the exclusive property of the have-nots, who seized upon the untested words as a buttress of their sense of hopelessness" or a "hiss of hatred in front of a television camera."[47]

In an earlier column, West does provide a portrait of the new generation of cottagers, one who embodies the characteristics she values: "She has met the crucial test. She has never felt sorry for herself. She has never let her blackness be a way of life. She has chosen to take part in the total human experience."[48] Her use of the gendered pronoun here is significant. Although the column went through many changes over the course of its forty-year tenure, its specific inception as "Cottager's Corner" provided a specifically gendered historiography grounded in the matrilineal history West valued from her childhood. West told Linsey Lee that "whenever I thought about home, although this was our summer home then, whenever I thought about home I thought about the Vineyard."[49] Even in Russia, West's thoughts turned island-ward: "It was September 1st, and I was in Russia, and I remember writing in the little journal that I kept, 'It is September 1st on the island,' and so forth and so on, and I remember the last line was, 'What is this compared to that? Nothing, nothing.'"[50]

Before, during, and after the time she wrote for the *Gazette*, Dorothy West continued to write stories set in the neighborhoods she covered in her column, primarily the Highlands and Oak Bluffs. When the column's name changed to "Oak Bluffs" in 1973 she expanded the scope per the name change; in actuality, however, the column continued to report primarily on local events. Because West's locality was the Highlands, the column continued to participate in the documentation and promotion of the black colony. A similar pattern arose in her short fiction, especially those penned for the *Daily News*. Stripped of discernible racial markers, "The Cottagers and Mrs. Carmody" gives a slice of Vineyard life from the perspective of a caretaker of a weekend cottage. Mrs. Carmody's perspective is that of a voyeur peering through a window onto a luscious spread of which she and her family cannot partake. She is painfully lonely. Above all, she misses the human contact shared during a scrumptious Thanksgiving dinner. Stories like "Mrs. Carmody" foreground class distinction rather than racial division.

West also used her experience covering the activities of the black community on the Vineyard landscape to shape her novel, *The Wedding*. Like many social columns, "Cottager's Corner" covered weddings, especially if the mother of the bride was a Cottager. For instance, thirty out-of-town guests attended Harriet Evans's wedding, and many cottagers were in attendance. An invitation to an island wedding bearing a postmark from Geneva, Switzerland, attests that the pull of the Vineyard extends across the Atlantic.[51] Of course, the impending nuptials of a daughter of the Highlands would be the main plot line for her final novel, which is not only set in the Highlands but also draws heavily on the landscape and geography of the island.

The notion of the Vineyard as a fixed timeless space is present in *The Wedding;* indeed, it is one of the major problems for the protagonists who wish to move forward and away from antiquated, exclusionary ideas about racial uplift and purity. Such conflicts are also at the heart of Toni Morrison's novel *Love*, which revisits several themes from her earlier novels including *Sula*—with its exploration of female relationships—and *Paradise*—in its critique of black nationalism and patriarchal articulations of masculinity. What primarily intrigues me about *Love* is Morrison's choice to set the majority of the action at a black-owned beach resort run by a man, Bill Cosey, who "wanted a playground for folk who felt the way he did, who studied ways to contradict history."[52] It is interesting to consider West's chronicles of the relative success of the Vineyard as a black resort with the rot, corruption, and envy that pervade and indeed bring down Morrison's imagined beachside hotel. Intraracial strife and the gender inequities work like poison to undermine the owner's short-lived dream:

> a place where [colored musicians] could walk in the front door, not the service entrance; eat in the dining room, not the kitchen; sit with guests, sleep in beds, not their automobiles, buses, or in a whorehouse across town. A place where their instruments were safe, their drinks unwatered, their talents honored so they didn't have to go to Copenhagen or Paris for praise. Flocks of colored people would pay to be in that atmosphere.[53]

Morrison could be describing the atmosphere at Shearer Cottage; yet, unlike Cosey's fictional hotel, Shearer and the community that grew up around it persist. West's columns give us clues as to why, but her fiction, especially *The Wedding*, allows the fractures and costs of preserving paradise to emerge.

To some extent the popularity of black women's fiction in the 1980s, spurred by the writings of Alice Walker, Gloria Naylor, Toni Morrison, and Terry McMillan, enabled the publication of West's final novel by cultivating an audience of readers interested in black women's writing and ready—almost—to read about the black middle class. The difference between the imagined Oval of the novel and the Highlands speaks to how West has mythologized her community.

8

Two Weddings

This movie is unique because I think it shows a world that most people have rarely seen: a world where black families are all highly educated, very successful, living in Martha's Vineyard.

–Oprah Winfrey, Introduction, *The Wedding*

Dorothy West's 1995 novel *The Wedding* evolves from the historiographical project undertaken in her *Vineyard Gazette* columns. It reprises an earlier attempt at a second novel set on the Vineyard entitled "Where the Wild Grape Grows" and represents the culmination of West's thematic interests and storytelling techniques shaped both by years of writing in diverse genres and by her role as the oral historian of her family and community. That familial narrative, which West recounts in interviews and in print, travels from South to North, slavery to freedom, from sharecropping on borrowed land to the acquisition of property. *The Wedding* parallels the constant movement between the present and the past in her oral narratives. In the novel, these digressions transform into flashbacks and reveries that intrude upon the novel's present. The complex tension between past events and present outcomes makes *The Wedding* a compelling and provocative tale about the path one family takes to monetary success. Mining her column for authentic content, West reveals how the institution of marriage cements social and financial security at a high personal cost. To acquire social and financial capital, the Clark Coleses, a fictional African American clan whose skin color reflects the color spectrum, mortgage their moral compasses.

In addition to building on the ethnographic aspects of "Cottager's Corner," *The Wedding* also advances West's interest in racializing the novel of manners, a genre of writing that focuses on a specific stratum of society and analyzes its behavioral codes within the private and public spheres of social life. Examples include Edith Wharton's novels, especially *The House of Mirth* and *The Custom of the Country*. Literary critic Nancy Bentley identifies in Wharton's writing a "double strategy" that both critiques and preserves "the authority of the turn-of-century leadership class," and West, influenced by Wharton's style, offers a similar dual perspective on midcentury social leadership. Bentley maintains that challenges to the old system of manners and class privilege inevitably "accommodate the very changes that class appeared to oppose."[1] Bentley's observation is similar to Mary Helen Washington's assessment that West was "both a fierce critic of the bourgeois life and a loyal daughter upholding the values of family and class."[2] If we consider *The Living Is Easy* as an ethnographic novel of manners that illuminates black Boston society, then *The Wedding* follows that society to their country homes or, more specifically to the language of Oak Bluffs, their cottages. Finally, although the cultural landscape of the Northeast spatially grounds both novels, the South retains a nostalgic hold on the characters. An important difference between the fictional representation of the Clark Coleses and the family portraits featured in "Cottager's Corner" focuses on narrative voice. West injects both narratives with humor, but she infuses the narrator of *The Wedding* with a cynicism absent from the more restrained voice she developed in her *Gazette* columns. Throughout her writing career, West wrote about what she saw in her own family and the environment in which she was reared. There is much that she admires, but there are also certain unspoken sacrifices she seeks to expose. To this end, *The Wedding* provokes self-reflection about the values we internalize and how historical forces can inform intimate desires.

Placing *The Wedding* in conversation with the television adaptation "Oprah Winfrey presents *The Wedding*" (1998) enriches my analysis of how the novel attempts to reveal a hidden world whose freemasonry is invisible to the uninitiated. Through the two "Weddings" I return to the site upon which my exploration of West's life and work began: on Dorothy West Avenue in the Highlands of Oak Bluffs, where fact and fiction, history and historiography merge through the unique geography of place. The televised version of the novel somewhat diminishes the specificity of the geography of the Highlands; however, it also reveals the challenge of representing "negro geography"—the peculiar stratifications of class and color that reduce the degrees of separation among middle-class and upper-class African Americans—on the small screen. West's depiction of the milieu of "the Oval" is critical to understanding how African Americans have negotiated the slippery terrain of race relations in the United States with varying degrees of success over the course of the twentieth century.

The accepted explanation for the long delay of West's sophomore novel is pragmatic: in the wake of the "second" Blacks Arts Movement of the mid-1960s to early 1970s that evolved in conjunction with the Black Power Movement, West feared that a novel centered on the black middle class set in Martha's Vineyard would be poorly received. *The Wedding* was not West's first attempt at a Vineyard novel: "Where the Wild Grape Grows" includes six chapters of what would have been a novel set on the Vineyard in the Oval. Verner D. Mitchell and Cynthia Davis suggest that the novel was a kind of "sequel" to *The Living Is Easy*: a novel about Rachel West's later years. Although the location is the same, "Wild Grape" focuses on the fraught relationship between two sisters, Jennie and Bit, and Jennie's friend Bea. With her narcissism and conniving sensibilities Jennie very much resembles an older, childless Cleo Judson. In their youth Jennie and her friend Bea are described as two of the "beauties of Brown Boston," drawing an even closer parallel to the persona of Rachel West that appears in her daughter's fiction and nonfiction. Incorporating familiar refrains from West's oral histories, "Wild Grape" uses and repeats sections from earlier stories by reiterating how class and color inform marital decisions. "Where the Wild Grape Grows" also provides yet another take on the tensions between the original Bostonian settlers of Highlands and the New Yorkers. Here, once again, West retells the story of the lost beach.

West told interviewers Deborah McDowell and Lorraine Roses in 1984 that she was working on a novel entitled "The Wedding" and another manuscript entitled "The White Tribe of Indians."[3] Potentially, unless the manuscript about the "white tribe of Indians" surfaces, "Where the Wild Grape Grows" would have been West's second novel; however, lack of interest on the part of publishers discouraged her from pursuing it further. According to West, Houghton Mifflin rejected the novel because it dealt with the black middle class. West felt that during the late 1960s and early 1970s "white publishers were very intimidated by militant blacks."[4] While West was concerned that black audiences would find a novel about upper-class blacks too assimilationist and bourgeois, some editors were concerned that it was too insular. Betty Arnoff at Doubleday suggested "that something more should be done with the white people who live on the island. Why don't Jenny and Bea ever have any dealings with them? I think you have a chance to deepen the story and give it some interesting details."[5] West put aside "Where the Wild Grape Grows" and poured her creative energy into her column. The result was a new novel that recycled many of the same themes and concerns about marriage, color, class, and property that have always preoccupied her writing. She submitted chapters of the "The Wedding" to Harper and Row who gave her a contract, but ultimately, the "revolution," as she refers to the Black Power Movement, kept her from finishing the novel.

West maintained an active writing life as a columnist and a regular contributor of fiction to the *Daily News* in the intervening years between the publication of *The Living Is Easy* (1948) and the emergence of *The Wedding* (1995). Former first lady Jacqueline Kennedy Onassis, another famous Vineyard resident and then an editor at Doubleday, was familiar with West's column. During the summers of 1992 and 1993, Onassis apparently visited West's Highland cottage every Monday to collect drafts and encourage West to keep writing.[6] *The Wedding* is dedicated to Onassis, who clearly had an interest in writing that dealt with the intimate, interracial history of the United States. While at Doubleday, Onassis also edited Barbara Chase Ribaud's historical novel *Sally Hemings*, a fictional book about Thomas Jefferson's African American mistress, who was also the mother of several of his children.

Critical reception of *The Wedding* was mostly positive. Several critics applauded the novel's complex narrative structure, which incorporates flashbacks that span more than one hundred years to trace the interlinking branches of the Coles family tree. Elizabeth Muther aptly describes "each transitional vehicle in West" as "an interpretative map—a miniature subtext, which for its vigor and directedness, enforces connections that become as imperative as the forward drive of the novel's strong suspense itself."[7] Muther refers to the flashbacks as "analepses" after Gérard Genette's definition of "any evocation after the fact that took place earlier than the point in the story where we are at any given moment" to distinguish them from cinematic flashbacks. While I agree with Muther's analysis of the function of the "analepses," I prefer the craft-based term reverie, and the cinematic and iconic connotations of the flashback provide a more useful way to think about how the novel's genealogical narrative integrates scenes from the past.[8] For readers, the long digressions away from the "contemporary" interracial romance may have been disconcerting. Some critics found the novel strangely out of touch with current ideas about racial identity. Valerie Smith and Ann Rayson both describe the end as unbelievable. Rayson goes further; she suggests that West "is promulgating a psycho-sexual essentialism of color and 'race' in 1995 that can probably be found in both the age of West and the age of the manuscript."[9] *The Wedding* is set in 1953, in the heart of the civil rights movement and exactly one year before the passing of *Brown v. Board of Education*, the decision that mandated the desegregation of public schools. Perhaps the difficulties of successfully evoking place and time reinforce the perceived artificiality of the novel and the television adaptation. *The Wedding* is set in one of the most explosive and racially charged decades in American history. The conflicts in *The Wedding* seem less urgent than the generational, transnational battles for civil rights and social justice. Indeed, West shared those concerns; they motivated her to suppress the novel until she could be assured of a more receptive climate.

In the novel's present, the plot turns on whether Shelby Coles will actually marry her fiancé Meade. We join Shelby just twenty-four hours before the much-anticipated nuptials, but the novel is primarily concerned with events that transpired throughout the previous hundred years. In short, the novel reflects upon how intimate relationships, especially calculated interracial and intraracial unions, have coalesced to create the Coleses: a successful, well-educated, phenotypically white African American family with a home on Martha's Vineyard.

A mere three years after its publication, Oprah Winfrey selected the novel for her second effort in her "Oprah Winfrey Presents" miniseries. Considering the popularity of recovered novels like Nella Larsen's *Quicksand* or Jessie Fauset's *Plum Bun* and the surge of black women's fiction produced by Toni Morrison, Gloria Naylor, Alice Walker, and Octavia Butler during the 1970s and 1980s, what made Winfrey select *The Wedding*? Certainly the explosion of black women novelists published during the later part of the twentieth century indicated that an audience existed for West's novel, but what made Oprah choose the recently published *The Wedding* over *The Living Is Easy* or other, more critically applauded and routinely taught texts of the era?

I believe Oprah selected *The Wedding* because she wanted to televise the "the Oval." Producing *The Wedding* provided her with an opportunity to showcase the exclusive enclave of affluent blacks who vacation on Martha's Vineyard. A community whose history and activities West had been faithfully recording first in "Cottager's Corner" and then in "Oak Bluffs" would enter popular culture. Like most television adaptations of novels *The Wedding*'s translation to the small screen would not be easy. The critically acclaimed filmmaker of *Killer of Sheep* (1977) and *To Sleep with Anger* (1990), Charles Burnett, was recruited to direct, and Lisa Jones, the author of *Bulletproof Diva: Tales of Race, Sex and Class* and the biracial daughter of poet-activist Amiri Baraka and Hettie Jones, wrote the script.

According to local lore, Oprah expressed disbelief when faced with the modest woodland plot of the Oval. The hundred-year-old cottages surrounding Highland Park did not live up to the Oval's grandeur in her imagination. Reportedly her response upon viewing the Highlands was: "*This* is the Oval?" According to Joyce Rickson, when Oprah arrived in the Highlands prior to the filming of *The Wedding* she reportedly expressed surprise at the modesty of the neighborhood:

J: And *The Wedding*, you know, you know the story about how Oprah came to see the Oval?

C: Oh, no I don't know that part. I haven't heard that part of it.

J: And she said "This is it?" because you've seen the Oval. And the Oval is nothing like what the Oval looks like in the movie, or probably described in the book.[10]

In *The Wedding*, West describes the Oval: "a rustic stretch of flowering shrubs and tall trees, designated on the old town maps in Highland Park. The narrow dirt road that circled it was Highland avenue. . . . A baker's dozen of cottages made a ring around the park. Some were small and plain of façade, others were bigger and handsomer (one, the Coles place, was called a mansion)." Her literary rendering of the Oval is both accurate and evocative of New England design principles of modesty and understatement. The "Oval" is a community founded not by corporate executives, but by teachers, caterers, and carpenters who acquired their property by stealth and determination. The claims of these early settlers made them first "the vanguard," and presently the "old guard," "the bulwark of colored society."[11] West imbues her opening depiction of the Oval with a tinge of satire that undermines the seriousness of titles like "Ovalite." As such, she draws on the specialized vocabulary she employed in her columns to capture the nuances of intraracial class stratification. Terms like "Highlands" and "Cottager" become "The Oval" and "Ovalite" in the novel.

Oprah's, and perhaps Burnett's, vision of the Oval was not a subtle parody of the community's exclusivity, but a celebration of black capitalist acquisition that required a grander venue that the rustic collection of cottages nestled in the Highlands. As a result, the film was shot in Wilmington, North Carolina, a setting that, while beautiful and dreamlike, is obviously not Martha's Vineyard or Cape Cod. Martha's Vineyard has been the site of several films, most notoriously *Jaws*, and the geography of Oak Bluffs from its Ocean Park gazebo to its historic cottage city is unmistakable. The proximity of the Wilmington studio Screen Gems probably made that site a likely location. Wilmington and its beaches are familiar because of their frequent appearance in motion pictures and on television. Another Martha's Vineyard movie, *The Inkwell* (1994), based on Trey Ellis's novel *Platitudes* (1988) and one of the first to highlight the black presence on the island, was also filmed in Wilmington. Directed by twenty-two-year-old Matty Rich and starring Larenz Tate, the film bore almost no resemblance to the novel, and critics decried it as shallow and amateurish. *The Inkwell*, while spotlighting Martha's Vineyard as the place where bourgeois blacks go to let their Afros down, offers only surface debates about black authenticity and class conflicts. A case in point is the tennis court showdown between the familiar stereotypes of the "Uncle Tom" and the "Revolutionary Negro." *Idlewild*, another film featuring an all-black resort, was also filmed in North Carolina.[12]

The choice of an inauthentic setting is a prelude to the film's failure to visually render two critical aspects of the novel: the architectural and geographic particularity of the Oval and the casting of the Clark Coleses, namely Shelby, Liz, Corinne, and Clark, as phenotypically "white" African Americans. The miniseries cast included Academy Award–winning actress Halle Berry as Shelby, Lynn Whitfield as Corinne, Eric Thal as Meade Howell, Cynda Williams as Liz, and Michael Warren as Clark Coles. What is puzzling to anyone familiar with the novel is the fact that the actors selected to portray the Clark Coleses are all visually identifiable as African American. As such, their behavior toward their "slightly darker" neighbors seems ridiculous. More important, one of the most pivotal flashbacks in the novel—when Shelby Coles goes missing for hours because the white islanders refuse to believe she is actually colored—cannot be rendered in the film.

In the novel West depicts Shelby Coles as the twin of her white grand-mother: "with rose-pinked skin, golden hair, and dusk-blue eyes."[13] Even among her light-skinned family members she is a throwback to her Caucasian ancestors; she is also named after her great-grandfather, Confederate colonel Lance Shelby. The movie focuses primarily on Shelby's pending interracial wedding to a white jazz player named Meade. In the novel, however, her character is merely a vehicle for the romantic plot under which the roots of the real story, the evolution of the family tree that serves as the frontispiece to the novel, emerges. With the exception of the little-girl-lost story, the novel's spotlight seldom shines on Shelby. She is important primarily in terms of what she represents to her various family members. In contrast, the casting of Halle Berry, one of America's most marketable, recognizable, and universally attractive actresses, required the film to build its narrative arc around her character. Thus the film omits the many digressing subplots that form the most compelling aspects of the novel.

What I call the "off-color" casting of the television version of *The Wedding* undermines a key concern of the novel and an idea that West reiterated in her *Gazette* columns: African Americans are a multiethnic, diverse group, and even those who could pass for white out of racial pride, among other reasons, choose not to.[14] Casting problems explain why novels like Nella Larsen's *Passing* have never been filmed: the two main characters are phenotypically white: one passes for white; the other lives as an African American. Even if there are few actresses available who would fit the bill—Jennifer Beals for example—their careers, like those of Fredi Washington and other early twentieth-century actresses whose appearance defied the visually understood grammar of blackness have been marked, if not sidelined, by their neither-nor status. Cinematic representation and the challenges facing unconventional black actresses were a particular concern of West's. For instance, she was friends with Fredi Washington. In addition to sharing a street with Fredi's sister Isabel Washington—a former Harlem chorine and the former wife of Adam Clayton Powell—West is photographed next to Fredi at a book-signing for *The Living Is Easy*. West's friendship with actress Edna Thomas secured her a small role in the London production of *Porgy*. She also intended to star in two film projects in Russia, though neither came to fruition.[15] "Cottager's Corner" enumerated the difficulties faced by actresses like Lillian Evanti (a renowned opera singer), Liz White (another neighbor who resided in the Twin Cottages), and Gladys Riddle, of whom West wrote: "whatever her potential it was constantly frustrated by producers and directors who said she was too fair to be Negro, which was hard for her to buy in a society that says one drop is enough for life membership."[16]

The aforementioned Jennifer Beals, the star of the 1983 cult classic *Flash-dance*, ironically faced similar challenges when she was cast as the passing figure Daphne Monet in the 1995 film *Devil in a Blue Dress*, which was based on Walter Mosley's novel. The film's director, Carl Franklin, was concerned that audiences who knew about her mixed-race background would read that biographical information into her portrayal of Monet, thus giving away the film's main plot twist: "I was concerned about her playing the role not because I did not trust her acting ability but because I knew she was part African American and I was concerned it would tip off the secret we were holding in the film." Aisha Bastiaans argues that *Devil in a Blue Dress* primes the audience to suspect and later believe Daphne Monet's racial transformation by relying on "visual and aural shorthand[s]" that manipulate the racial perceptions of the audience.[17] The shorthands include associating sexualized and exotic imagery with Monet. First, the film opens with a pan shot over Archibald J. Motley's painting *Bronzeville by Night* and lingers on a naked, fair-skinned, racially ambiguous woman in a window in the corner of the painting. Later, a character introduces Monet before Beals even appears on screen as a woman with a penchant for "jazz, pig's feet, and dark men."[18]

If the director feared that audiences familiar with Beals's ethnicity would not be fooled by her portrayal of Daphne Monet, it is likely that audiences privy to Halle Berry's well-publicized biracial background (she is the daughter of a white mother and a black father) reinforced her portrayal of a woman who "on one side is the great granddaughter of slaveholders and on the other is the great granddaughter of slaves." In the novel, Shelby is a product of systematic, atavistic decisions to achieve higher-class status through marrying light-skinned partners with the desired result of returning not to the ancestry of the slaves, but to that of the slaveholders. From Gram's perspective, Shelby's wedding to Meade ensured the family's "return to its origination, the colored blood drained out, degree by degree, until none was left, either known or remembered."[19] The novel then chronicles how the Clark Coleses acquired their color, class status, and property. The stories of the relationships narrated in the novel inevitably intertwine all three markers of success.

Director Charles Burnett also deploys racial shorthand and strategic pairings of actors to achieve a class/color division that would otherwise not be as readily apparent. While the complexions of actors cast as the Coleses do not resemble West's character descriptions, the film uses other methods to distinguish them as elite and distinct from other African Americans in the movie.[20] Lute McNeil, Linc Odis, and the housekeepers Emmaline and Gigi are all slightly darker skinned than the actors portraying the Coleses. That contrast, however slim it may be, works to establish the ridiculousness of enforcing an intraracial color line—a point that is in line with West's satirical exposé of intraracial color prejudice in her novel. The Coleses' housemaid Emmaline tells

Gigi, McNeil's housekeeper who in the book, but not the movie, is also his sex partner, that "it's all high yella around here." Emmaline's dialogue codes the Coleses as "high yella" and also implies that the appellation is synonymous with black education and achievement. Tellingly, this is not language used in West's novel, but a term scriptwriter Lisa Jones has borrowed from black vernacular discourse. The connotations of "high yella" are subjective; in vernacular culture "high yella" is also used as a feminized noun—"I got me a high yella at home"—rather than an adjective.[21] To convey the understated colorism that the novel simultaneously critiques and upholds, the film incorporates these incidents as shorthand to manipulate spectators' visual understanding of race. Another example unique to the film that conveys Gram's refusal to accept or even touch Laurie's brown daughter is the scene where she tells Laurie that she has purchased a bonnet to hide the little girl's "nappy" hair.

The film also capitalizes on the image of Halle Berry as a singularly beautiful actress whose screen presence tends to overwhelm her character. Throughout the film, Berry is shot in a manner that inscribes her as the carefree 1950s image of a woman bicycling. Her on-screen costume, when she is not being fitted for her wedding dress, includes a variety of pastel, short-sleeve blouses that she has tied above her navel. More than a fifties fashion statement, her attire and bobbed wig, a marked departure from Berry's signature short haircut that she wore in her earlier films, establishes her as a bronze version of the typical postwar woman. An early scene follows the pink-clad Berry rushing on basket-laden bicycle to meet her fiancé's ferry. From the ferry disembarks a racially diverse group of passengers who signify the island's status as an interracial space. These images of Berry and the bucolic setting reinforce the film's melodramatic appeal and appear to emulate 1950s films like Douglas Sirk's *Imitation of Life*, a reinterpretation of Fannie Hurst's novel and the 1932 film by John Stahl starring Fredi Washington. The stylized and often overly dramatic conversations between Shelby and her various family members recall the satirical and melodramatic confrontations in *Imitation of Life* (1959) between Lana Turner, Sandra Dee, and Susan Kohner, who plays the prodigal daughter passing for white.

The mobility of the bicycle as a vehicle identified with feminist freedom also appears as a trope in West's novel *The Living Is Easy*.[22] Cleo first encounters Bart Judson when she crashes into him on her bicycle; Bart is immediately entranced. The lecherous nephew of Cleo's guardian gave her the bicycle hoping that she would "break every bone in her body and destroy her beauty, if not herself" thus relieving him of his interracial attraction for her. Instead, the bicycle sends her flying into her future husband, who drowns "helplessly in her welling eyes and tumbled hair."[23] The frame of Berry cycling appears in the opening credits of each sequence of the film following the commercial advertisement. The sequence of moving photographs evokes the experience of flipping through a photo album. The effect suggests that a television movie is itself a collection of snapshots or memorabilia from a bygone era, which amplifies the feeling that the film takes place outside of reality. That kind of nostalgic fantasy produces a film more in line with Oprah's vision of an upper class informed by southern as opposed to northern sensibilities and locales.

The film also uses sex, or rather the lack of it, to separate and distinguish the Coleses from the other African Americans in the film. By desexualizing Shelby and Corinne the film highlights the idea that asexuality, combined with both light skin and proper family connections, makes a female partner an asset. For instance, the flashbacks in film and novel portray Gram as anxious to marry off Corinne while she is still a virginal prize. She fears the "primitive behind the pale skin" and believes that "some girls should marry young or come to grief as unwed mothers." Thus the debutante Corinne supplants Clark's first love, a dark-skinned scholarship student named Sabina, who is the double of Rachel, his current mistress. In the novel both Sabina and Rachel are as beautiful as, if not more lovely than, Corinne: "a paler woman pales by comparison. Not everyone can see it, but those who can know there is no beauty like that of a brown-skinned woman when she is beautiful: the velvet skin, the dark hair like a cloud, the dark eyes like deep wells to drown in."[24] Despite their earthy beauty, they lack light skin and familial wealth: the crucial elements that make the film version of Corinne, as she states with bitterness, an "asset."

The novel also includes several scenes of lovemaking that are completely absent from the movie. One element that distinguishes *The Wedding* from West's other fiction is her incorporation of sexuality and intimacy. The most passionate scene takes place between Schoolteacher and Isaac (Clark's parents). Interestingly enough, the language that precedes their sexual act is the language of religious conversion. Isaac is drawn to his wife when she "began to moan, not in pain but in passion. She was in the throes of an old-time religious conversion, a convulsive surrender to Christ free of Episcopalian restraints, her naked spirit kneeling and praying for union with his." Schoolteacher's "ecstasy" fires Isaac's desire, and their lovemaking becomes sacred: "In the crescendo of her conversion, she witnessed the revelation, the word made flesh, Christ coming toward her in the visible body of the man. If he but touched her, she would be redeemed."[25] The irony is that the morning after their passionate act, Schoolteacher awakens to find that Isaac has died. That the most passionate act of marital lovemaking in the novel results in death speaks to the elusiveness of physical, emotional, and intellectual compatibility in the world of the novel.

In contrast to the fleeting passion of her paternal grandparents or the illicit affairs of her parents, Meade and Shelby's relationship is portrayed as ascetic; in both the novel and the television movie Shelby is a virgin, and the couple barely touches. This leaves room for Lute McNeil to move in with his predatory sexuality. In the film, he appears as a devoted father—an opportunistic social climber yes, but handsome and desirable nonetheless. His well-cast on-screen daughters span the color spectrum. Like their counterparts in the novel they resemble "children from a painter's easel."[26] However, the story of Lute's systematic seduction and physical abuse of a succession of impoverished immigrant women and prostitutes before finally marrying the blue-blooded Brahmin Della is left out of the film. The novel's portrayal of Lute's contempt for the girls' three different mothers and his indiscriminate sexual appetite prompts readers to view his relationship with his daughters as disturbing and deviant. Even the innocent task of braiding his daughter's hair takes on incestuous overtones. In one scene after Lute "bound Tina's hair in braids" he kisses her: "Impaling the love on that lifted face, Lute kissed Tina so hard that her teeth caught in the flesh of her lip, and a little trickle of blood filled her throat with nausea. As she clambered over Lute's knee to give her place to Muffin, he caught her in a bear hug that took her breath away. She gasped from the pain of it. Her ribs felt crushed."[27]

In the novel Lute's dangerous love for his daughters is unnaturally propri-etary and oppressive. Additionally, Tina's uncanny resemblance to Shelby makes his attentive parenting even more suspect. Tina is as white as if not whiter than his immigrant wife, whom he refers to as "the polack," reinforcing his grotesque character and foreshadowing his role in the horrific death of his supposedly beloved child. In the movie, the brief hair-braiding scene is much more innocently framed, and Lute is insistent that his role is only temporary and that women are the most adept at this intimate act.

Discussing her choice to marry Linc, a dark-skinned doctor, Liz Coles reveals her feelings about giving birth to a brown child without the "protective coloring of the Coleses."[28] The shield of a near-white skin presumably has kept the Coles family safe and prosperous, but an incident from Shelby's childhood reveals that the protective coloring is not inviolable. In chapter 7, the barking of Jezebel, Lute's dog, prompts a moment of reverie that takes Shelby back to when she was six years old and lost her way while following a puppy out of the Oval. Although her family immediately notified the authorities, Shelby remained lost for several hours because the people she encountered misrecognized her, owing to their fixed perceptions of what a colored child from the Oval area looked like: "The sickness of the search was that so many people saw Shelby, but they were not looking for such a child. They were looking for a colored child, which meant they were looking for what they knew to be a colored child—dark skin, dark hair, and Negroid features." At no point in her many encounters outside the Oval does anyone connect the blond, blue-eyed Shelby with the colored child described as wearing a "yellow dress and red sandals." The similarity in attire did not "strike them as anything more than a remarkable coincidence. Every little girl had a pair of red shoes." Brought up in the insularity of the Oval, Shelby has never had to wonder or question her identity before this point. She and her community understood who she was, but when she wanders outside that community she falls not under the jurisdiction of Jim Crow, but under the New England liberalism that refuses to acknowledge its own prejudice and fixed ideas of racial categories. Even when Shelby tells a woman that her name is "Coles," she is met with disbelief. To ascertain her true racial identity a woman rubs Shelby's hair between her fingers saying, "You see, it's real gold, it didn't rub off. It's real hair—it stayed on her scalp. God may have given some coloreds light skin, but He never gave them blond hair."[29] The implication of this farcical act is that God, and not selective genetic engineering, is responsible for the distribution of genetic traits like hair texture/color and eye color. Shelby passes the test—her hair is "real gold" and not counterfeit—which proves that African Americans can access divinely bestowed racial characteristics, but the novel attests that the method of acquisition is often violent. For instance, one of Shelby's ancestors, Preacher, is spared from the fever which kills his family because "half his blood was the blood of his mother's master, a hard-drinking Irishman who had broken his mother's hymen by divine right upon purchasing her, before mating her with one of his bucks to increase his herd of livestock, which recurring plagues were depleting."[30] In turn, Preacher would wed a "butternut woman" with the same parentage and "protective coloring" as his own, thus continuing a selective "breeding" process that chillingly recalls slaveowners' systematic practices of putting prized male slaves out to stud and raping female slaves to increase their property.

In her *Gazette* columns West is ever attentive to the multitude of skin tones, hair textures, and eye color present among the cottagers, though she rarely hints at how such traits were acquired. Instead, her colorful descriptions resemble a paean to black beauty. Her observations form a primer that educates the white residents of Oak Bluffs on the permeability of racial identity and identification and the strange, persistent arithmetic of the one-drop rule. Perhaps West's intention was to prevent incidents like the one that happens to Shelby?

The terrifying experience of being lost in whiteness, of passing outside the Oval, renders Shelby "limp and white and mute." Only when she is returned to the Oval does she come back to life: "When they drove into the Oval, her name began to sing, soaring to a crescendo burst out of screen doors and running after the car on legs stout and thin, repeating itself over and over. There was no uncertainty. She had her identity back; she was Shelby, one and indivisible, a girl with real hair."[31] West had a talent for rendering the world from the point of view of the child; she employed this technique wonderfully in her characterization of Judy in *The Living Is Easy*.

Similarly, throughout *The Wedding* children's viewpoints lend tenderness and poignancy to the novel.

Shelby's prolonged disappearance is critical to understanding the novel's commentary about color and boundaries of race. The so-called "protective coloring of the Coleses" does not keep Shelby safe; in fact, it endangers her. The scene captures the fragility of the world of the Oval. Despite their success, the Ovalites recognize the vulnerability of their invisible boundaries, and thus they fervently guard their gates: "Though money was as important in the Oval as in any other upper-class community, it was not the determining factor in distinguishing between majors and minors. The distinction was so subtle, the gradations so fine drawn, that only an Ovalite knew on which level he belonged, and an outsider sometimes wasted an entire summer licking the wrong boot."[32] Those subtle gradations turn out to be impossible to relate in the television adaptation of *The Wedding*. The scene of Shelby's disappearance cannot be filmed because Halle Berry is obviously identifiable as a woman of color. When she tries to relate the event to Meade, it makes little sense. The movie Shelby remembers:

SHELBY: There were reports going around the island that there was a lost little colored child. A policeman finally found me and brought me back to the Oval. I was so happy to be home. No more funny faces staring at me asking me if I was that lost little colored child.

MEADE: I'm just glad you got home okay.

SHELBY: Yeah. It's funny. I don't even know why I told you that story really. Some things just kind of stick with you I guess.

MEADE: I know what made you think about it. My parents.

Within the racial context established by the film, this story relays what happens when a person of color, even a child, steps outside the established boundaries of black and white; this story reifies the distinction between the Oval and the rest of the island as primarily a color distinction. Yet the truncated story given to Meade loses the complexity of how and why Shelby, when she ventured out of a context where her body was legible, was lost. She admits that she has no idea why she tells Meade the story, and we don't know either. The story is not immediately provoked by any particular incident. Meade and Shelby are walking on a jetty of rocks jutting out to the ocean, and she says apropos of nothing that she remembers following a dog out of the Oval. Meade, however, simultaneously dismisses the significance of what she is trying to tell him by expressing relief that she was found and fixes the meaning of the story by telling her that what provoked her remembrance was his parents' refusal to attend their wedding. Meade's interpretation of the incident reduces it to a story about a young child innocent of the deceptive geography of race who goes missing when she crosses the color line she didn't know existed. Because the made-for-television adaptation has narrowed the plot of the novel to an interracial romance this exchange parallels Shelby's decision to once again transgress the color line by marrying outside her race.

Another key question posed by the novel that cannot be taken up in the film, given Berry's off-color casting, is whether Shelby will pass for white once she marries Meade. As Muther observes, and as the story of the little lost colored girl emphasizes, "others cannot see [Shelby] as black out of context." When she crossed that "infinite distance between two worlds and two concepts of color" Shelby moved outside the semiotics of race.[33] Rather than capture the subtle dance of the black colony's unobtrusive integration the movie has to include standard examples of discrimination, such as the scene where Shelby is kept waiting in the lobby of a restaurant because the hostess does not think to ask if she is the "fiancée" Meade is expecting. The discrimination and heightened scrutiny that Shelby and Meade face as an interracial couple in the restaurant in the television version were nonexistent in the world of the novel, where only in the Oval is their racial identity understood as non-white. By becoming engaged to Shelby, Meade, whose skin is no whiter than his fiancée's, forfeits his claim to whiteness: his identification is strained by both his parents' refusal to attend the wedding and his identification with the racialized category of an unemployed jazz musician. The implicit and explicit explorations of racial identity posed by the novel—for example, will Shelby insist upon her cultural blackness or will she yield to the demands of Gram, spurred by the historical maneuvers of generations of ancestors, and pass into whiteness—cannot be voiced in the television movie. Nor can the uneasy and controversial conclusion of the novel be staged on the small screen.

Part one of the miniseries contains only two flashbacks: the story of Corinne's parents' interracial marriage and her own marriage to Clark. The first episode of the miniseries relies on the romantic hook: Will Shelby marry Meade or fall for Lute? This is the driving plot of the miniseries, but it is a red herring in the novel. Meade is off-stage for the majority of the novel. He appears only in a recent flashback set in an island jazz club. This scene is woven into the movie's present because Meade is a primary character. Additionally, the movie features several scenes where Meade plays the piano for Shelby or Emmaline. These scenes seem to demonstrate his successful acquisition of cultural blackness demonstrated by his espousal of jazz (black music) and his authenticating black fiancée.

The film versions of Meade and Shelby fit the iconic profile of interracial pairings that fueled jazz's barrier-crossing potential in the 1950s and 1960s. In fact, they resemble one of most famous of these "interracial couplings": Chet and Halema Baker. Chet Baker's moody rendition of "My Funny Valentine" and his James Dean good looks grasped the imagination of photographer William

Claxton and subsequently American popular culture. Claxton's photography established Baker as a cultural icon of the 1950s. Baker's image was associated with the "birth of the cool," an idea that captures the nonchalance of modernity and the insouciance of jazz culture.[34] In Claxton's photograph, Halema Alli Baker looks soulfully outward, her short dark curly head leaning against Chet's knee. Her sundress emphasizes her dark skin and eyes while the light streaming in from the window behind the couple creates identical shadows on their bare arms. Chet is captured in profile gazing down at Halema's head. Between them lies the trumpet, its shiny brass almost phallic.[35]

Could West have had this photograph in mind when she imagined Meade as a jazz musician? Meade is described as playing the piano with a "cold, cool fire." To establish credibility he must woo his audience into accepting his position as "a white man in an otherwise all-colored band." His position as a boundary-crossing outlier makes him good match for Shelby, who admits that she fell in love with Meade's music first. Meade was an ideal partner because he "poured his passion into his music" and "played that [piano] like he was giving birth." Meade is more of an idea than an actual presence in the novel. He functions as a foil for Lute, who works with his hands as a carpenter and who uses his physicality to overwhelm women. Shelby describes their differences in nonracialized terms: "How different Lute and Meade were, Shelby thought. Lute was a craftsman, a man whose life was dedicated to old patterns, old forms, forms he followed with remarkable precision—forms that Meade rejected out of hand. Meade was an artist, a trailblazer."[36] Meade is the visionary; Lute is the automaton. In the movie, the two are contrasted primarily in terms of race to emphasize the sensationalism of an interracial love triangle. In fact, part one concludes after Lute and Shelby share an illicit kiss on the beach, a scene that reinforces the movie's suspense hinging upon which man will win Shelby's heart. After the kiss, Shelby runs away in horror. She leaves Lute standing alone in the sand while "to be continued" appears on the screen.

Part two of the miniseries restages several familial flashbacks from the novel. We see the mistakes made by Clark's parents without the passionate death-causing lovemaking in the book. But the action stalls as the second installment of the miniseries moves slowly toward a climactic ending that sharply diverges from the novel. The movie ends as expected with Shelby's fairytale Vineyard wedding to Meade, but it defies the novel's main irony. Though the novel's plot is ostensibly driven by Shelby's anticipated wedding as the event of the year and the culmination of years of genetic engineering, that wedding is tragically usurped by the horrific and graphic death of Lute McNeil's daughter Tina. In the novel, there is a funeral instead of a wedding. This fitting conclusion emphasizes that the family's previous unions resulted in marriages that lead to the characters' physical and/or psychological death.

The novel establishes the marriage as entrapment, a motif evoked from the outset by describing the Coleses' "glassed-in porches, against which many birds had dashed themselves to death." Descriptions like this reiterate the placement of the Coleses: while part of the Oval, they actually exceed, rather than lead, the vanguard. Unlike the other cottages, the Coles house is more properly called "a mansion." Located at a "dead end," its landscaped lawns stand out for the wrong reasons; their place may be the "prize piece of the Oval," but it is also its barometer of excess because they are too near to their white "counterparts."[37] Rather than a kitschy, comfy, seaside cottage with an open porch covered with rockers, the Coleses' stately white mansion evokes the antebellum architecture of the big house. Indeed, relationships shaped by the peculiar, southern institution of slavery haunt the house and its inhabitants, despite its northern locale.

The film concludes with the expected, triumphant interracial wedding capped by Shelby's pronouncement that "color and class are false distinctions; love was not. In the summer of 1953, I married for love." In the novel, Shelby only "thank[s] God that it is not too late for her and Meade" when she perceives Lute's diabolic plan, revealed only by the sacrifice of an innocent who is Shelby's double: "Tina's hair was golden brown, shot through with silvery strands. Her long-lashed eyes were gray-blue."[38] Additionally, the movie's benediction inserts "class" as a false distinction; in fact, while West's novel may undermine notions of superiority based on color, the class barriers do not succumb to the same toppling. Certainly there may be exceptions to class-based discrimination, but those lines are not overcome. Lute's behavior fulfills the Ovalites' expectations and confirms that Lute is merely an interloper in a borrowed cottage. To stage on television the wedding that the novel leaves out, Tina cannot die because "it would be impossible to stage a full blown wedding on screen after a child's death."[39] Furthermore, as the movie excises Lute's pathological misogyny and single-minded desire for revenge on the inhabitants of the Oval, it would not be clear why Tina has to die.

The television revision of the ending becomes even more disturbing given the controversy surrounding the novel's publication. Apparently reviewers received galleys before the book was finished. Henry Louis Gates Jr. brought his copy to West who was astonished: "There can't be galleys yet," she said. "I haven't finished the book. It doesn't have an ending." Under the pressure of Gates's intervention, Doubleday postponed the publication date, and West rewrote the ending. There are conflicting stories about who actually wrote the first ending. It is possible that Scott Moyers, Onassis's editorial assistant, actually "stitched together the last chapter using [West's] original outline."[40]

The particular timelessness of the Vineyard setting makes it a difficult novel for late twentieth-century audiences to unpack. The novel's uneasy translation to the small screen reflects the difficulty of representing African Americans cinematically. Although I have not found access to viewership numbers, it is telling that, unlike several of Oprah's other television movies—often based on novels from her celebrated book club—neither a DVD nor a VHS version of *The Wedding* is available for purchase. Questions of authenticity and the historic distrust of affluent blacks complicate representations of middle-class and upper-class blacks and confound the reception of films that focus on these types of communities. It is also difficult to determine which elements of the film resulted from Lisa Jones's screenplay and which were the result of Charles Burnett's directorial decisions. I find it intriguing that Jones, a columnist for the *Village Voice* who often wrote about colorism and her own biracial background, was chosen to adapt the novel. Even more prescient is the irony that her father, Amiri Baraka, arguably a primary architect of the Black Arts Movement and the Black Aesthetic, contributed to the cultural climate that prompted West to suppress the novel for so long. That Baraka's daughter, who was born out of an interracial union he renounced when he famously separated himself from the Beat poets and changed his name from Leroi Jones to Imamu Amiri Baraka, would emphasize a happier ending may also reflect her own hopes for the viability of interracial unions.

To render West's novel as a 1950s melodrama in the style of Douglas Sirk with its commentary of the falsity of color and class boundaries and by allowing Shelby to provide the narrative voice-over, we lose what Muther characterizes as the "crackling electrical humor" of the novel's narrator and the irony she brings to her caricatures of both the Ovalites and the ancestors brought to life through the flashbacks. The dreamlike, almost technicolor cinematography of "Oprah Winfrey Presents *The Wedding*" reinforces the world of the Oval as a utopic space that exists outside everyday life.

West's novel develops the historiographical impulse of her *Gazette* columns into an intricate and scathing story. The television version augments many goals set out by West's columns: it gives visibility to the achievements of African Americans by revealing a separate, but equally flawed, world that exists alongside the other vacation communities on Martha's Vineyard. The miniseries misses, however, the collective nostalgia and communal feeling expressed by actual Vineyard residents and West's much harsher fictional assessment of behavior of the "Ovalites" and their painful family histories.

As West's swansong, *The Wedding* is not exactly a satisfying sequel to the promise of her first novel. But it does mark the evolution of her writing career: from a precocious short story writer inspired by her family's history and the roots they put down in Boston and Oak Bluffs, to the spunky ingénue who sets off to Russia with such optimism, to a maturing editor and crossover fiction writer who at last becomes a novelist, to the social columnist and community organizer, to the lay historian finally recognized as the last survivor of that glittering good time in Harlem. Ann Rayson identifies the "puzzle" of *The*

Wedding as "why West is using and even promoting worn stereotypes about class, color, and sexuality when geneticists have demolished old theories of genetic inheritance residing in race."[41] I find it appropriate that *The Wedding* bears many of West's trademarks—her satirical voice, her empathy and skill at capturing a child's perspective, but also her persistent obsession with skin color and class anxiety she never truly exorcised from either her fiction or her life. If it discomforts readers to have those anxieties laid bare, perhaps it is because, however easy it might be to dismiss the themes and motivations of the characters in *The Wedding* as antiquated, they still strike a chord of recognition evident in debates about multiculturalism and biraciality in the twenty-first century. Though contemporary conversations about class stratification in the black community—particularly the widening gap between the underclass and the middle class in terms of education, income, and residential location—have little to do with a person's skin hue, it is difficult to sever how success is encoded from a color-sensitive vocabulary in both public and private discourse.

Film critics and other students of popular culture have noted a precipitous rise in the popularity of ambiguously or ethnically flexible actors and actresses who, like the nineteenth-century literary figures of the mulatto/a, serve the mediating role that the entertainment industry finds viable. As our vocabulary around racial representation becomes more nuanced, it is possible that a twenty-first-century version of *The Wedding* would be cast very differently. That does not mean, however, that it would be any more faithful to the novel. Whatever its flaws, the novel and its accompanying miniseries put the spotlight back on West. Without her "weddings," West may have remained in relative obscurity, known primarily as the eccentric columnist of her island community. Instead, the two *Wedding*s catapulted her back into the public eye, where her work was finally encountered by the broad audience she always desired.

Coda

"Winter on Martha's Vineyard"

A woman walks toward the Inkwell in the early hours as the sun draws a path over the still-excited waters of the harbor. I think of her moving always at a vigorous pace. Even if it is winter on the Vineyard, and West is in the winter of her life, along her way to greet the morning she lifts a hand to her girlhood friends, the daughters of other old Vineyard families who grew up in the same sphere of defiant privilege. She gives a thumbs-up to Lois Mailou Jones, painting furiously at her easel, desperate to catch a certain quality of light before the true morning dawns. She casts a backward glance at her cousin Helene, who sits on her memorial bench in the Highlands composing a companion sonnet to "A Southern Road." Once she turns onto Circuit Avenue, Wally, Zora, Countee, Lang, and Claude give her a collective fist pump from their café seats: "You are the last one, Dorothy," they say. She nods and continues toward the beach.

It is the fate of many writers to labor in obscurity, but West was lucky enough to enjoy a festschrift atmosphere that allowed her to once again reshape the narrative of her life in a way that still managed to avoid illuminating the lacunas in her interviews or her autobiographical fiction. Along with the critics, she also proclaimed herself the last surviving writer of the Harlem Renaissance.

In his introduction to *The Last Leaf of Harlem*, Lionel Bascom compares Dorothy West to the unnamed narrator in Ralph Ellison's *Invisible Man*. He writes: "Dorothy West had gone underground and remained there until Henry Louis 'Skip' Gates from Harvard and Jackie Onassis found her living again on Martha's Vineyard."[1] In following West's writing beyond the Harlem Renaissance it is clear that she was not an invisible woman. As a columnist, short story writer, and vibrant presence within Oak Bluffs, she continued to write for the entirety of her life. Nor was she undiscovered. The interviews she gave with

Lorraine Roses, Genii Guinier, Katrine Dalsgård, Deborah McDowell, and Linsey Lee, and the black feminist scholarship that exploded during the late 1980s and the early 1990s belie the idea that she was invisible until "rediscovered" by Onassis, who, by the way, religiously read her column in the *Gazette*.[2]

I do not claim to have rediscovered Dorothy West, but, after living with her voice and her work for several years, I have come to appreciate the tension between the intimacy of life-writing and the imaginative palette of fiction. They converge in the mind of the biographer/literary critic in a way that is both confounding and illuminating. West also wore the hat of a social historian/columnist, and in this genre she most successfully fused her politics, poetics, and passion. Depending on the viewfinder we choose, West is either a closeted lesbian revolutionary or a color-struck grand dame of a bygone era. Her multiple identities offer many provocative insights on how color and class worked among the black elite of the Northeast. Her articulation of the performative nature of class provides a sophisticated nexus for understanding the particular status of people of African descent in North America and the global/local implications of blackness in the diaspora. In this biography I did not intend to paint a complete portrait of the writer and her work, but I hoped to offer a glimpse into the multiple geographies she inhabited and how those spaces shaped, and were shaped by, her writing.

In "Winter on Martha's Vineyard" West writes that "best of all the remembering was the reliving of the opening of the cottage."[3] She proceeds to describe in detail the rituals of returning to a beloved space and how, through careful acts of unveiling, the space becomes animated, awakened from its dusty hibernation to once again become a domestic sanctuary. For me, reading West is like the opening of a summer cottage. I enter a world that is both familiar and foreign, beautiful in its race pride and terrible in its racial prejudice. Like the returning cottager who takes an inventory of what has been changed and what has remained unaltered, I marvel at and am unsettled by how American culture has been dramatically transformed and how easily it ignores its past.

In "Winter," West confronts her own mortality. When she wrote it, she was just approaching middle age. She couldn't know that she would, in fact, live to fulfill her witticism that there was "magic in island living" and "no one died but the ancients." There's a certain prophetic urgency in this piece. In the context of current concerns about the preservation of the planet's most precious and sublime spaces, her evocation of the natural environment has a palpable pulse. You can feel the spray of the icy wave and hear the hoarse screeching of the gulls. In this vignette, West has turned her attention away from the fleeting summer to the season in which "ice laid a trap for the old." With every winter comes the distinct possibility of death for the island's elderly permanent residents. "Winter" could serve as a cautionary tale for those with dreams of retiring on the island in "summer houses without cellars, where the pipes were above ground instead of buried in it." But the story also affords an opportunity for quiet contemplation.[4]

After hearing me give a talk about Dorothy West at the University of Wisconsin–Madison Institute for Research in the Humanities, an audience member asked me to describe my personal connection to West. He wanted to know if I as so many biographers do, had become personally identified with my subject. Like West, I am an only child, a woman, an African American, and a writer; my subject position makes me, like West, acutely sensitive to the color, class, and gender divisions that make up the social hierarchies of our increasingly global society. I am not a Bostonian. I am not even a New Englander; however, we do, ultimately, come from the same place. My class anxiety centers on the widening economic gap between African Americans and other citizens of this country and between the shrinking African American middle class and the persistent problems that plague low-income and impoverished African Americans. Many of the small gains accomplished during the 1990s have been undone by the downturn of the economy in the early twenty-first century. I do not promise that the solution to such class divisions can be found in West's fiction and nonfiction, but studying her life and her work has helped me gain a deeper understanding of how African American culture performs and represents class. Understanding the fictions of class is as important as understanding empirical, economic classifications based on income level. After all, we are a country in which a minority holds more than 80 percent of the wealth; this minority is invisible to a middle class that labors under the delusion that they can move up the social ladder through hard work, only to learn, as Edith Wharton's heroine Lily Bart finally does, that the ones least able to afford the bill often foot it.

Given those stark realities, in researching and writing *Dorothy West's Paradise* I sought to understand the evolution of intraracial class and color divisions over the course of the twentieth century. West was part of a movement that hoped to change our social reality through artistic activism. I am an ardent believer in the power of the production and experience of art to have transformative effects. In following the artist's path we explore what it means to be human and how as human beings we shape and are shaped by our environment. The island in West's writing appears to be "an unaltered place." In reality, it is, like our planet, ever evolving. It is also under siege. African American discourse is riddled with the rhetoric of utopia—that elusive promised land we are never sure we will reach, but where we imagine our children will finally catch the brass ring. Dorothy West's paradise may not be a utopia, but the desire for utopia is not easily dismissed, nor should it be derided as mere bourgeois yearning. The election of Barack Obama in 2008 has prompted us to radically rethink what black nationalism means when the nation is led by an African American president. Studying West and the black communities she wrote about broadens our understanding of how a "boutique" black nationalist community might look. There is no reason to believe that West would endorse such an experiment, but through her columns she certainly covered it.

I return to Shelby Coles's final statement at the end of the novel *The Wedding*. Shelby concludes, or rather, insists, "Color was a false distinction; love was not."[5] Her assertion is undermined not only by her omission of class as a category that needs toppling but also by the confusion and ambivalence surrounding the ending. Advocates of postracial discourse would endorse Shelby's verdict, but even those who like to think racial discrimination is no longer a determining or prevailing factor in our lives (there's strong evidence to suggest that for many it still is) cannot pretend that we are postclass as well. I wonder if, as we become postracial, our class stratifications and classifications become even more firmly racialized than they already are. For a not-yet-postracial, class-divided society, reading Dorothy West presents an opportunity to explore the pressures of heteronormative gender roles and how geography, architecture, and space interact with the constitution of class from the perspective of a Bostonian by way of Oak Bluffs, Moscow, Harlem, South Carolina, and, of course, Africa. Through Dorothy West we as readers can lay claim to (if not a state or sovereign territory) a cottage, a beach, and maybe, just maybe, a "land of milk and honey to which the old returned to taste its elixir on their tongues."[6]

NOTES

INTRODUCTION

1. For a thorough discussion of Emma Dunham Kelley-Hawkins's misidentification and revaluation within the field of African American literature, see Cherene Sherrard-Johnson and P. Gabrielle Foreman, "Racial Recovery, Racial Death: An Introduction in Four Parts," *Legacy: A Journal of American Women Writers* 24.2 (2007): 157–170; Holly Jackson, "Mistaken Identity: What If a Novelist Celebrated as a Pioneer of African-American Women's Literature Turned Out Not to Be Black at All?" *Boston Globe*, 20 February 2005, D1, D3; Katherine E. Flynn, "A Case of Mistaken Racial Identity: Finding Emma Dunham (née Kelley) Hawkins," *National Genealogical Society Quarterly* 94 (2006): 5–22.

2. Dorothy West, "Winter on Martha's Vineyard," in *Where the Wild Grape Grows: Selected Writings, 1930–1950*, ed. Verner D. Mitchell and Cynthia Davis (Amherst: University of Massachusetts Press, 2005), 162.

3. For more on Helene Johnson, see *This Waiting for Love: Helene Johnson, Poet of the Harlem Renaissance*, ed. Verner D. Mitchell (Amherst: University of Massachusetts Press, 2000).

4. Hermione Lee, *Edith Wharton* (New York: Knopf, 2007), 214–215.

5. Joseph Willson, *Sketches of the Higher Classes of Colored Society in Philadelphia by a Southerner*, ed. Julie Winch (1841; reprint, University Park: Pennsylvania State University Press, 2000), 87.

6. Samuel Otter, "Frank Webb's Still Life: Rethinking Literature and Politics through the Garies and Their Friends," *American Literary History* 20.4 (Winter 2008): 732.

7. Candice Jenkins, *Private Lives, Proper Relations: Regulating Black Intimacy* (Minneapolis: University of Minnesota Press, 2007), 13.

8. West, "The Legend of Oak Bluffs," in *Where the Wild Grape Grows*, 34.

9. Ibid.

10. The 2005 film, however, was set and filmed in the South.

11. W.E.B. Du Bois, "Hopkinsville, Chicago and Idlewild," *Crisis* 22.4 (August 1921): 158–160.

12. Robert Stepto, *Blue as the Lake: A Personal Geography* (Boston: Beacon, 1998).

13. "Auction for Johnson Villa: Lake Geneva Millionaires Get a Chance to Outbid Johnson," *Chicago Daily Tribune*, 27 December 1912, 2.

14. Robert C. Hayden, *African Americans on Martha's Vineyard: A History of People, Places, and Events*, 2d ed. (Boston: Select Publications, 2005), xiii.

15. Stephen Carter, *The Emperor of Ocean Park* (New York: Knopf, 2002), 1.

16. The Pease study includes an analysis of several black communities in Canada, the efforts of the American Colonization Society to resettle blacks in Liberia, and Port Royal, a settlement on the South Carolina Sea Islands. William H. Pease and Jane H. Pease, *Black Utopia: Negro Communal Experiments in America* (Madison: State Historical Society of Wisconsin, 1963), 18.

17. Michel Foucault, "Of Other Spaces," *Diacritics* 16.1 (Spring 1986): 24, 27.

18. Audre Lorde, *Zami, a New Spelling of My Name: A Biomythography* (New York: Persephone Press, 1982).

19. Elisabeth Petry, *At Home Inside: A Daughter's Tribute to Ann Petry* (Jackson: University of Mississippi, 2009), 51, 53.

20. Kevin Gaines, *Uplifting the Race: Black Leadership, Politics, and Culture in the Twentieth Century* (Chapel Hill: University of North Carolina Press, 1996), 14.

21. Flannery O'Connor, "Revelation," in *The Complete Stories* (New York: Farrar Straus Giroux, 1971).

22. Shirley Elizabeth Thompson, *Exiles at Home: The Struggle to Become American in Creole New Orleans* (Cambridge, Mass.: Harvard University Press, 2009), 117.

23. Plaçage was a system of concubinage that placed young women of color, known as placeés, with white protectors who in exchange for sexual favors supplied housing, a stipend, and education for any offspring.

24. Guillory cited in Ariela Gross, "Litigating Whiteness: Trials of Racial Determination in the Nineteenth-Century South," *Yale Law Journal* 108.1 (October 1998): 109–188, 112.

25. Dorothy West, "Cottager's Corner," *Vineyard Gazette*, 22 August 1969, 2-A.

26. West, "Cottager's Corner," 9 August 1968.

27. Gross, "Litigating Whiteness," 65.

28. Thompson, *Exiles at Home*, 139, 140.

29. Ibid., 168.

30. Dorothy West, *The Wedding* (New York: Doubleday, 1995), 2.

31. Christopher Stoddard, *A Centennial History of Cottage City: 1880–1980* (Oak Bluffs, Mass.: Oak Bluffs Historical Commission, 1980), 48.

32. Thompson, *Exiles at Home*, 117.

33. Ibid., 78.

34. Dorothy West, Interviews with Linsey Lee, Oral History Division, Martha's Vineyard Museum, 21 January 1982, 13

35. Dorothy West to Rachel West, in *Where the Wild Grape Grows*, 191.

36. West, Interview with Linsey Lee, 21 January 1982.

37. West, *The Wedding*, 74.

CHAPTER 1. A "LEGEND OF OAK BLUFFS"

1. Candice Jenkins, "Pure Black: Class, Color, and Intraracial Politics in Toni Morrison's *Paradise*," *Modern Fiction Studies* 52.2 (2006): 270–296.

2. Ibid., 272.

3. Toni Morrison, *Paradise* (New York: Plume, 1997), 8.

4. Dorothy West to Linsey Lee, Interviews with Dorothy West, Oral History Division, Martha's Vineyard Museum, 21 January 1982, 19–20.

5. Ibid., 18.

6. Jill Nelson, *Finding Martha's Vineyard: African Americans at Home on an Island* (New York: Doubleday, 2005), 8.

7. Ibid., 18.

8. Edgartown's restrictive covenants led blacks to settle in Oak Bluffs.

9. Elaine Weintraub, *Lighting the Trail: The African American Heritage of Martha's Vineyard* (Elaine Weintraub, 2005) 78.

10. From its founding as a Methodist camp meeting site, Cottage City, as it was called until 1907 when the name changed to Oak Bluffs, combined the secular and sacred as construction expanded outside the campgrounds and more visitors came who did not worship at the Iron Tabernacle in Wesleyan Grove.

11. Kevin Gaines, *Uplifting the Race: Black Leadership, Politics and Culture in the Twentieth Century* (Chapel Hill: University of North Carolina Press, 1996), 75.

12. Russ Rymer describes an eccentric black woman who is the keeper of the beach's cultural memory as "a radical black feminist ecological activist" in *American Beach: A Saga of Race, Wealth, and Memory* (New York: HarperCollins, 1998). See also Marsha Dean Phelts, *An American Beach for African Americans* (Gainesville: University Press of Florida, 1997).

13. Jeff Wiltse, *Contested Waters: A Social History of Swimming Pools in America* (Chapel Hill: University of North Carolina Press, 2007), 2.

14. Ibid., 123, 3.

15. Ibid., 212.

16. Mixed-gender pools demanded racial segregation because whites feared that the more muscular physiques of black men would undo notions of racial superiority. Wiltse writes that "racial segregation at municipal pools also likely resulted from white concerns that black men displaying their bodies at highly visible public spaces would undermine white supremacy" (134).

17. Sutton Griggs's utopian novel, *Imperium e Imperio* (1899) takes a strong stance against amalgamation. Gaines, *Uplifting the Race*, 126.

18. Gaines, *Uplifting the Race*, 5.

19. Dorothy West, Interview with Linsey Lee, 25 February 1983, 21.

20. Dorothy West, "Fond Memories of a Black Childhood," in *The Richer, The Poorer: Stories, Sketches and Reminiscences* (New York: Doubleday, 1995), 137.

21. Wiltse, *Contested Waters*, 140, 210.

22. Dorothy West, "Where the Wild Grape Grows," in *Where the Wild Grape Grows: Selected Writings, 1930–1950*, ed. Verner Mitchell and Cynthia Davis (Amherst: University of Massachusetts Press, 2005), 136–137.

23. West, *The Living Is Easy* (1948; reprint, New York: Feminist Press, 1982), 40.

24. West, "Fond Memories of a Black Childhood," in *The Richer, The Poorer*, 174.

25. Ibid, 174.

26. Joyce Rickson, Interview with the author, Vineyard Haven, Massachusetts, July 2008.

27. Gaines, *Uplifting the Race*, 89.

28. West, "Where the Wild Grape Grows," in *Where the Wild Grape Grows*, 137

29. Psyche Williams-Forson, *Building Houses Out of Chicken Legs: Black Women, Food, and Power* (Chapel Hill: University of North Carolina Press, 2006). Williams-Forson draws

on oral histories, cookbooks, personal memories, and literature to examine the symbolic value of chicken beyond its stereotypical connotations.

30. Dorothy West, Interview with Linsey Lee, 21 January 1982.

31. Williams-Forson, *Building Houses Out of Chicken Legs*, 108.

32. West, *The Living Is Easy*, 167.

33. Williams-Forson, *Building Houses Out of Chicken Legs*, 116.

34. Adelaide Cromwell, "The History of Oak Bluffs as a Popular Resort for Blacks," *Dukes County Intelligencer, Special Edition* (October 1997): 61.

35. Ibid., 62.

36. Robert Hayden, *African Americans on Martha's Vineyard and Nantucket: A History of People, Places, and Events* (Boston: Select Publications, 1999), 11–12.

37. Jill Nelson, *Finding Martha's Vineyard: African Americans at Home on an Island* (New York: Doubleday, 2005), 175.

38. West, "Fond Memories of a Black Childhood," in *The Richer, The Poorer*, 174.

39. Dona Brown, *Inventing New England: Regional Tourism in the Nineteenth Century* (Washington, D.C.: Smithsonian Institution Press, 1995), 84.

40. West, "Cottager's Corner," 14 August 1970.

41. Morrison, *Paradise*, 138.

42. Lois Mailou Jones, Interview with Linsey Lee, 17 September 1983.

43. Barbara Townes, Interview with Linsey Lee, 13 August 1983.

44. Colson Whitehead, *Sag Harbor* (New York: Doubleday, 2009), 77.

45. Ibid., 78.

46. Ibid.

47. George Levesque, *Black Boston: African American Life and Culture in Urban America, 1750–1860* (New York: Garland, 1994), 8.

48. Ibid., 474.

49. The *Vineyard Gazette* extensively covered the investigation of the 1969 drowning of a young woman riding in the car with Senator Edward Kennedy when he drove off a bridge on Chappaquiddick Island.

50. Stanley Nelson, *A Place of Our Own*, prod. and dir. Stanley Nelson, 60 minutes, A Firelight Media Production for Independent Lens on PBS, 2004, DVD.

51. West, "The Legend of Oak Bluffs," in *The Richer, the Poorer*, 240–241.

52. Tritobia Benjamin and Lois Mailou Jones, *The Life and Art of Lois Mailou Jones* (San Francisco, Calif.: Pomegranate Art Books 1994), 5. Significantly, 25 Pacific Avenue is not a Highlands address; the house can be found in the "Gold Coast" adjacent to Inkwell Beach.

53. Carter, *The Emperor of Ocean Park* (New York: Knopf, 2002), 400.

54. Hayden, *African Americans*, 2.

55. Nelson, *Finding Martha's Vineyard*, 7.

CHAPTER 2. CHILDHOOD SKETCHES

1. During West's childhood and adolescence the West family lived in a variety of Boston residences, including 10 Cedar Street and 23 Worthington Street; the Brookline address is the one West primarily references as her childhood home.

2. Sidonie Smith, "Construing Truths in Lying Mouths: Truthtelling in Women's Auto-biography," *Studies in the Literary Imagination* 23.2 (Autumn 1990): 163.

3. West, *The Living Is Easy* (1948; reprint, New York: Feminist Press, 1982), 302.

4. The Black Women's Oral History Project of Radcliffe College (1970–1981) interviewed seventy-two black women born from the 1870s through the 1920s to make available "a body of resource material on the lives and contributions of black women in the twentieth century, especially the years prior to the Civil Rights Movement." This valuable resource of oral "life stories" covers much the same period of time as this study.

5. ·Dorothy West to Linsey Lee, Interviews with Dorothy West, Oral History Division, Martha's Vineyard Museum, Martha's Vineyard Historical Society, 21 January 1982.

6. West, "Rachel," in *The Richer, The Poorer: Stories, Sketches and Reminiscences* (New York: Doubleday, 1995), 168.

7. West, Interview with Linsey Lee, 5 May 1994, 16.

8. Smith, "Construing Truths," 161–162.

9. Michelle Cliff, *Claiming an Identity They Taught Me to Despise* (Watertown, Mass.: Persephone, 1980), 11.

10. McGrath, "Afterword," *This Waiting for Love: Helene Johnson, Poet of the Harlem Renaissance*, ed. Verner D. Mitchell (Amherst: University of Massachusetts Press, 2000), 123.

11. Ibid.

12. Du Bois, *The Souls of Black Folk* (London: A. Constable, 1905), 1.

13. West, "Rachel," 172, 171.

14. Elizabeth Fox-Genovese, "Myth and History: Discourse of Origins in Zora Neale Hurston and Maya Angelou Author(s)," *Black American Literature Forum* 24.2 (Summer 1990): 221–235

15. For an in-depth discussion of signification in African American discourse, see Henry Louis Gates Jr., *The Signifying Monkey: A Theory of African American Literary Criticism* (New York: Oxford, 1988).

16. James Olney, "Autobiography and the Cultural Moment: A Thematic, Historical and Bibliographic Introduction," in *Autobiography: Essays Theoretical and Critical*, ed. James Olney (Princeton, N.J.: Princeton University Press, 1980), 15.

17. Alice Deck, "Autoethnography, Zora Neale Hurston, Noni Jabavu, and Cross-Disciplinary Discourse," *Black Literature Forum* 24.2 (Summer 1990): 238.

18. Ibid., 243.

19. Ibid., 238.

20. Biddy Martin, "Lesbian Identity and Autobiographical Difference(s)," in *Life/Lines: Theorizing Women's Autobiography*, ed. Bella Brodzi and Celeste Schenck (Ithaca, N.Y.: Cornell University Press, 1988), 77.

21. Rickson, Interview with the author, July 2008, Martha's Vineyard, Mass.

22. Dalsgård, "Alive and Well and Living on the Island of Martha's Vineyard: An Interview with Dorothy West," *The Langston Hughes Review* 12.2 (Fall 1993): 40.

23. Toni Morrison, "The Site of Memory," in *Inventing the Truth*, ed. William Zinsser (New York: Houghton Mifflin, 1995), 113.

24. Partricia Marks, *Bicycles, Bangs, and Bloomers: The New Woman in the Popular Press* (Lexington: University Press of Kentucky, 1990), 174.

25. The preponderance of ambiguously raced and/or mixed-race heroines that appeared in early African American literature served a variety of functions for writers and readers and in popular culture. Some functioned as surrogates to attain empathy with a reading audience that was predominately white and female; others troubled the notion of a fixed racial identity through their transgressions back and forth across the color line.

26. Rickson, Interview with the author.

27. West frequently denies this in her interviews. Interview with Linsey Lee, 23 June 1982.

28. West, "The Purse," in *The Richer, The Poorer*, 18.

29. Joyce Jackson Rickson is both a distant cousin by marriage and an adopted cousin who became a member of West's extended family. She and her brother often spent their summers on the Vineyard at the home of Rachel West.

30. Cromwell, Interview with the author, July 1998, Vineyard Haven, Martha's Vineyard, Mass.

31. The family tree assembled by Mitchell and Davis lists nineteen children of Benjamin Benson and Helen Pease Benson: Robert, William, David, Ella, Carrie, Rachel, Mayme, Isabella, Minnie, Benjamin, Jessie, Scotter, Eugene, Scipio, Emma, Belton, Sarah, Malcolm, and Ruth. This list may not include the children whom "Mama" Benson lost that West mentions in her interviews, hence the discrepancy among determining an accurate number of children. See *Where the Wild Grape Grows*, Appendix II.

32. West, "The Purse," 184.

33. Ibid., 185.

34. West, Interview with Linsey Lee, 25 February 1983, 17.

35. West, "The Purse," 192–193.

36. Ibid.

37. West, Interview with Linsey Lee, 25 February 1983, 22.

38. In Henry Louis Gates Jr.'s series "African American Lives" he traced the DNA of several famous African Americans, like actor Don Cheadle, who believed they had Native American ancestry. In many cases, the DNA evidence contradicted the oral family histories of black and Indian intermingling. Gates found in many cases that the ancestry was European American, rather than Native American. For the relevant episode, see http://www.pbs.org/wnet/aalives/profiles/cheadle.htm.

39. West, Interview with Linsey Lee, 5 May 1994, 4.

40. West, Interview with Linsey Lee, 23 June 1928, 5.

41. Dalsgård, "Alive and Well," 40.

42. West, "At the Swan Boats," in *Where the Wild Grape Grows*, 60, 62.

43. West, "The Gift," in *The Richer, The Poorer*, 177.

44. Ibid., 182.

45. West, Interview with Linsey Lee, 23 June 1982, 5.

46. West, Interview with Linsey Lee, 23 January 1982, 5.

47. West, Interview with Linsey Lee, 21 January 1982.

48. West, Interview with Linsey Lee, 23 June 1982, 6.

49. Ibid.

50. Genii Guinier, "Interview with Dorothy West," Black Women's Oral History Project Interviews, Harvard University, 39.

51. "and the little boy, Melvin, who had blond hair . . ." West, Interview with Linsey Lee, 25 February 1983, 27.

52. Rickson, Interview with the author.

53. West, Interview with Linsey Lee, 25 February 1983, 22.

54. West, *The Living Is Easy*, 172, 39, 229, 74, 44.

55. West, Interview with Linsey Lee, 7 July 1982, 13.

56. Genii Guiner, "Interview with Dorothy West," 63.

57. Ibid., 40.

58. For a thorough, fictional meditation on how "blue eyes" represent the apex of white beauty and appeal and how the desire for them leads to a complete destruction of the vulnerable psyches of African American girls, see Toni Morrison's novel *The Bluest Eye* (New York: Holt, Rinehart, & Winston, 1970).

59. West, "Fond Memories of a Black Childhood," 171.

60. McGrath, "Afterword," 124.

61. Ibid., 124.

62. Rickson's maiden name was Jackson.

63. Rickson, Interview with the author, July 2008, Martha's Vineyard.

64. Mitchell and Davis, "Introduction," *Where The Wild Grape Grows*, xiv.

65. Gordon later became an ardent Marxist; he traveled to Russia were he contributed to the *Moscow Daily News*, and when he returned to the states he freelanced for the *Daily Worker*. Gordon was a pioneering journalist, but his membership in the communist party worked to suppress his influence and work on behalf of Afro-America.

66. Eugene Gordon, "Negro Society," *Scribner's Magazine* 88 (August 1930): 134–142.

67. Ibid., 135.

68. Adelaide Cromwell, *The Other Brahmins: Boston's Black Upper Class 1750–1950* (Fayetteville: University of Arkansas Press, 1994), 206.

69. J. Walter Stevens, *Chip on My Shoulder* (Cambridge, Mass.: Meador Publishing Company, 1946), 80.

70. Miss Elliot may have been based on Georgina Brown, who held a dancing school and organized piano recitals for African American children. Cromwell, *The Other Brahmins*, 161.

71. West, Interview with Linsey Lee, 21 January 1982, 18.

72. McGrath, "Afterword."

73. Rickson, Interview with the author, July 2008, Martha's Vineyard.

74. West, Interview with Linsey Lee, 23 June 1982, 21. Cromwell is the author of many books, including sociological studies and family histories; she was also one of West's oldest friends. Cromwell first came to the island around 1944 as a young bride; her husband, like so many young students, worked on the ferries and became introduced to the Highlands community in Oak Bluffs. She spent time with West and through her became introduced to Barbara Townes and Lois Mailou Jones.

CHAPTER 3.   DOROTHY WEST'S "TYPEWRITER"

1. West, "Introduction," *The Richer, The Poorer: Stories, Sketches, and Reminiscences* (New York: Doubleday, 1995), 2.

2. Ibid.

3. Alain Locke, *The New Negro: An Interpretation* (New York: Boni and Liveright, 1925), 14.

4. Although West was her parents' only child, her huge extended family included her mother's siblings and step-siblings. The aunt who buys the magazine is most likely Minnie—one of West's "other-mothers."

5. In some interviews West remembers the magazine title correctly as *Opportunity*. She shared second prize with Zora Neale Hurston's "Muttsy," while first prize went to Arthur Huff Fauset for "Symphonesque." Other honorees included Claude McKay, Georgia Douglas Johnson, Anita Scott Coleman, and Wallace Thurman.

6. Locke, *The New Negro*, 14.

7. West, *The Richer, The Poorer*, 2. West's first publications appeared in the *Boston Post*. It's likely that her early stories, though published in New York–based magazines, were written when she was still living in Boston.

8. Verner D. Mitchell and Cynthia Davis, "Introduction: Dorothy West and Her Circle," in *Where the Wild Grape Grows: Selected Writings, 1930–1950,* ed. Verner D. Mitchell and Cynthia Davis (Amherst: University of Massachusetts Press, 2005), 18.

9. Laurie Champion, "Social Class Distinctions in Dorothy West's *The Richer, the Poorer,*" *The Langston Hughes Review* 161.2 (Fall 1999/Spring 2001): 48.

10. West, "The Typewriter," *The Richer, The Poorer*, 9.

11. Ibid., 16, 15, 13, 9, 14.

12. The politics of respectability refers to a strategy to counter negative stereotypes and perceptions of African Americans. Espousing respectability through exceptional behavior, manners, and morality allowed African Americans (especially women) to redefine their self-image outside the racist discourse of American culture. The flipside of such a strategy is that it often resulted in intraracial policing of gender and sex roles that consequently reaffirmed rigid categories of identity. On the ideology of uplift Kevin J. Gaines writes: "Consequently, through uplift ideology, elite blacks also devised a *moral economy* of class privilege, distinction, and even domination *within the race*, often drawing on the patriarchal gender conventions as a sign of elite status and "race progress." *Uplifting the Race: Black Leadership, Politics and Culture in the Twentieth Century* (Chapel Hill: University of North Carolina Press, 1996), 17.

13. West, "An Unimportant Man," *The Richer, The Poorer*, 137.

14. Ibid., 138, 139.

15. Verner D. Mitchell, ed., *This Waiting for Love: Helene Johnson, Poet of the Harlem Renaissance* (Amherst: University of Massachusetts Press, 2000), 5.

16. Jean Toomer, *Cane* (New York: Boni and Liveright, 1923), 27.

17. West, "An Unimportant Man," *The Richer, The Poorer*, 142.

18. Most likely a reference to Clarence Darrow: ACLU member and lawyer in the infamous "Scopes" trial. Ibid., 155.

19. Ibid., 145, 139.

20. Candice M. Jenkins, *Private Lives, Proper Relations [Regulating Black Intimacy]* (Minneapolis: University of Minnesota Press, 2007), 43.

21. West, "An Unimportant Man," *The Richer, The Poorer*, 148.

22. Ibid., 153–154, 160.

23. "Hannah Byde," in *Where the Wild Grape Grows*, 81, 80.

24. Ironically, as Hortense Spillers notes, "the unsexed black female and the supersexed black female embody the very same vice, cast the very same shadow, inasmuch as both are an exaggeration—at either pole—of the uses to which sex might be put." Spillers, "Interstices: A Small Drama of Words," *Pleasure and Danger: Exploring Female Sexuality*, ed. Carol Vance (London: Routledge, 1984), 85.

25. Ibid., 81, 82.

26. Marita Bonner, "On Being Young—A Woman—and Colored," in *Double Take: A Revisionist Harlem Renaissance Anthology*, ed. Venetria K. Patton and Maureen Honey (New Brunswick, N.J.: Rutgers University Press, 2001), 110.

27. West, "Hannah Byde," in *Where the Wild Grape Grows*, 79.

28. Ibid., 79, 81, 80.

29. Dorothy West to Linsey Lee, Interviews with Dorothy West, Oral History Division, Martha's Vineyard Museum, July 1982, 7.

30. Xiomara Santamarina, "Reclassifying Group Identity: Nineteenth Century African American Chroniclers of the Higher Classes" (Lecture, University of Wisconsin–Madison, 24 April 2008).

31. Tricia Rose, *Longing to Tell: Black Women Talk about Sexuality and Intimacy* (New York: Farrar Straus Giroux, 2004), 10.

32. Ibid.

33. Despite flirtations with men like Claude McKay and Langston Hughes, West's longest intimate relationship appears to have been with her coeditor of the *Challenge*, writer Marian Minus. West, *Where the Wild Grape Grows*, 18.

34. Roderick Ferguson argues that a "queer of color" analysis challenges heteronormative discourse by examining "African American culture as a site of contradiction." *Aberrations in Black: Towards a Queer of Color Critique* (Minneapolis: University of Minnesota Press, 2003), 26.

35. Amritjit Singh, ed., *The Collected Writings of Wallace Thurman: A Harlem Renaissance Reader* (New Brunswick, N.J.: Rutgers University Press, 2004), 119.

36. Wallace Thurman, *Infants of the Spring* (Boston: Northeastern University Press, 1992), 231.

37. West, "Elephant's Dance: A Memoir of Wallace Thurman," in *Where the Wild Grape Grows*, 170–171.

38. Wallace Thurman, Letter to Dorothy West, August 1929, in *Collected Writings*, 172.

39. West, "Elephant's Dance," 169.

40. Thurman, "The Blacker the Berry," in *Collected Writings*, 449.

41. West, Interview with Linsey Lee, 5 May 1994, 16.

42. Ibid.

43. Zora Neale Hurston, Letter to Dorothy West, 5 November 1928, *Zora Neale Hurston: A Life in Letters*, ed. Carla Kaplan (New York: Doubleday, 2002), 130.

44. See Mitchell and Davis, "Introduction," *Where the Wild Grape Grows*; and Sharon Jones, *Rereading the Harlem Renaissance: Race, Class, and Gender in the Fiction of Jessie Fauset, Zora Neale Hurston, and Dorothy West* (London: Greenwood, 2002).

45. West, *The Living Is Easy*, 14.

46. Ibid., 12.

47. Hurston, "Drenched in Light," in *The Portable Harlem Renaissance Reader*, ed. David Levering Lewis (New York: Viking, 1994), 700.

48. Zora Neale Hurston, Letter to Charlotte Osgood Mason, 6 July 1932, in *Zora Neale Hurston*, 262–263.

49. Jayna Brown, *Babylon Girls: Black Women Performers and the Shaping of the Modern* (Durham, N.C.: Duke University Press, 2008), 146–147.

50. These two popular offshoots of the cakewalk have sexually provocative elements.

51. Zora Neale Hurston, *Color Struck*, in *Zora Neale Hurston: Collected Plays*, ed. Jean Lee Cole and Charles Mitchell (New Brunswick, N.J.: Rutgers University Press, 2008), 43.

52. Zora Neale Hurston, Letter to Dorothy West, 5 November 1928, in *Zora Neale Hurston*, 130.

CHAPTER 4.   TO RUSSIA WITH LOVE

1. Deborah E. McDowell, "Conversations with Dorothy West," in *Harlem Renaissance Reexamined: A Revised and Expanded Edition*, ed. Robert Russ and Victor Kramer (Troy, N.Y.: Whitson, 1997), 293.

2. Gilmore's history of the trip differs from the others in that she identifies Thompson's critical role as an organizer of the group and includes an examination of Lovett Fort-Whiteman, the first American-born black communist.

3. Kate Baldwin, *Beyond the Color Line and the Iron Curtain: Reading Encounters between Black and Red 1922–1963* (Durham, N.C.: Duke University Press, 2002), 108.

4. Other black women also visit Russia at various times in history. Mary Seacole describes her experience as a nurse during the Crimean war in *The Wonderful Adventures of Mrs. Seacole in Many Lands* (1857), and Audre Lorde shares her brief recollections from the African-Asian Writers Conferences in "Notes from a Trip to Russia" (1976). Thanks to Athan Bass for drawing to my attention the self-published Charlotte Bass's *Forty Years: Memoirs from the Pages of a Newspaper* (1960). Bass was editor of the *California Eagle* and a vice-presidential candidate for the Progressive Party in 1952.

5. Francine Hirsch, *Empire of Nations: Ethnographic Knowledge and the Making of the Soviet Union* (Ithaca, N.Y.: Cornell University Press, 2005), 273.

6. Ironically, at the same time that they "took a firm stand against biological determinism" they also oppressed people with "'wrong' ethnic origins." Ibid., 16.

7. Andrea Lee, *Russian Journal* (New York: Random House, 2006), 4.

8. Joy Gleason Carew, *Blacks, Reds and Russians: Sojourners in Search of the Soviet Promise* (New Brunswick, N.J.: Rutgers University Press, 2008), 1.

9. Christopher Miller's articulation of "Africanist" as a discourse similar to but also distinct from Edward Said's concept of Orientalism and Toni Morrison's identification of the Africanist presence within American literature informs my understanding of the term "Africanist" as a set of mythic, stereotypical, or projected understandings of the black subject. Christopher Miller, *Blank Darkness: The Africanist Discourse in French* (Chicago: University of Chicago Press, 1985). Toni Morrison, *Playing in the Dark: Whiteness and the Literary Imagination* (Cambridge, Mass.: Harvard University Press, 1992).

10. Arnold Rampersad, *The Life of Langston Hughes*, Vol. 1: *1902–1941, I, Too, Sing America* (New York: Oxford University Press, 1986), 244.

11. Nancy Prince, *A Narrative of the Life and Travels* (1853; reprint, New York: Oxford University Press, 1968), 23.

12. Ibid., 29.

13. Cheryl Fish writes, "While sewing was considered an acceptable and 'genteel' profession for black women it was known to be among the worst-paying jobs, regardless of race." *Black and White Women's Travel Narratives: Antebellum Explorations* (Gainesville: University Presses of Florida, 2004), 4.

14. Prince, *A Narrative of the Life and Travels*, 27.

15. Ibid., 28

16. Jennifer Steadman, *Traveling Economies: American Women's Travel Writing* (Columbus: Ohio State University Press, 2007), 5.

17. Despite her success in business, Prince always emphasized her domestic concerns—though she peculiarly omits any discussion of her married life. We know that she opens an orphanage: "My time was taken up in domestic affairs; I took two children to board, the third week after commencing housekeeping and increasing their numbers." Prince, *A Narrative of the Life and Travels*, 38–39.

18. Ibid., 38.

19. Hughes, quoted in Baldwin, *Beyond the Color Line and the Iron Curtain*, 95.

20. Claire Nee Nelson, "Louise Thompson Patterson and the Southern Roots of the Popular Front," in *Women Shaping the South: Creating and Confronting Changes*, ed. Angela Boswell and Judith N. McArthur (Columbia: University of Missouri Press, 2006), 216.

21. Ibid.

22. "Southern Terror," *Crisis* 41.11 (November 1934): 327–338.

23. Katrine Dalsgård, "Alive and Well and Living on the Island of Martha's Vineyard: An Interview with Dorothy West," *The Langston Hughes Review* 12.2 (Fall 1993): 39.

24. Zora Neale Hurston, Letter to Charlotte Osgood Mason, 6 July 1932, *Zora Neale Hurston: A Life in Letters*, ed. Carla Kaplan (New York: Doubleday, 2002), 262–263.

25. Hughes, *The Big Sea* (New York: Knopf, 1940), 85.

26. Glenda Gilmore, *Defying Dixie: The Radical Roots of Civil Rights (1919–1950)* (New York: Norton, 2008), 135.

27. Dalsgård, "Alive and Well," 35.

28. Ibid., 35.

29. Louise Thompson Patterson, "Louise Thompson Patterson Memoirs: Trip to Russia—1932," draft 1, 18. Box 20, October–November 1994, Special Collections and Archives, Robert W. Woodruff Library, Emory University.

30. Hughes, *The Big Sea*, 93.

31. Ibid., 95.

32. Ibid.

33. Jack El-Hai, "Black and White and Red," *American Heritage* 42.3 (1991): 86.

34. Dalsgård, "Alive and Well," 35.

35. Ibid., 35.

36. Gilmore, *Defying Dixie*, 146–147.

37. Patterson, "Trip to Russia," draft 2, 9.

38. Gilmore, *Defying Dixie*, 135. In the documentary *Louise Thompson Patterson: In Her Own Words* (dir. Louise Massiah. 18 minutes. 2002. Third World Newsreel), Patterson mentions Thurman in the briefest of side notes.

39. West continued to hold a grudge against Thompson for information she had provided to Nathaniel Huggins, which he included one of the first studies of the Harlem Renaissance. Dorothy West to Genii Guinier, Interview, Black Women's Oral History Project, Harvard University, 27.

40. *As I Remember It: Portrait of Dorothy West*. Directed by Salem Mekuria. 1991. DVD. 56 minutes. Distributed by Women Make Movies.

41. West, "An Adventure in Moscow," *The Richer, The Poorer*, 207.

42. McDowell, "Conversations with West," 287.

43. West, "Voices," *Challenge* 1.2 (September 1934): 31.

44. West, writing under "Mary Christopher," "Room in Red Square," *Challenge* 1 (March 1934): 10.

45. I find that Julia Mickenberg's concept of revolutionary tourism aptly describes certain aspects of West's sojourn in Russia. "In Love with Russia: U.S. Women, Sexual Revolution, and Revolutionary Tourism, 1905–1945," Jay C. and Ruth Hall Lecture, University of Wisconsin–Madison, January 2010.

46. West, "Room in Red Square," 10.

47. Ibid., 19.

48. Helene Johnson, Letter to Dorothy West, 8 December 1932, *This Waiting for Love: Helene Johnson: Poet of the Harlem Renaissance*, ed. Verner D. Mitchell (Amherst: University of Massachusetts Press, 2000), 115.

49. Glimore, *Defying Dixie*, 137.

50. West, "Room in Red Square," 11.

51. Lee, *Russian Journal*, 6.

52. Dalsgård, "Alive and Well," 34.

53. West, "Room in Red Square," 14.

54. Ibid., 15.

55. Dorothy West, Letter to Rachel West, 29 June 1932, in *Where the Wild Grape Grows: Selected Writings, 1930–1950*, ed. Verner D. Mitchell and Cynthia Davis (Amherst: University of Massachusetts Press, 2005), 186.

56. Steadman, *Traveling Economies*, 5.

57. Langston Hughes, *I Wonder as I Wander* (New York: Hill and Wang, 1956), 73.

58. West, Letter to Rachel West, 29 June 1932, *Where the Wild Grape Grows*, 186.

59. Lewis fell in love with a German diplomat and joined him in Berlin after the film's postponement. In 1933, she writes her friend Dorothy West to join her in Germany where "Life was Divine," apparently unaware of Hitler's rise to power. Lewis later married Henry Moon. Gilmore, *Defying Dixie*, 158.

60. Ibid., 103.

61. Hughes credits Mildred's influence with Count Oumansky, the Soviet head of foreign press relations for the Kremlin, for enabling his tour to "the Urals and travel almost to the Chinese Border." Hughes, *I Wonder as I Wander*, 103.

62. Dorothy West, Letter to Langston Hughes, 27 October 1932, in *Where the Wild Grape Grows*, 189.

63. Mildred apparently had an affair with Constantine Oumansky. See Gilmore, *Defying Dixie*, 492 n184; also Hughes, *I Wonder as I Wander*, 104.

64. West, "Russian Correspondence," *Challenge* 1.2 (September 1934): 15.

65. Hughes, *I Wonder as I Wander*, 103.

66. West, "Russian Correspondence," 15.

67. Ibid., 20.

68. Patterson, "Trip to Russia," draft 1, 53.

69. Ibid., 59.

70. West, "Russian Correspondence," 15.

71. West, Letter to Rachel West, 6 March 1933, in *Where the Wild Grape Grows*, 192.

72. Rampersad, *The Life of Langston Hughes*, 265, 288.

73. West, Letter to Langston Hughes, 26 May 1933, in *Where the Wild Grape Grows*, 194.

74. West, Letter to Rachel West, 6 March 1933, in *Where the Wild Grape Grows*, 192.

75. West, Letter to Langston Hughes, 26 May 1933, in *Where the Wild Grape Grows*, 195.

76. West, Letter to Langston Hughes, 25 May 1933, in *Where the Wild Grape Grows*, 194.

77. Hughes, *I Wonder as I Wander*, 93.

78. West, "An Adventure in Moscow," in *The Richer, the Poorer*, 207.

79. Hughes, *I Wonder as I Wander*, 88.

80. Gilmore, *Defying Dixie*, 142. Discord resulting after the cancellation of the film drove permanent wedges between Thompson and Moon, Poston and Lewis.

81. West, Letter to Rachel West, 6 March 1933, in *Where The Wild Grape Grows*, 191.

82. Lee, *Russian Journal*, 166.

83. Ibid., 167.

84. Claude McKay, "Soviet Russia and the Negro," quoted in Baldwin, *Beyond the Color Line*, 280.

85. Patterson, "Trip to Russia," October/November 1994, draft 1, 40.

86. Ibid., 18.

87. Ilya Ilf and Evgeny Petrov, *Ilf and Petrov's American Road Trip: The 1935 Travelogue of two Soviet Writers*, ed. Erika Wolf; with texts by Aleksandr Rodchenko and Aleksandra Ilf; trans. Anne O. Fisher (New York: Cabinet Books, 2007), 127.

88. Lee, *Russian Journal*, 147.

89. Ibid., 15.

90. Ibid., 8.

91. Ibid., xi

92. Ibid., xii.

93. Ibid., 7, 3, 32.

94. Ibid., 33.

95. Baldwin argues that Hughes's excised essay "offers three important challenges to existing scholarship in these areas: it disputes not only the masculine but the hetero-normative bias of the black veil as engaged by critical discourse on the topic; it offers a point of entry to rethink the exclusively female focus of postcolonial discussions of the veil; and it confronts the othering of the discourse of the Muslim veil as external

to the disciplining of non-Muslim U.S. bodies in 1930s." Baldwin, *Beyond the Color Line and the Iron Curtain*, 108.

96. Ibid., 122.

97. Lee, *Russian Journal*, x.

98. Hirsch defines "diaspora nationalities" as "peoples who comprised national minorities in the Soviet Union but had homelands outside of Soviet borders." Hirsch, *Empire of Nations*, 275.

99. Prince, *A Narrative of the Life and Travels*,

100. West, Letter to Rachel West, July 1932, in *Where the Wild Grape Grows*, 188.

101. Hughes, *I Wonder as I Wander*, 83.

102. Lee, *Russian Journal*, 40.

103. West, Letter to Langston Hughes, 2 February 1934, in *Where the Wild Grape Grows*, 201.

104. West, Letter to Langston Hughes, n.d., in *Where the Wild Grape Grows*, 203.

CHAPTER 5. NEW CHALLENGES

1. West often changes the amount and/or currency of money she received. The important point is that the sum was substantially larger than what others in her group received as severance pay. The money helped her bankroll the journal.

2. Dorothy West, Letter to James Weldon Johnson, 23 October 1933, in *Where the Wild Grape Grows: Selected Writings, 1930–1950*, ed. Verner D. Mitchell and Cynthia Davis (Amherst: University of Massachusetts Press, 2005), 198–199.

3. Edward Bishop, "Re:Covering Modernism—Format and Function in the Little Magazines," in *Modernist Writers and the Marketplace*, ed. Ian Willison, Warick Gould, and Warren Chernaic (New York: St. Martin's, 1996), 287.

4. Anne Carroll, *Word, Image, and the New Negro* (Bloomington: Indiana University Press, 2005), 211.

5. Ibid., 196.

6. Helene Johnson, "A Southern Road," *Fire!!* (1926; Westport, Conn.: Negro Universities Press, 1970), 17.

7. Langston Hughes, Letter to Dorothy West, 22 February 1934, in *Where the Wild Grape Grows*, 201.

8. Dorothy West, "Dear Reader," *Challenge* (March 1934): 39.

9. James Weldon Johnson, "Foreword," *Challenge* (March 1934): 2

10. West, Letter to James Weldon Johnson, 23 October 1933, in *Where the Wild Grape Grows*, 198.

11. Michelle Gordon, "Black Literature of Revolutionary Protest from Chicago's South Side: A Local Literary History, 1931–1959" (Ph.D. diss., University of Wisconsin–Madison, 2008), 71.

12. Arna Bontemps, as quoted in West, "Dear Reader," *Challenge* (March 1934): 39.

13. West, "Dear Reader," *Challenge* (January 1936): 38.

14. Dorothy West, "Voices," *Challenge* 1.2 (September 1934): 39.

15. Dorothy West, Letter to Langston Hughes, 2 February 1934, in *Where the Wild Grape Grows*, 200.

16. Brown maintains that Hopkins defined romance as "a state of existence that persisted in the face of oppression." Her journalism linked history and her concept of romance together to create a "powerful race romance." Lois Brown, *Pauline Elizabeth Hopkins: Black Daughter of the Revolution* (Chapel Hill: University of North Carolina Press, 2008), 291–292, 456.

17. Hopkins's pseudonyms include her mother's maiden name, Sarah A. Allen, and J. Shirley Shadrach.

18. Hannah Wallinger, *Pauline E. Hopkins: A Literary Biography* (Athens: University of Georgia Press, 2005), 59. The politics behind Hopkins's departure are too complex to relate in detail here, but they are thoroughly analyzed by Lois Brown and Hannah Wallinger in their respective biographies.

19. Wallinger, *Pauline E. Hopkins*, 83.

20. Katrine Dalsgård, "Alive and Well and Living on the Island of Martha's Vineyard: An Interview with Dorothy West," *The Langston Hughes Review* 12.2 (Fall 1993): 39.

21. West, "Cook," *Challenge* (March 1934): 28.

22. Dorothy West, "Dear Reader," *Challenge* (April 1937): 41.

23. Ibid.

24. Michel Fabre, *The Unfinished Quest of Richard Wright* (New York: Morrow, 1973), 142.

25. Margaret Walker, *Richard Wright, Daemonic Genius: A Portrait of the Man, a Critical Look at His Work* (New York: Warner, 1988), 91.

26. "New Challenge Now On Stands," *Amsterdam News*, 13 November 1937, 9.

27. West, "Dear Reader," *Challenge* (April 1937): 41.

28. Gordon, "Black Literature of Revolutionary Protest," 45.

29. Richard Wright, "Blueprint for Negro Writing," *New Challenge* (Fall 1937): 53.

30. Ibid., 60.

31. Ibid., 62.

32. West, "New Challenge," 4.

33. Zora Neale Hurston, Letter to Dorothy West, 24 March 1934, in *Zora Neale Hurston, A Life in Letters*, ed. Carla Kaplan (New York: Doubleday, 2002), 296.

34. Marian Minus, Review of *Their Eyes Were Watching God*, by Zora Neale Hurston, *New Challenge* (Fall 1937): 87.

35. Wright, "Blueprint," 62.

36. Wright, Review of *Their Eyes Were Watching God*, by Zora Neale Hurston [1937], in *Zora Neale Hurston: Critical Perspectives Past and Present*, ed. Henry Louis Gates Jr. (New York: Amistad, 1993).

37. William Maxwell, *New Negro, Old Left: African-American Writing and Communism between the Wars* (New York: Columbia University Press, 1999), 157.

38. Dalsgård, "Alive and Well," 38.

39. Deborah McDowell, "Conversations with Dorothy West," in *Harlem Renaissance Reexamined: A Revised and Expanded Edition,* ed. Robert Russ and Victor Kramer (Troy, N.Y.: Whitson, 1997), 292.

40. Marian Minus, Letter to Dorothy West, 21 October 1936, in *Where the Wild Grape Grows*, 208–209.

41. Marian Minus, "Present Trends of Negro Literature," *Challenge* (April 1937): 9.

42. Dorothy West, "Pluto" [1938], in *The Last Leaf of Harlem: Selected and Newly Discovered Fiction by the Author of The Wedding*, ed. Lionel Bascom (New York: St. Martin's, 2008), 91.

43. Dorothy West, Letter to Langston Hughes, 7 September 1934, in *Where The Wild Grape Grows*, 203.

44. West, "Temple of Grace," in *The Last Leaf of Harlem*, 108.

45. West, "Mammy," in *The Richer, The Poorer: Stories, Sketches and Reminiscences* (New York: Doubleday, 1995), 44–45.

46. Ibid., 45.

47. Ibid, 48.

48. Ibid, 52.

49. "West, "The Penny," in *The Richer, The Poorer*, 81.

50. Dalsgård, "Alive and Well," 43.

51. McDowell, "Conversations with Dorothy West," 296.

CHAPTER 6. *THE LIVING IS EASY*

1. In response to Katrine Dalsgård's query about Yale library's listing of West under Mildred Wirt, West replied, "I did use another [pseudonym]. But it was not Mildred Wirt. I used my father." "Alive and Well and Living on the Island of Martha's Vineyard: An Interview with Dorothy West," *The Langston Hughes Review* 12.2 (Fall 1993): 43. West admitted to using Jane Isaac, after her father Isaac West. Her fictional and nonfictional contributions to *The Challenge* were published under the pseudonyms Mary Christopher and Jane Isaac.

2. Cherene Sherrard, "'This Plague of Their Own Locusts': Space, Property, and Identity in Dorothy West's *The Living Is Easy*," *African American Review* 38.4 (Winter 2004): 609–624.

3. James Weldon Johnson Collection, Yale University's Beinecke Manuscript and Research Library. JWJ MSS WEST, Folder labeled "Mildred Wirt."

4. Susan Tomlinson, "An Unwonted Coquetry: the Commercial Seductions of Jessie Fauset's *The Chinaberry Tree*," in *Middlebrow Moderns: Popular American Women Writers of the 1920s*, ed. Lisa Botshon and Meredith Goldsmith (Boston: Northeastern University Press, 2003), 230.

5. Deborah E. McDowell, "Conversations with Dorothy West," in *Harlem Renaissance Reexamined: A Revised and Expanded Edition*, ed. Robert Russ and Victor Kramer (Troy, N.Y.: Whitson, 1997), 296.

6. Bill Chase, "All Ears," *New York Amsterdam News*, 15 May 1948, 9.

7. *Corpus Christi Caller-Times*, 16 May 1948, 30.

8. Henry Lee Moon, review of *The Living Is Easy*, by Dorothy West, 55.10 *Crisis:* 308.

9. "New Book Tells of Boston Life," *Atlanta Daily World*, 19 May 1948, 2.

10. "Global News Digest," Albert Barnett, *Chicago Defender (National Edition)*, 28 August 1948, 15.

11. Moon, review of Dorothy West's *The Living is Easy*, 308.

12. Edward Wagenknecht, "Negroes Are Just People, Novel Shows," *Chicago Daily Tribune*, 4 July 1948, G8.

13. Seymour Krim, "Boston Black Belt," *New York Times*, 16 May 1948, BR5.

14. Dalsgård, "Alive and Well," 33.

15. Dorothy West, *The Living is Easy* (1948; New York: Feminist Press, 1982), 40.

16. Cynthia Davis and Verner Mitchell, "Introduction," *Where the Wild Grape Grows: Selected Writings, 1930–1950* (Amherst: University of Massachusetts Press, 2005), 26.

17. Linsey Lee, Interviews with Dorothy West, Oral History Division, Martha's Vineyard Museum, 23 June 1983, 13.

18. West, *The Living Is Easy*, 9, 3.

19. Genii Guinier, "Interview with Dorothy West," Black Women's Oral History Project Interviews, Harvard University, Cambridge, Mass., 75.

20. Farrah Griffin, *"Who Set You Flowin'": African American Migration Narrative* (New York: Oxford University Press, 1995), 83.

21. Lawrence Rodgers, "Dorothy West's The *Living Is Easy* and the Ideal of Southern Folk Community," *African American Review* 26 (Spring 1992): 167.

22. See Wall and Hull on how scholars' periodization of Harlem Renaissance literature often excluded women artists. It is ironic that Wall does not include a chapter on Dorothy West in her landmark study, *Women of the Harlem Renaissance*.

23. During the Harlem Renaissance, female journal editors came under harsh scrutiny. Just as critics attempted to undermine Jessie Fauset's authority while she was editor of the *Crisis*, Wallace Thurman detracted from West's editorial efforts: "Challenge lacks significance or personality-it is too pink tea and la de da" (quoted in Cromwell, "Afterword," 355). West weathered the storm, however, by standing up to the leadership of the Communist Party who sought to use the *New Challenge* as an organ of the party.

24. McDowell, "Conversations with Dorothy West," 291.

25. *New York Times*, 16 May 1948.

26. West, *The Living Is Easy*, 38

27. Ibid., 53.

28. For additional discussions that challenge definitions of time and space as static categories, see Doreen Massey, *Space, Place, and Gender* (Minneapolis: University of Minnesota Press, 1994).

29. See Griffin's discussion of migration narratives in *"Who Set You Flowin'?"* See also Bret Williams, "The South in the City," *Journal of Popular Culture* 16 (1982): 30–41, which examines the cultural adaptation of migrants to a new locale: "Migrants bring to cities an expressive culture deeply rooted in another place. Because expressive culture is crucial in defining place, they must revise the often-inappropriate aesthetics of home and join them to the more embracing commercial and popular media" (206).

30. West, *The Living Is Easy*, 143.

31. Houston Baker, "Critical Memory and the Black Public Sphere," *Public Culture* 7 (1994): 10.

32. West, *The Living Is Easy*, 143.

33. Ibid., 113, 105 193.

34. Ibid., 182.

35. Willard Gatewood, *Aristocrats of Color* (Bloomington: Indiana University Press, 1990), 153.

36. West, *The Living Is Easy*, 6, 7.

37. Ibid., III, II2.

38. Gillian Rose, *Feminism and Geography: The Limits of Geographical Knowledge* (Minneapolis: University of Minnesota Press, 1993), II8.

39. West, *The Living Is Easy*, 130.

40. Ibid., 5, 49.

41. Ibid., 5.

42. In some parts of the West End, four-fifths of the households took in relatives or lodgers in early twentieth-century Boston. Sarah Deutsch, *Women in the City: Gender, Space, and Power in Boston, 1870–1940* (New York: Oxford University Press, 2000), 28.

43. Ibid., 40, 46, 48.

44. The interaction between black (im)migrants and Irish and Italian immigrants is central to Marita Bonner's "A Sealed Pod," a story that inverts conventional assumptions about phenotypes of race and ethnicity. In this story, after a resident of black Frye Street is murdered by her Italian American lover, the black community agrees that Davy, Violette's black lover, killed her. Meanwhile Joe Tamona, her true murderer, escapes to the outskirts of the city among the "old country Italians," where he "forg[et]s" to speak English. Marita O. Bonner, *Frye Street and Environs* (Boston: Beacon, 1987), 143.

45. Ibid., 105.

46. West, *The Living Is Easy*, 209, 207, 205.

47. Ibid., 101. According to Noel Ignatiev, Irish people, who had formed an oppressed race in England, were initially supportive of racial equality and class solidarity with black workers with whom they were first lumped by "established" whites when they arrived at the end of the nineteenth century. At one point Irish were referred to as "niggers turned inside out." Conversely, blacks were deemed "smoked Irish." *How the Irish Became White* (New York: Routledge, 1996), 41. As early as the census of 1850, which first included mulatto as a racial category, there was indication of black-Irish intermarriage.

48. Benedict Anderson, *Imagined Communities: Reflections on the Origin and Spread of Nationalism* (London: Verso, 1991), 153.

49. West, *The Living Is Easy*, 25, 135. Circa 1890, the majority of black upper-middle-class Bostonians, who were overwhelmingly light-skinned, objected to the term Negro; they saw themselves as a kind of in-between group, somewhat ambiguous, certainly a better class of "coloreds." Gatewood, *Aristocrats of Color*, 110.

50. West, *The Living Is Easy*, 221.

51. Ibid., 92.

52. Gambling in the West End was predominately run by African Americans. See Roger Lane, *Policing the City: Boston 1822–1885* (Cambridge, Mass.: Harvard University Press, 1967), 214.

53. Bonner, "On the Altar," in *Frye Street*, 233.

54. Bonner, "On the Altar," in *Frye Street*, 243.

55. West, *The Living is Easy*, 177, 211, 53.

56. Ibid., 318.

57. See Roger Lane, *Policing the City*, on public outrage at abortionists in 1870s Boston (186).

58. In Nella Larsen's *Passing*, passing characters Clare and Gertrude express their fear of producing a dark-skinned child. Similarly, in Jessie Fauset's dark *Comedy: American Style* Olivia Blanchard blames her family's inability to pass completely into whiteness on her son Oliver's golden brown skin.

59. West, *The Living Is Easy*, 31.

60. Carol Allen, *Black Women Intellectuals: Strategies of Nation, Family and Neighborhood in the Works of Pauline Hopkins, Jessie Fauset and Marita Bonner* (New York: Garland, 1998).

61. West, *The Living Is Easy*, 31, 97, 35.

62. Deustch, *Women in the City*, 55.

63. West, *The Living Is Easy*, 70–71.

64. Rose, *Feminism and Geography*. Rose argues that in the 1980s "spatial structure [was] seen not merely as an arena in which social life unfolds but as a medium through which social life is produced and reproduced" (19). Rose also discusses ways that time-geography presumes a transparent, universal space based on white western heterosexual concepts that "violently [police]" the boundaries of public space to exclude women and Others (62). She asserts that "concepts of place and space are implicitly gendered in geographical discourse," and, I would add, explicitly raced (62). A critical illustration of this kind of policing in *The Living Is Easy* is exemplified when the bronze-skinned Simeon Binney is accused of interracial dating when in fact he is chaperoning his fair-skinned sister in Harvard Square.

65. Ibid., 70.

66. Massey, *Space, Place and Gender*, 8.

67. West, *The Living Is Easy*, 118, 308.

68. Ann duCille, *The Coupling Convention: Sex, Text, and Tradition in Black Women's Fiction* (New York: Oxford University Press, 1993), 112.

69. West, *The Living Is Easy*, 91.

70. Eugenia Peretz, "The 'IT' Parade," *Vanity Fair*, September 2000, 314.

71. West, *The Living Is Easy*, 266, 245.

72. Ibid., 50, 249.

73. Ibid., 317.

74. Jennifer Wilks, *Race, Gender and Comparative Black Modernism, Suzanne Lacascade, Marita Bonner, Suzanne Césaire, Dorothy West* (Baton Rouge: Louisiana State University Press, 2008), 168.

75. West, *The Living Is Easy*, 318, 316.

76. Wilks, *Race, Gender, and Comparative Black Modernism*, 173.

77. In *Paradise*, fifteen families who share the coal-black skin known as "8-rock" found a town called Haven, later reinvented as Ruby (193). These dark-skinned southern migrants had been banned in 1890 from a settlement in Oklahoma: light-skinned blacks had warned, "Come prepared or not at all" (in an event recorded in their town annals as the "Disallowing," 13, 195). In response to their exclusion, the town fathers established an exclusive community in which they were the privileged, the chosen, and the patriarchs.

78. West, *The Living Is Easy*, 171, 154.

79. duCille, *The Coupling Convention*, 115.

80. Ward Just, "How the Other Half Lives," Review of *The Emperor of Ocean Park*, by Stephen Carter, *New York Times Book Review*, 9 June 2002, 11.

CHAPTER 7.   COTTAGER'S CORNER

1. Dorothy West, "Cottager's Corner," *Vineyard Gazette*, 24 July 1970.

2. In addition to being a predominantly African American homeowners' association, the Cottagers are distinct from typical neighborhood associations in that not all of the members necessarily live in close proximity to one another. Moreover, given the aggressive role that homeowners and/or neighborhood associations have historically played in enforcing restrictive covenants designed to keep out people of color and other groups, the founding of a black women's homeowners organization is particularly significant.

3. I focus specifically on the years when West's column was entitled "Cottager's Corner." See James Robert Saunders and Renae Nadine Shackelford's *Dorothy West's Martha's Vineyard: Stories, Essays, and Reminiscences by Dorothy West Writing in the "Vineyard Gazette"* (Jefferson, N.C.: McFarland, 2001) for a selection of articles from the duration of the column.

4. West, "Cottager's Corner," 23 June 1982, 7.

5. West, *Dorothy West's Martha's Vineyard*, 26.

6. West, "Cottager's Corner," 15 August 1969.

7. West, "Cottager's Corner," 21 July 1972.

8. Dorothy West, Interview with Linsey Lee, Oral History Division, Martha's Vineyard Museum, 21 January 1982, 12. It is very difficult for Lee to get West to articulate the main purpose of the organization. She continues to veer off on tangents, and Lee has to repeatedly ask her to explain the groups' activities. West vaguely discusses raising money for a hospital and how the dues increased over the years before Lee gives up and allows the interview to continue in another direction. This pattern characterizes nearly all interviews with West that have not been heavily edited for coherence. See also Jill Nelson on the exclusivity of the club.

9. Current Cottagers describe their work as "quiet activism." According to the web site their "mission is to promote education, a sense of cultural pride and the value of service to the community for the people of the Island." http://www.cottagerscornermv.org/aboutus.html.

10. Adelaide Cromwell wrote the afterword to the reprint of the Feminist Press edition of *The Living Is Easy*. A professor and sociologist, her book *The Other Brahmins* offers an invaluable examination of class dynamics in the African American community. She is a rigorous scholar and one of the few friends with whom West remained on good terms toward the end of her life. Although West thought Cromwell would have made a terrible biographer, I found her insights on West and the island during our conversation in July 2008 intriguing and essential to piecing together the unique history of the black presence and West's role within that community.

11. Cromwell, Interview with the author, July 2008, Martha's Vineyard.

12. Robert Hayden, *African Americans on Martha's Vineyard and Nantucket: A History of People, Places, and Events* (Boston: Select Publications, 1999).

13. Noliwe Rooks, *Ladies' Pages: African American Women's Magazines and the Culture That Made Them* (New Brunswick, N.J.: Rutgers University Press, 2004), 20.

14. West, "Cottager's Corner," 10 September 1971.

15. Nella Larsen, *Quicksand*, (1928), in *Quicksand and Passing*, ed. Deborah McDowell (New Brunswick, N.J.: Rutgers University Press, 1986), 59.

16. West, "Cottager's Corner," 5 September 1969.

17. Telephone conversation with the author, Oak Bluffs, Martha's Vineyard, 14 July 2008.

18. Isabel Washington Powell, *Adam's Belle: A Memoir of Love Without Bounds* (Springfield: DBM Press, LC, 2008), 100.

19. Ibid.

20. Ibid., 125.

21. Hayden, *African Americans on Martha's Vineyard*, 12.

22. West, Interview with Linsey Lee, 1 January 1982, 1.

23. Jacqueline Holland, "The African American Presence on Martha's Vineyard," Martha's Vineyard Historical Society, *Dukes County Intelligencer*, special edition (October 1977): 16.

24. Rickson, Interview with the author, July 2008, Martha's Vineyard, Mass.

25. West, "Cottager's Corner," 14 August 1970.

26. West, *Dorothy West's Martha's Vineyard*, 62.

27. West, "Cottager's Corner," 5 May 1994, 8.

28. Dorothy West, Interview with Nancy Safford, 23 August 1973, Oral History Division, Martha's Vineyard Museum.

29. Lois Mailou Jones to Linsey Lee, 17 September 1993, Oral History Division, Martha's Vineyard Museum.

30. Edward Brooke, *Bridging the Divide: My Life* (New Brunswick, N.J.: Rutgers University Press, 2007), 49.

31. Ibid., 50.

32. West, "Fond Memories," in *The Richer, The Poorer: Stories, Sketches, and Reminiscences* (New York: Doubleday, 1995), 173.

33. Lois Mailou Jones to Linsey Lee, 17 September 1993, Oral History Division, Martha's Vineyard Museum.

34. Elaine Cawley Weintraub and Carrie Camillo Tankard, then vice president of the Martha's Vineyard Chapter of the NAACP, were instrumental in establishing the African American History Trail. The trail is a "physical entity consisting of a series of identified sites commemorating the history of people of color on Martha's Vineyard." Weintraub, "Introduction," *Lighting the Trail: The African American Heritage of Martha's Vineyard* (Elaine Weintraub, 2005), xxii.

35. Sarah Biggers, Entry on "89 Ocean Avenue," in The Cottagers Inc. Twenty-sixth Annual House Tour, Descriptions by Dr. Bettye Baker.

36. West, Interview with Linsey Lee, 21 January 1982.

37. The most striking aspect of Moretti's approach to setting includes the meticulous maps that illustrate his spatial arguments. His maps of Jane Austen's novels trace her characters and plotlines through various locales and in and out of particular social milieus. Franco Moretti, *Atlas of the European Novel, 1800–1900* (London: Verso, 1999), 20.

38. West, "The Sun Parlor," in *The Richer, The Poorer*, 195, 243. "I was always referred to as sis or sister." Joyce Rickson, Interview with the author, July 2008, Martha's Vineyard.

39. West, "The Sun Parlor," in *The Richer, The Poorer*," 243.

40. "Boston as the Paradise for the Negro," *Colored American Magazine* 7.5 (May 1904): 309.

41. West, "Cottager's Corner," 31 August 1971.

42. Jill Nelson, *Finding Martha's Vineyard: African Americans at Home on an Island* (New York: Doubleday, 2005), 98.

43. West, "Cottager's Corner," 12 July 1968.

44. Ibid.

45. West, "Cottager's Corner," 31 August 1971.

46. West, "Cottager's Corner," 5 September 1969.

47. West, "Cottager's Corner," 30 August 1968.

48. West, "Cottager's Corner," 31 August 1971.

49. West, "Cottager's Corner," 23 June 1982.

50. Ibid.

51. Saunders and Shackelford, *Dorothy West's Martha's Vineyard*, 22.

52. Toni Morrison, *Love* (New York: Knopf, 2003), 103.

53. Ibid., 102.

CHAPTER 8.   TWO WEDDINGS

1. Nancy Bentley, *The Ethnography of Manners: Hawthorne, Wharton, and James* (New York: Cambridge University Press, 1995), 102.

2. Ann Rayson, "Sexuality, Color, and Class in Dorothy West's *The Wedding*," *The Langston Hughes Review* 16.1–2 (Fall/Spring 1999–2001): 221.

3. Deborah E. McDowell, "Conversations with Dorothy West," in *Harlem Renaissance Reexamined: A Revised and Expanded Edition*, ed. Robert Russ and Victor Kramer (Troy, N.Y.: Whitson, 1997); Lorraine Elena Roses and Ruth Elizabeth Randolph, *Harlem Renaissance and Beyond: Literary Biographies of 100 Black Women Writers, 1900–1945* (Boston: G. K. Hall, 1990)

4. McDowell, "Conversations with Dorothy West," 299.

5. Betty Arnoff, Letter to Dorothy West, 2 April 1951, in *Where the Wild Grape Grows*, 210.

6. Jacqueline Onassis's editorial assistant at Doubleday, Scott Moyers, confirms accounts that during the time West was finishing *The Wedding* Onassis drove down from her house in Chilmark to visit West in her cottage in Oak Bluffs: "If Jackie hadn't paid those weekly visits the book would never have been finished, and that book, *The Wedding,* is a real classic." Quoted in Sarah Bradford, *America's Queen: The Life of Jacqueline Kennedy Onassis* (New York: Viking, 2000), 411.

7. Elizabeth Muther, "The Racial Subject of Suspense in Dorothy West's *The Wedding*," *Narrative* 7.2 (May 1999): 198.

8. Ibid., 210.

9. Ann Rayson, "Sexuality, Color and Class in Dorothy West's *The Wedding*," *The Langston Hughes Review* 16.1–2 (Fall/Spring 1999–2001): 224.

10. Joyce Rickson, Interview with the author, July 2008, Martha's Vineyard.

11. Dorothy West, *The Wedding* (New York: Doubleday, 1995), 2.

12. Idlewild is a historically black resort town in Michigan.

13. West, *The Wedding*, 4.

14. Off-color casting speaks to debates around colorblind casting in film and theater. The discussion around colorblind casting in the theater industry came under scrutiny during a conversation between August Wilson and Lloyd Richards. Wilson advocated a separate black theater and was against the practice of colorblind casting.

15. See "Dorothy West Signs For Another Film," *The New York Amsterdam News*, 25 January 1933, 8.

16. The recent popularity of what Mary Beltrán calls "off white" actresses like Jessica Alba and Rosario Dawson suggest that this type of casting may be changing. The 2001 film adaptation of Anne Rice's *Feast of All Saints*, a novel about the octoroon/quadroon/mulatta women who danced at the famous New Orleans' Octoroon Balls and formed contractual agreements with wealthy white men, featured several racially ambiguous actresses who could have played the Coles family as West described them in her novel. Nicole Lyn, an actress with African and Chinese ancestry, played the role of Marie, the phenotypically white daughter of a plantation owner and his mixed race mistress, played by Gloria Reuben.

17. Aisha Bastiaans, "Detecting Difference in *Devil in a Blue Dress*: The Mulatta Figure, Noir, and the Cinematic Reification of Race," in *Mixed-Race Hollywood*, ed. Mary Beltrán and Camilla Fojas (New York: New York University Press), 235, 246.

18. Motley's *Bronzeville by Night*, which serves to evoke the historically black vitality of Los Angeles Central Avenue, actually portrays a street in Chicago. Motley's paintings are often used out of their specific context. One of his most famous paintings is often used to evoke a Harlem speakeasy although it depicts an international jazz club in Paris. Additionally, the use of Motley in the opening shot is particularly suggestive since he specialized in painting portraits of ambiguously raced women.

19. West, *The Wedding*, 49.

20. An example of successful off-color casting includes casting Denzel Washington as the light-skinned, freckled, red-haired Malcolm X. Although Malcolm's physical appearance was critical to his understanding of his identity, his persuasiveness as a radical leader, and his iconic status in black popular culture, Washington's ability to capture his vocal range, attitude, and the cadence of his speech allowed him to convincingly inhabit Malcolm X in Spike Lee's biopic. Washington's performance earned him an Academy Award nomination for best actor, though the film was otherwise snubbed.

21. This line is spoken by the Stepin Fetchit character in the Broadway musical *Bring in Da Noise, Bring in Da Funk*.

22. Patricia Marks, *Bicycles, Bangs, and Bloomers: The New Woman in the Popular Press* (Lexington: University Press of Kentucky, 1990), 174.

23. Dorothy West, *The Living Is Easy* (1948; reprint, New York: Feminist Press, 1982), 31.

24. West, *The Wedding*, 97, 109.

25. Ibid., 172, 173.

26. Ibid., 12.

27. Ibid., 18.

28. Ibid., 93.

29. Ibid., 62, 63, 71.

30. Ibid., 115.

31. Ibid., 73.

32. Ibid., 7.

33. Muther, "The Racial Subject," 201, 62.

34. The idea of "the birth of the cool" takes its name from Miles Davis's *The Birth of the Cool,* a compilation album released in 1957. The album marks a major development in post-bebop jazz and included many innovations such as incorporating instruments like the French horn and the tuba that were previously unknown in jazz.

35. Ironically, Halema was frequently misidentified as part black, colored, or Negro. She is actually Pakistani. Chet Baker's career was marked by tragedy; he died in 1998 from a fall from a hotel window in Amsterdam.

36. West, *The Wedding*, 220, 209, 219.

37. Ibid., 2, 3.

38. Ibid., 12.

39. Muther, "The Racial Subject," 208.

40. David Streitfield, "Dorothy West, Renaissance Woman: She Faded from Sight with the Harlem Artists of the '20s, but the Final Chapter Had Yet to Be Written," *Washington Post*, 6 July 1995.

41. Rayson, "Sexuality, Color, and Class," 220.

CODA

1. Lionel Bascom, ed., *The Last Leaf of Harlem: Selected and Newly Discovered Fiction by the Author of The Wedding* (New York: St. Martin's, 2008), xxxi.

2. Ibid., 411.

3. Ibid., 165.

4. Dorothy West, "Winter on Martha's Vineyard," in *Where the Wild Grape Grows: Selected Writings, 1930–1950,* ed. Verner D. Mitchell and Cynthia Davis (Amherst: University of Massachusetts Press, 2005), 164, 163.

5. Dorothy West, *The Wedding* (New York: Doubleday, 1995), 240.

6. West, "Winter on Martha's Vineyard," 166.

BIBLIOGRAPHY

WORKS BY DOROTHY WEST

"An Adventure in Moscow." In *The Richer, The Poorer: Stories, Sketches, and Reminiscences,* 205–210. 1985. Reprint, New York: Doubleday, 1995. 205–210

"At the Swan Boats." In *Where the Wild Grape Grows: Selected Writings, 1930–1950,* ed. Verner D. Mitchell and Cynthia Davis, 57–62. Amherst: University of Massachusetts Press, 2005.

"Cook." [as Jane Isaac]. *Challenge* (March 1934): 28–36.

"The Cottagers and Mrs. Carmody." In *The Last Leaf of Harlem: Selected and Newly Discovered Fiction from the Author of The Wedding,* ed. Lionel Bascom. New York: St. Martin's Press, 2008.

"Elephant's Dance." In *The Richer, The Poorer: Stories, Sketches, and Reminiscences.* 1970. Reprint, New York: Doubleday, 1995.

"The Five Dollar Bill." [as Mary Christopher.] *Challenge* (June 1936): 35–40.

"Fond Memories of a Black Childhood." In *The Richer, The Poorer: Stories, Sketches, and Reminiscences,* 171–176. New York: Doubleday, 1995.

"The Gift." In *The Richer, The Poorer: Stories, Sketches, and Reminiscences,* 177–180. 1984. Reprint, New York: Doubleday, 1995.

"Hannah Byde." In *Where the Wild Grape Grows: Selected Writings, 1930–1950,* ed. Verner D. Mitchell and Cynthia Davis, 79–85. Amherst: University of Massachusetts Press, 2005. *The Last Leaf of Harlem: Selected and Newly Discovered Fiction by the Author of The Wedding,* ed. Lionel Bascom. New York: St. Martin's, 2008.

"The Legend of Oak Bluffs." In *The Richer, The Poorer: Stories, Sketches, and Reminiscences,* 235–242. 1980. Reprint, New York: Doubleday, 1995.

The Living Is Easy. 1948. Reprint, New York: Feminist Press, 1982.

"Mammy." In *The Richer, The Poorer: Stories, Sketches, and Reminiscences,* 43–52. 1940. Reprint, New York: Doubleday, 1995.

"The Penny." In *The Richer, The Poorer: Stories, Sketches, and Reminiscences, 1930–1950,* ed. Verner D. Mitchell and Cynthia Davis, 77–82. New York: Doubleday, 1995.

"Pluto." In *Where the Wild Grape Grows: Selected Writings, 1930–1950,* ed. Verner D. Mitchell and Cynthia Davis, 102–104. Amherst: University of Massachusetts Press, 2005.

"Rachel." In *The Richer, The Poorer: Stories, Sketches, and Reminiscences,* 167–170. New York: Doubleday, 1995.

The Richer, The Poorer: Stories, Sketches, and Reminiscences. 1940. Reprint, New York: Doubleday, 1995.

"Room in Red Square." [as Mary Christopher]. *Challenge* 1.1 (March 1934): 10–15.

"Russian Correspondence." [as Mary Christopher]. *Challenge* 1.2 (September 1934): 14–20.

"Selected Letters." In *Where the Wild Grape Grows: Selected Writings, 1930–1950*, ed. Verner D. Mitchell and Cynthia Davis, 179–212. Amherst: University of Massachusetts Press, 2005.

"The Sun Parlor." In *The Richer, the Poorer: Stories, Sketches, and Reminiscences*, 201–204. New York: Doubleday, 1995.

"The Typewriter." In *The Richer, The Poorer: Stories, Sketches, and Reminiscences*, 9–18. 1926. Reprint, New York: Doubleday, 1995.

"An Unimportant Man." In *The Richer, The Poorer: Stories, Sketches, and Reminiscences*, 137–160. 1928. Reprint, New York: Doubleday, 1995.

The Wedding. New York: Doubleday, 1995.

Where the Wild Grape Grows: Selected Writings, 1930–1950, ed. Verner D. Mitchell and Cynthia Davis. Amherst: University of Massachusetts Press, 2005.

"Winter on Martha's Vineyard." In *Where the Wild Grape Grows: Selected Writings, 1930–1950*, ed. Verner D. Mitchell and Cynthia Davis, 160–166. Amherst: University of Massachusetts Press, 2005.

ARCHIVES AND SPECIAL COLLECTIONS

Dorothy West Papers, Schlesinger Library, Radcliffe Institute, Harvard University, Cambridge, Mass.

James Weldon Johnson Collection. Yale University Beinecke Manuscript and Rare Book Library, New Haven, Conn.

Louise Thompson Patterson Memoirs: Trip to Russia—1932, Draft 1–3. Box 20. Special Collections and Archives, Robert W. Woodruff Library, Emory University Atlanta, GA.

Martha's Vineyard Gazette Archives, Edgartown, Mass.

Oral History Archives, Martha's Vineyard Museum, Martha's Vineyard Historical Society, Edgartown, Mass.

INTERVIEWS

Christian, Anita. Personal Interview. July 2008, Oak Bluffs, Martha's Vineyard, Mass.

Cromwell, Adelaide. Personal Interview. July 2008, Vineyard Haven, Martha's Vineyard, Mass.

Guinier, Genii. "Interview with Dorothy West." Black Women's Oral History Project Interviews, Schlesinger Library, Radcliffe Institute for Advanced Study, Harvard University, Cambridge, Mass.

Lee, Linsey. Interviews with Dorothy West and Lois Mailou Jones., Oral History Division, Martha's Vineyard Museum, Edgartown, Mass.

Rickson, Joyce. Personal Interview. July 2008, Martha's Vineyard, Mass.

Roses, Lorraine Elene. "Interviews with Black Women Writers: Dorothy West at Oak Bluffs, MA, July 1984." *Sage* 2.1 (Spring 1985): 47–49.

Stafford, Nancy. Interview with Dorothy West. Oral History Division, Martha's Vineyard Museum, Edgartown, Mass.

BOOKS AND ARTICLES

Allen, Carol. *Black Women Intellectuals: Strategies of Nation, Family, and Neighborhood in the Works of Pauline Hopkins, Jessie Fauset, and Marita Bonner.* New York: Garland, 1998.

Anderson, Benedict. *Imagined Communities: Reflections on the Origin and Spread of Nationalism.* London: Verso, 1991.

Anzaldua, Gloria. *Borderlands: La Frontera, the New Mestiza.* San Francisco: Spinsters, 1987.

As I Remember It: Portrait of Dorothy West. DVD. Directed by Salema Mekuria. 56 minutes. Distributed by Women Make Movies, 1991.

"Auction for Johnson Villa: Lake Geneva Millionaires Get a Chance to Outbid Johnson." *Chicago Daily Tribune,* 27 December 1912, 2.

Baker, Houston. "Critical Memory and the Black Public Sphere." *Public Culture* 7 (1994): 3–33.

Baldwin, Kate. *Beyond the Color Line and the Iron Curtain: Reading Encounters between Black and Red, 1922–1963.* Durham, N.C.: Duke University Press, 2002.

Bascom, Lionel, ed. *The Last Leaf of Harlem: Selected and Newly Discovered Fiction by the Author of The Wedding.* New York: St. Martin's, 2008.

Bass, Patrick Henry. "Working It!" *Essence,* December 2000, 120–127.

Bastiaans, Aisha. "Detecting Difference in *Devil in a Blue Dress*: The Mulatta Figure, Noir, and the Cinematic Reification of Race." In *Mixed-Race Hollywood*, ed. Mary Beltrán and Camilla Fojas, 223–247. New York: New York University Press, 2008.

Benjamin, Tritobia Hayes, and Lois Mailou Jones. *The Life and Art of Lois Mailou Jones.* San Francisco: Pomegranate Books, 1994.

Bishop, Edward. "Re:Covering Modernism—Format and Function in the Little Magazines." In *Modernist Writers and the Marketplace*, ed. Ian Willison, Warick Gould, and Warren Chernaic. New York: St. Martin's, 1996.

Bonner, Marita O. *Frye Street and Environs.* Boston: Beacon, 1987.

———. "On Being Young—A Woman—and Colored." In *Double Take: A Revisionist Harlem Renaissance Anthology*, ed. Venetria K. Patton and Maureen Honey. New Brunswick, N.J.: Rutgers University Press, 2001.

"Boston as the Paradise for the Negro." *Colored American Magazine* 7.5 (May 1904): 309–317.

Bradford, Sarah. *America's Queen: The Life of Jacqueline Kennedy Onassis.* New York: Viking, 2000.

Brooke, Edward. *Bridging the Divide: My Life.* New Brunswick, N.J.: Rutgers University Press, 2007.

Brown, Dona. *Inventing New England: Regional Tourism in the Nineteenth Century.* Washington, D.C.: Smithsonian Institution Press, 1995.

Brown, Jayna. *Babylon Girls: Black Women Performers and the Shaping of the Modern.* Durham, N.C.: Duke University Press, 2008.

Brown, Lois. *Pauline Elizabeth Hopkins: Black Daughter of the Revolution.* Chapel Hill: University of North Carolina Press, 2008.

Carew, Joy Gleason. *Blacks, Reds and Russians: Sojourners in Search of the Soviet Promise.* New Brunswick, N.J.: Rutgers University Press, 2008.

Carroll, Anne. *Word, Image, and the New Negro.* Bloomington: Indiana University Press, 2005.

Carter, Stephen. *The Emperor of Ocean Park.* New York: Knopf, 2002.

Champion, Laurie. "Social Class Distinctions in Dorothy West's *The Richer, The Poorer*." *The Langston Hughes Review* 161.2 (Fall 1999/Spring 2001): 39–49.

Chesnutt, Charles. *The Wife of His Youth and Other Stories of the Color Line.* Ridgewood, N.J.: Gregg Press, 1967.

Chodorow, Nancy. *The Reproduction of Mothering: Psychoanalysis and the Sociology of Gender.* Berkeley: University of California Press, 1978.

Cromwell, Adelaide. "Afterword." In *The Living Is Easy,* 349–364. 1948. Reprint, New York: Feminist Press, 1982.

Cromwell, Adelaide. "The History of Oak Bluffs as a Popular Resort for Blacks." *The Dukes County Intelligencer, Special Edition* (October 1997): 61.

———. *The Other Brahmins: Boston's Black Upper Class, 1750–1950*. Fayetteville: University of Arkansas Press, 1994.

Dalsgård, Katrine. "Alive and Well and Living on the Island of Martha's Vineyard: An Interview with Dorothy West." *The Langston Hughes Review* 12.2 (Fall 1993): 39–45.

Deck, Alice. "Autoethnography, Zora Neale Hurston, Noni Jabavu, and Cross-Disciplinary Discourse." *Black American Literature Forum* 24.2 (Summer 1990): 237–256.

Deutsch, Sarah. *Women in the City: Gender, Space, and Power in Boston, 1870–1940*. New York: Oxford University Press, 2000.

Du Bois, W.E.B. "Hopkinsville, Chicago and Idlewild." *Crisis* 22.4 (August 1921): 158–160.

duCille, Ann. *The Coupling Convention: Sex, Text, and Tradition in Black Women's Fiction*. New York: Oxford University Press, 1993.

Fabre, Michel. *The Unfinished Quest of Richard Wright*. New York: Morrow, 1973.

Ferguson, Roderick. *Aberrations in Black: Towards a Queer of Color Critique*. Minneapolis: University of Minnesota Press, 2003.

Fish, Cheryl. *Black and White Women's Travel Narratives: Antebellum Explorations*. Gainesville: University Presses of Florida, 2004.

Foucault, Michel. "Of Other Spaces," *Diacritics* 16.1 (Spring 1986): 22–27.

Fox-Genovese, Elizabeth. "Myth and History: Discourse of Origins in Zora Neale Hurston and Maya Angelou Author(s)." *Black American Literature Forum* 24.2 (Summer 1990): 221–235.

Frazier, E. Franklin. *Black Bourgeoisie*. New York: Free Press, 1957.

Gaines, Kevin J. *Uplifting the Race: Black Leadership, Politics, and Culture in the Twentieth Century*. Chapel Hill: University of North Carolina Press, 1996.

Gatewood, Willard. *Aristocrats of Color*. Bloomington: Indiana University Press, 1990.

Gilmore, Glenda. *Defying Dixie: The Radical Roots of Civil Rights (1919–1950)*. New York: Norton, 2008.

Gordon, Michelle. "Black Literature of Revolutionary Protest from Chicago's South Side: A Local Literary History, 1931–1959." Ph.D. diss., University of Wisconsin–Madison, 2008.

Graham, Lawrence. *The Senator and the Socialite: The True Story of America's First Black Dynasty*. New York: HarperCollins, 2006.

Griffin, Farrah. *"Who Set You Flowin'?": The African American Migration Narrative*. New York: Oxford University Press, 1995.

Gross, Ariel. "Litigating Whiteness: Trials of Racial Determination in the Nineteenth-Century South." *Yale Law Journal* 108.1 (1998): 109–188.

Guillory, Monique. "Under One Roof: The Sins and Sanctity of the New Orleans Quadroon Balls." In *Race Consciousness*, ed. Judith Jackson Fossett and Jeffrey A. Tucker, 67–92. New York: NYU Press, 1997.

Hayden, Robert. *African Americans on Martha's Vineyard and Nantucket: A History of People, Places, and Events*. Boston: Select Publications, 1999.

Hirsch, Francine. *Empire of Nations: Ethnographic Knowledge and the Making of the Soviet Union*. Ithaca, N.Y.: Cornell University Press, 2005.

Holland, Jacqueline. "The African American Presence on Martha's Vineyard." *The Dukes County Intelligencer*. Martha's Vineyard Historical Society. Special Edition. October 1997, 1–24.

Hughes, Langston. *I Wonder as I Wander*. New York: Hill and Wang, 1956.

Hull, Gloria T. *Color, Sex, and Poetry: Three Women Writers of the Harlem Renaissance*. Bloomington: Indiana University Press, 1987.

Hurston, Zora Neale. *Color Struck*. In *Zora Neale Hurston: Collected Plays*, ed. Jean Lee Cole and Charles Mitchell. New Brunswick, N.J.: Rutgers University Press, 2008.

——. "Drenched in Light." In *The Portable Harlem Renaissance Reader*, ed. David Levering Lewis. New York: Viking, 1994.

——. *Their Eyes Were Watching God*. New York: Perennial Library, 1990.

Ignatiev, Noel. *How the Irish Became White*. New York: Routledge, 1996.

Ilf, Ilya, and Petrov Evgeny. *Ilf and Petrov's American Road Trip: The 1935 Travelogue of Two Soviet Writers*, ed. Erika Wolf. Texts by Aleksandr Rodchenko and Aleksandra Ilf; translated by Anne O. Fisher. New York: Cabinet Books, 2007.

James, Joy. *Transcending the Talented Tenth: Black Leaders and American Intellectuals*. New York: Routledge, 1997.

Jenkins, Candice M. *Private Lives, Proper Relations [Regulating Black Intimacy]*. Minneapolis: University of Minnesota Press, 2007.

——. "Pure Black: Class, Color, and Intraracial Politics in Toni Morrison's *Paradise*." *Modern Fiction Studies* 52.2 (Summer 2006): 270–296.

Johnson, Helene. *This Waiting for Love: Helene Johnson, Poet of the Harlem Renaissance*, ed. Verner D. Mitchell. Amherst: University of Massachusetts Press, 2000.

Jones, Sharon. *Rereading the Harlem Renaissance: Race, Class, and Gender in the Fiction of Jessie Fauset, Zora Neale Hurston, and Dorothy West*. Westport, Conn.: Greenwood, 2002.

Just, Ward. "How the Other Half Lives." Review of *The Emperor of Ocean Park*, by Stephen Carter. *New York Times Book Review*, 9 June 2002, 11.

Kaplan, Carla. *Zora Neale Hurston: A Life in Letters*. New York: Doubleday, 2002.

Keckley, Elizabeth. *Behind the Scenes or, Thirty Years a Slave, and Four Years in the White House*. 1868. Reprint, New York: Oxford University Press, 1988.

Knopf, Marcy, ed. *The Sleeper Wakes: Harlem Renaissance Stories by Women*. New Brunswick, N.J.: Rutgers University Press, 1993.

Lane, Roger. *Policing the City: Boston 1822–1885*. Cambridge, Mass.: Harvard University Press, 1967.

Lee, Andrea. *Russian Journal*. 1979. Reprint, with Introduction and Foreword. New York: Random House, 2006.

Lee, Hermione. *Edith Wharton*. New York: Knopf, 2007.

Levesque, George. *Black Boston: African American Life and Culture in Urban America, 1750–1860*. New York: Garland, 1994.

Locke, Alain. *The New Negro*. New York: Boni and Liveright, 1925.

Lorde, Audre. "Notes from a Trip to Russia" (1976). In *Sister Outsider: Essays and Speeches*. Trumansburg, N.Y.: The Crossing Press, 1984.

——. *Zami, a New Spelling of My Name: A Biomythography*. New York: Persephone Press, 1982.

Louise Thompson Patterson: In Her Own Words. Directed by Louise Massiah. 18 minutes. Third World Newsreel, 2002.

Marks, Patricia. *Bicycles, Bangs, and Bloomers: The New Woman in the Popular Press*. Lexington: University Press of Kentucky, 1990.

Massey, Doreen. *Space, Place, and Gender*. Minneapolis: University of Minnesota Press, 1994.

Martin, Darnell. *Their Eyes Were Watching God*. ABC, 2005.

McDowell, Deborah E. "Conversations with Dorothy West." In *Harlem Renaissance Re-examined: A Revised and Expanded Edition*, ed. Robert Russ and Victor Kramer, 265–282. Troy, N.Y.: Whitson, 1997.

Miller, Christopher. *Blank Darkness: The Africanist Discourse in French*. Chicago: University of Chicago, 1985.

Mitchell, Verner D., and Cynthia Davis, eds. *Where the Wild Grape Grows: Selected Writings, 1930–1950*. Amherst: University of Massachusetts Press, 2005.

Moretti, Franco. *Atlas of the European Novel, 1800–1900*. London: Verso, 1999.

Morrison, Toni. *Love*. New York: Knopf, 2003.

———. *Paradise*. New York: Plume, 1997.

———. "The Site of Memory." In *Inventing the Truth*, ed. William Zinsser, 103–124. New York: Houghton Mifflin, 1995.

Muther, Elizabeth. "The Racial Subject of Suspense in Dorothy West's *The Wedding*." *Narrative* 7.2 (May 1999): 194–212.

Nelson, Claire Nee. "Louise Thompson Patterson and the Southern Roots of the Popular Front." In *Women Shaping the South: Creating and Confronting Changes*, ed. Angela Boswell and Judith N. McArthur, 204–228. Columbia: University of Missouri Press, 2006.

Nelson, Jill. *Finding Martha's Vineyard: African Americans at Home on an Island*. New York: Doubleday, 2005.

Nelson, Stanley. *A Place of Our Own*. Produced and directed by Stanley Nelson. DVD. 60 minutes, A Firelight Media Production for Independent Lens on PBS, 2004.

Norton, Lois, and James Norton. *Black Bostonians: Family Life and Community Struggle in the Antebellum North*. New York: Holmes & Meier, 1979.

O'Connor, Flannery. "Revelation." In *The Complete Stories*. 488–509. New York: Farrar Straus Giroux, 1971.

Olney, James, ed. *Autobiography: Essays Theoretical and Critical*. Princeton, N.J.: Princeton University Press, 1980.

Otter, Samuel. "Frank Webb's Still Life: Rethinking Literature and Politics through the Garies and Their Friends." *American Literary History* 20.4 (Winter 2008): 732–752.

Pease, William, and Jane Pease. *Black Utopias: Negro Communal Experiments in America*. Madison: State Historical Society of Wisconsin, 1963.

Peretz, Evgenia. "The 'IT' Parade." *Vanity Fair*, September 2000.

Petry, Elisabeth. *At Home Inside: A Daughter's Tribute to Ann Petry*. Jackson: University of Mississippi Press, 2009.

Phelts, Marsha Dean. *An American Beach for African Americans*. Gainesville: University Presses of Florida, 1997.

Powell, Isabel Washington, with Joyce Burnett. *Adam's Belle: A Memoir of Love without Bounds*. Springfield, Va.: DBM Press, 2008.

Prince, Nancy. *A Narrative of the Life and Travels of Mrs. Nancy Prince Written by Herself*. Collected Black Women's Narratives, ed. Henry Louis Gates Jr. 1853. Reprint, New York: Oxford University Press, 1988.

Rampersad, Arnold. *The Life of Langston Hughes*, Vol. 1: *1902–1941, I, Too, Sing America*. New York: Oxford University Press, 1986.

Randolph, Ruth Elizabeth, and Lorraine Elena Roses. "Marita Bonner: In Search of Other Mothers' Gardens." *Black American Literature Forum* 21 (1987): 165–183.

Rayson, Ann. "Sexuality, Color and Class in Dorothy West's The Wedding." *The Langston Hughes Review* 16.1–2 (Fall/Spring 1999–2001): 32–37.

"Return from Sag Harbor," *Chicago Defender, 15 September 1923, 9, col.7*.

Rodgers, Lawrence. "Dorothy West's The *Living Is Easy* and the Ideal of Southern Folk Community." *African American Review* 26 (Spring 1992): 161–172.

Rooks, Noliwe. *Ladies' Pages: African American Women's Magazines and the Culture That Made Them.* New Brunswick, N.J.: Rutgers University Press, 2004.

Rose, Gillian. *Feminism and Geography: The Limits of Geographical Knowledge.* Minneapolis: University of Minnesota Press, 1993.

Rose, Tricia. *Longing to Tell: Black Women Talk about Sexuality and Intimacy.* New York: Farrar Straus Giroux, 2003.

Roses, Lorraine Elena, and Ruth Elizabeth Randolph. *Harlem Renaissance and Beyond: Literary Biographies of 100 Black Women Writers, 1900–1945.* Boston: G. K. Hall, 1990.

Rymer, Russ. *American Beach: A Saga of Race, Wealth and Memory.* New York: HarperCollins, 1998.

Santamarina, Xiomara. "Reclassifying Group Identity: 19th Century African American Chroniclers of the Higher Classes." Lecture delivered at the University of Wisconsin–Madison, 24 April 2008.

Saunders, James Robert, and Renae Nadine Shackelford. *Dorothy West's Martha Vineyard: Stories, Essays, and Reminiscences by Dorothy West Writing in the "Vineyard Gazette."* Jefferson, N.C.: McFarland, 2001.

Seacole, Mary. *The Wonderful Adventures of Mrs. Seacole in Many Lands.* 1857. New York: Oxford University Press, 1998.

Sherrard, Cherene. "'This Plague of Their Own Locusts': Space, Property, and Identity in Dorothy West's *The Living Is Easy.*" *African American Review* 38.4 (Winter 2004): 609–624.

Sherrard-Johnson, Cherene. "Dorothy West's Typewriter: A Short Story of the Harlem Renaissance." Special Issue on the Twenties. Anglo American Issue. *Letterature D'America* 124 (2009): 55–78.

Singh, Amritjit, and Daniel M. Scott III, eds. *The Collected Writings of Wallace Thurman: A Harlem Renaissance Reader.* New Brunswick, N.J.: Rutgers University Press, 2004.

"Southern Terror." *Crisis* 41.11 (November 1934): 327–338.

Spillers, Hortense. "Interstices: A Small Drama of Words." In *Pleasure and Danger: Exploring Female Sexuality*, ed. Carol S. Vance. Boston: Routledge, 1984.

Steadman, Jennifer Bernhardt. *Traveling Economies: American Women's Travel Writing.* Columbus: Ohio State University Press, 2007.

Stepto, Robert. *Blue as the Lake: A Personal Geography.* Boston: Beacon Press, 1998.

Stoddard, Chris. *A Centennial History of Cottage City: 1880–1980.* Oak Bluffs, Mass.: Oak Bluffs Historical Commission, 1980.

Streitfield, David. "Dorothy West, Renaissance Woman: She Faded from Sight with the Harlem Artists of the '20s, but the Final Chapter Had Yet to Be Written." *Washington Post*, 6 July 1995.

Thompson, Shirley Elizabeth. *Exiles at Home: The Struggle to Become American in Creole New Orleans.* Cambridge, Mass.: Harvard University Press, 2009.

Thurman, Wallace. *Infants of the Spring.* Boston: Northeastern University Press, 1992.

Tomlinson, Susan. "An Unwonted Coquetry: the Commercial Seductions of Jessie Fauset's *The Chinaberry Tree.*" In *Middlebrow Moderns: Popular American Women Writers of the 1920s*, ed. Lisa Botshon and Meredith Goldsmith, 227–243. Boston: Northeastern University Press, 2003.

Toomer, Jean. *Cane.* New York: Boni and Liveright, 1923.

Walker, Margaret. *Richard Wright, Daemonic Genius: A Portrait of the Man, a Critical Look at His Work.* New York: Warner, 1988.

Wall, Cheryl. *Women of the Harlem Renaissance*. Bloomington: Indiana University Press, 1995.

Wallinger, Hannah. *Pauline E. Hopkins: A Literary Biography*. Athens: University of Georgia Press, 2005.

Washington, Isabel, with Joyce Burnett. *Adams Belle:A Memoir of Love with Bounds*. Springfield, Va.: DBM Press, LC, 2008.

Washington, Mary Helen. "I Sign My Mother's Name: Alice Walker, Dorothy West, Paule Marshall." In *Mothering the Mind: Twelve Studies of Writers and Their Silent Partners*, ed. Ruth Perry and Martine Brownley Watson, 142–163. New York: Holmes & Meier, 1984.

Weintraub, Elaine Cawley. *Lighting the Trail: The African American Heritage of Martha's Vineyard*. N.p.: Elaine Weintraub, 2005.

Whitehead, Colson. *Sag Harbor: A Novel*. New York: Doubleday, 2009.

Wilks, Jennifer. *Race, Gender, and Comparative Black Modernism: Suzanne Lacascade, Marita Bonner, Suzanne Césaire, Dorothy West*. Baton Rouge: Louisiana State University Press, 2008.

Williams, Bret. "The South in the City." *Journal of Popular Culture* 16 (1982): 30–41.

Williams-Forson, Psyche. *Building Houses Out of Chicken Legs: Black Women, Food, and Power*. Chapel Hill: University of North Carolina Press, 2006.

Willson, Joseph. *Sketches of the Higher Classes of Colored Society in Philadelphia by a Southerner*, ed. Julie Winch. 1841. Reprint, University Park: Pennsylvania State University Press, 2000.

Wiltse, Jeff. *Contested Waters: A Social History of Swimming Pools in America*. Chapel Hill: University of North Carolina Press, 2007.

INDEX

abortion and colorism, 140
activist authors, 115
actresses, 164, 156, 172–174
African American: artists, 36; autobiography, 43; avant-garde, 105; fiction,
6–8, 115, 123, 194n25; food culture,
29–30; oral culture, 108; sororities, 150;
women, images of, 65, 152; women's
club movement, 7, 148–150. *See also*
black culture; black women; black
writers
"African American Lives" [television
series], 194n38
African Americans: diversity, 173;
self-image, 196n12; in Russia, 101;
sociological studies, 54–56; upper
class, *see* black elite
African-Asian Writers Conferences,
198n4
"Africanist" [term] (Miller), 198n9
Africanist art, in Russia, 80
Africans in Russia, 98
Alba, Jessica, 211n16
Allen, Carol, 140
Allen, Eloise Downing, 31, 150
Alpha Kappa Alpha, 150
ambiguously raced women, 194n25,
211n18
American Communist Party. *See* Communist Party
American South. *See* South
American women, business ventures, 83
"analepses" (Genette), 170
Aquinnah, 36, 161
aracial stories, 122
architecture, 15–17
Arnoff, Betty, 169
art: in magazines, 106; of Martha's Vineyard, 159; and social change, 108
artistic activism, 60, 69, 115, 129, 187
asexuality, as social asset, 176
aspirations, class vs. personal, 64
autobiographical fiction, 127
autobiography, 39, 43
autoethnography, 44
Azurest (Sag Harbor, N.Y.), 33–34

Baker, Chet, 180–181
Baker, Halema Alli, 180–181, 212n35
Baker, Houston, 132
Baldwin, Kate, *Beyond the Color Line and
the Iron Curtain*, 78, 96, 201–202n95
Ballou, Phoebe, 36, 157, 160
"banana kings," 50–51
Baraka, Amiri, 183
Barthe, Richmond, *(Portrait of a Woman)
A'Lelia Walker* [painting], 125
Bascom, Lionel, ed., *The Last Leaf of
Harlem*, 119, 122, 185
Bass, Charlotte, 198n4
Bastiaans, Aisha, 174
beaches, 26
Beals, Jennifer, 174
beauty, standards of, 46–47
Beltrán, Mary, 211n16
Benjamin, Jessica, 145
Bennett, Gwendolyn, 62
Benson, Helen Pease, 47–48
Benson family, 194n31
Bentley, Nancy, 167–168
Berry, Halle, 173, 174, 175
bicycle, as symbol, 45, 140, 175
"biomythography" (Lorde), 10
bisexuality, 71
black actresses, 173, 174
black America, on film, 84
Black and White [film], 77, 86
black art, 36, 106, 110–111
Black Arts Movement; local movements,
105; poetry, 106; second phase (1960s
and 1970s), 114, 168
black bourgeoisie, 56; codes, 74–75, 144;
self-segregation, 133
black Brahmins, social boundaries, 132–137
black community, diversity, 152; imagined, 164
black conservatives, 132–133
black culture: class hierarchies, 61; and
food, 29–30, 63; and nostalgia, 72;
satirized, 74; and social change, 34–35;
stereotypes, 30, 87; and writing, 115.
See also African American oral culture;
black folk culture; cultural blackness

ABOUT THE AUTHOR

CHERENE SHERRARD-JOHNSON is currently professor of English at the University of Wisconsin–Madison where she teaches nineteenth- and twentieth-century American and African American literature, cultural studies, and feminist theory. She is the author of *Portraits of the New Negro Woman: Visual and Literary Culture in the Harlem Renaissance* (Rutgers University Press, 2007) and the editor of a new, annotated edition of Jessie Redmon Fauset's last novel, *Comedy: American Style* (Rutgers University Press, 2009).